DRAFT YEAR
BRENDAN GAUNCE

JOHN MATISZ & HOCKEYPROSPECT.COM

FORWARD

I first saw Brendan Gaunce during his OHL Draft eligible season. He was playing Minor Midget AAA for the Markham Waxers. Unlike a few seasons earlier when I watched his older brother Cameron, a 1990 birthdate, Brendan's team was a far cry from the powerhouse that his older brother played on. Cameron Gaunce had teammates named Stamkos and Del Zotto. Brendan did not.

Brendan still managed to take advantage of his situation with the Waxers. He had no shortage of icetime and had a great OHL Draft season. The productive season led to him being selected by the Belleville Bulls early in the 1st round of the draft.

I watched Brendan early and often in his OHL career. He impressed me with a great start to his rookie season. Brendan is what I call a 'coaches' player. As a coach myself for almost 20 years, you begin to appreciate players, like Brendan, who just 'get it'. Brendan is a player who coaches can rely on to be another voice, an extension of the coach. Brendan is the type of player who would help a rookie who is making a mistake before the coach noticed. It's easy to see the 'Captain like' qualities in Brendan Gaunce.

I met Brendan's father while I was coaching against Cameron Gaunce in Junior 'A'. When I started thinking about possible players to ask to be our subject for this book, I ended up making just one phone call. I reached out to the Gaunce family and after 48 hours, we had our player to follow. I had only met Brendan once before this past season. I only needed that one chat to know he was our guy. Based on that chat and my previous dealings with the Gaunce family, I knew he would be great for this book. He was.

I wish all of you readers could meet Brendan, but this book will give you a peek into who he is and how he goes about both his hockey life and personal life. I am not a writer. I scout hockey and have coached hockey for many years. I needed a talented young writer who would be willing to take this project on. I needed a junior hockey fan and an NHL Draft fan. I found him.

Back in May 2011 I had a request from a young writer to bring one of our NHL Draft Guides to the Memorial Cup in Mississauga. The young writer was of course, John Matisz. John and I chatted for a short time at one of the tournament games and then went our separate ways. This is 2012 however, the twitter age is in full force. It was easy to find John a few months later to ask him if he wanted to write a book about a high-end prospect as he made his way through his draft season. If memory serves, John said yes right there and then.

I explained my idea to John. I told him in order to make the book a true account he would need to talk to Brendan OFTEN. John understood and did an amazing job of speaking to Brendan week after week after week. I can tell you that from the few times I chatted with Brendan this year, he was not your average teenager when it came to conversation. I can recall one chat more than others. A few OHL trades had just been completed, including Jack Campbell, who was traded to the Soo Greyhounds. Brendan and I traded info from our sources about that trade and many others which were in the rumour state. I can only imagine how the chats between Brendan and John would have evolved from August to the following June.

I'll finish by saying that this project turned out the way I had hoped. John Matisz worked diligently on this book. Brendan, his family and his agents made this book enjoyable to produce. I hope you enjoy it.

Mark Edwards
Founder & Director of Scouting
HockeyProspect.com
First Round Scouting Inc.

TABLE OF CONTENTS

ACKNOWLEDGMENTS

On behalf of John and myself, a massive thank-you goes out to the entire Gaunce family (Brendan, Stephen, Julie, Ally and Cameron) for their incredible help in putting this book together. He would also like to acknowledge Brendan's agent, Paul Capizanno, as well as the entire Belleville Bulls organization, for their support.

Stick-taps to the following people for offering their time in order to be important secondary sources: Gary Roberts, Sean Monahan, Malcolm Subban, Jake Grimes, George Burnett, Lindsay Hofford, Paul Titanic, Matt Sands, Josh Sweetland, David Foot, Samantha Moore, Brandon Pantaleo, Mike Gouglas, Luke Judson.

Finally, thanks to John Matisz for his commitment to this book and the effort he put into it each and every week.

Mark Edwards

1

"B"

Amidst the Yardmen Arena faithful in early January 2012, a very ordinary-looking man sits quietly in between a messy collection of season ticket holders.

Though he's the lone member of his party, no one really notices. The game is on, and the Belleville Bulls are on the power-play.

Aware of his surroundings and its implications, the man refrains from chatting too much, too overtly. He doesn't want anyone to know his name, intentions, religious affiliations, what he puts in his coffee. Anything true and telling may somehow blow his cover, which could bust open his anonymity.

All of this brings a smile to his middle-aged face.

He's a true hockey guy, an insurance broker by day, yes, but an indisputable puckhead away from the office.

Unlike the proponents in his seating block, the man is a tad biased.

Make that about as biased as one can be. His allegiance, in the most ancient meaning of the word, is towards a particular player.

But he won't let anyone know that. Not today. He left that outward enthusiasm at home, roughly 190 kilometres west, down Highway 401 towards Toronto.

The worst thing he could do is blurt out a comment with any sort of personal flare. He doesn't want to blow his cover. Cheering is reserved for his living room, where he can freely moan and applaud alongside his wife and canine companion.

Instead, his blockmates decide to verbalize their disgust in the apparent incompetence the home team has displayed on the power-play this evening. One booster, taking aim at one of Belleville's assistant captains, hollers at the top of his lungs.

"C'mon, Gaunce, smarten up out there," he yelps.

Although he's chomping at the bit to ring the beer-fuelled fan's neck, the man, sitting two seats over, refrains from saying a peep.

He's irate but refrains from taking any sort of action. It wouldn't be proper.

He sits with the Yardmen commoners because he can, not because he has to.

Deep down he knows what it's like. He knows the feeling of being a die-hard supporter of a sports club, only to be seemingly robbed by the team's lack of oomph on a certain night. He knows what it feels like to live and breathe the colours of one's favourite franchise in one's favourite league.

He won't let the displeased fan disrupt his night. If it were him, he'd be ticked off too, paying hard-earned cash to watch a club underachieve.

Because of this, he stares straight ahead, continuing to turn the hockey intelligence wheels inside his head. The wheels produce inner dialogue that will come in handy once his second son of three children, the baby of the family, meets him and his wife after the game.

Brendan Gaunce will vent to him, like any 17-year-old would after losing for the third outing in a row.

A proud Papa, but also a clear-thinking Papa, Stephen Gaunce— the one-man party amidst the Yardmen Arena faithful that night—always tells it like it is.

Offering words of encouragement, he rarely speaks in a negative tone or in a way that would prevent future such conversations. Rather, he speaks to his son with realism in his eyes. He accompanies the comforting look with a primal, parental-laden tone in his voice. He is very much a people's person, and simultaneously a son's dad.

This down-to-earth nature is part of the reason why he sits with a clan of strangers when his ultra-talented son is on display, essentially asking for criticism with every missed pass or poorly calculated movement.

He doesn't want to be wined and dined. He's not interested in that. He wants the atmosphere. He wants to feel the rawness of being next to a Bulls booster.

And, quite frankly, he doesn't care about any harsh words thrown his—and his son's—way. If it's deserved, it's just that: Deserved.

That's the thing—it's the Gaunce way to look the other way.

***

After growing up in modest families on the east coast of Canada, the parents of Brendan Gaunce eventually landed in the Toronto suburb of Markham, Ontario. It's been their hometown since 1994, the year Brendan was born.

There, they don't live a lavish lifestyle, nor do they wish they did. They're not high-profile bankers, paediatricians, or judges. And that's perfectly fine with them.

They don't frequent Ontario's picturesque Muskoka cottage country in the summer just because they can. Nor do they have a three-car garage to leave largely unused.

Their Havanese dog, Rocky, is not spoiled beyond belief—just a little bit. They're not excessive in their spending either, and prefer to keep it that way. They don't ask for much, and intend to stay true to those values.

After all, they're not looking to stand out.

"We're not special, we're just normal," Julie says plainly.

Like a romantic comedy's script, Stephen and Julie —two of more than 80,000 in the city of Saint John, New Brunswick, at the time —did not cross paths until after high school.

Julie, formerly of the surname Kingston, wed Stephen Gaunce in 1983. The celebration was a culmination of two same-town born and raised teens that had the world in front of them.

Stephen, who is a year older, had barely graduated Saint Mary's University. Also a Saint Mary's alumnus, Julie's May graduation was a mere flicker in the year's events, as the couple's wedding fell a week after.

Armed with ambitious diplomas that read 'Bachelor of Commerce-General Business' (Stephen), and 'Bachelor of Commerce-Accounting' (Julie), they fled five provinces westward.

Together, they were ready to start a life-long two-person voyage.

In Calgary, Alberta, home of the Stampede, a sales-privy Stephen worked his magic as an entry-level insurance company employee. The property and casualty insurance game was his first introduction to the real world.

Three quick years passed before the couple moved almost directly north of Cowtown, to the humble community of Red Deer.

Their time spent in the hometown of the Western Hockey League's Rebels franchise was remarkably short. Eighteen months later, with their bags barely unpacked, it was off to Ontario.

Stephen was recruited by corporate big wigs in the Greater Toronto Area. A move to suburb Ajax was the next pit stop in the couple's early-marriage suitcase life.

Aside from a temporary transfer to the 'nickel capital of the world,' Sudbury, Ontario, the Gaunce clan has lived in the GTA. Since 1988, the family's breadwinner has been with the same insurance brokerage based out of Markham.

When asked to reflect back on their now 24-year relationship with the city, the Gaunces don't have a single regret. Like virtually all parents, they're attached to the nostalgia and countless memories.

Since the family settled in the bedroom community, the city has sprouted out of the ground and into the sky.

Julie can't help but shake her head at the immense urban sprawl centre Markham has become. A commuter hub by definition, it is not designed for relentless traffic jams post-rush hour.

But it happens, and it's a fact of life.

The head-shaking is all in fun. Julie wouldn't trade their spot for the world.

Especially when her and Stephen reminisce about their time on Penny Crescent. One story always seems to come up.

"He used to be John Vanbiesbrouck. He couldn't say it though, he'd say 'John Vanbeeksbrook,'" Stephen laughs, as he reveals one of his favourite memories of his son's childhood in Markham, imitating the now-retired NHL goaltender.

Born eight pounds, eight ounces at Sudbury General Hospital, late in the morning of March 25, 1994, Brendan Stephen Gaunce was a bit bigger than the norm right out of the womb.

The average weight of a North American newborn is 7.5 pounds, meaning the youngest child of three in the family was ready to fit in with the big kids immediately.

And he did.

Using his plastic OshKosh car as the so-called zamboni during road hockey games, the boy everyone called 'B' was a playful nuisance in the neighbourhood from as early as four years old.

Being seven years younger than sister Allyson and four years behind brother Cameron, B certainly had his work cut out for him if he wanted to be a part of the group.

"That's how annoying he was," Julie says, hardly containing a massive grin. "He would try so hard to be a big kid that he came off extra annoying to them."

As one of the main houses facing the only opening of their street's cul-de-sac, the Gaunce's home was placed perfectly to accommodate road hockey games.

Julie and Stephen could keep an eye on the kids through the front window, and the eager hockey enthusiasts were able to go about their business until their parents went to bed. It was a win-win situation.

In Brendan's eyes, it gave him valid excuse to stay up way past his bedtime. After all, he would be playing outside, getting some fresh air and quality exercise.

However, on the odd occasion, it wasn't all roses for the tyke of the group. As a four-year-old playing with mainly 8-10 year olds, the youngest Gaunce boy was on his own.

He didn't have a buddy to console with when he was picked last, nor did he have the comfort of another toddler's faults to make him feel less inadequate. He was just there, the kid brother who got in the way more than anything.

A punishment for being the naïve, piny little squirt of the group was to play goalie. In the spirit of fitting in, Brendan figured it only made sense to take them up on their seemingly one-sided offer.

There was nothing to lose, he thought.

So, B anxiously accepted. He dropped to the pavement and laid on his stomach so someone close by could strap on the neighbourhood set of goalie pads.

Those moments of preparation were succeeded by pain.

He took wrist shots from two-feet away, slap shots from five. He braved shots near the privates. He brushed off rubber balls to the noggin.

Penny Crescent was his own Maple Leaf Gardens. The cul-de-sac's light fixtures put a spotlight on the Hockey Night in Canada atmosphere the group of Markham kids had created.

As a whole, Brendan enjoyed the exhilaration of being treated as an equal in front of Grade 2's and 3's. Except he didn't have a clue how to play goalie—he was supposed to be one of the players.

Whoops.

And there was one rule that seemed to throw things right off kilter.

"That was the rule the big kids had," Stephen remembers. "They would always say, 'If you want to play with us, that's fine, but you can't cry.'"

Like any toddler putting his heart and soul into a game of road hockey against players who have walked the earth for a half-decade longer, B cried.

Who wouldn't? He was pelted with a rubber ball time and time again, with relentless velocity.

Conscious of the outlined fate of showing weakness in front of the big kids, the Gaunce house became Brendan's sanctuary.

A shot to the face would send him running up the steps and into the inside foyer. A quick cry later and he was leaping over the front steps onto the driveway, ready for more orange ball-induced pain.

"As a little kid, I remember him getting balls blasted at him during road hockey games. Cameron and some other guys were riffling shots at him in net, constantly," Paul Titanic, a long-time family friend, says.

Luckily for B, he had two elder siblings.

One was his protective brother Cameron. Mindful of his little brother's vulnerability, Cameron straddled the line between being the watchful eye and being a kid himself.

"It was me in net for a little bit. And then luckily when a couple of the younger kids came around, like Brendan, I no longer had to do it," Cameron says.

Eventually Brendan was off the hook himself.

"I feel he was pretty mature," Cameron says. "He kind of had to be. Growing up on Penny, he was always the youngest by a few years. I was the closest to him in age, but there were kids literally 10 years older than him playing."

Along the way, Brendan's maturity level wasn't always up to par with the older kids. This brought about the occasional confrontation between him and Cameron.

It's almost a duty for brothers to fight, both physically and verbally, when growing up under the same roof. It happens in every family, everywhere.

The Gaunce boys were no exception to the convention. And they certainly weren't strangers to each other, despite the age gap.

"They would be playing with all the other kids then the two of them would go into the garage and whack it out, then open the door and go out and play again," Ally recalls, adding the two youngsters would go at it both publicly and behind closed doors.

Out on the street, with Brendan behind the mask and Cameron fully enthralled in a never-ending intra-neighbour road hockey rivalry, there wasn't much time for watching the little guy.

Cameron was his own unit, and would step in if he needed to, but it's not as if he was B's full-time protector. He was busy taking care of himself, scoring imaginary Game 7 overtime goals.

That sort of mothering role was reserved for the female sibling, Ally.

"I always watched over Brendan like he was my own," she says softly. "He and I were the closest siblings growing up."

Brendan came into the world when she was seven. It's not uncommon for parents to span their offspring out over 7-10 years, but in a generation of 1-2 kids per family, it's also not necessarily the standard.

Ally revelled in the responsibility.

Together, Brendan and Ally watched Cameron learn the ropes of that stick and puck sport at the local rink.

It was obvious from the tender age of four that Brendan had an infatuation with the game of hockey. The whole crawling stage each baby experiences was followed by a brief stint where he learned how to walk, before skating came into the picture.

After taking beginner's lessons through a city learn-to-skate program as a two-year-old, it was house league time.

Skip ahead two seasons and an ever-growing B was ready to challenge some older kids once again. This time it would be on the ice, as he made the Markham Waxers novice AA team.

His first year of competitive hockey was against players a year older than him, seeing as Brendan, six, was supposed to be enlisted in the local Tyke program.

Like virtually all eventual Ontario Hockey League players, Brendan showed earnest promise from the get-go of his minor hockey career.

There are surely late bloomers out there, but that wasn't the path Brendan was on.

Aside from above-average skill development over a short period of time, Brendan's size was a determining factor when the Gaunces made the important decision of letting Brendan try-out for novice.

Back then, it wasn't all about hockey. Brendan was drawn to numerous sports, and flourished in most.

As a natural ball sport lover, basketball and volleyball fit into his mindset and ability range while attending Edward T. Crowle Public School in Markham. Track and field and cross-country also checkered his sporting schedule throughout the early school years.

Towards the end of his elementary school career, the volleyball court, running track, hockey rink and soccer pitch weren't satisfying every one of Brendan's needs.

He wanted to familiarize himself with a different stage of display, a more artsy one.

While it wasn't as if he was dropping one hobby for another, acting helped Brendan open up.

As well, it helped him prove he wasn't a one-dimensional kid.

His teacher for both Grade 7 and 8 at Edward T. Crowle, Samantha Moore, was impressed with Brendan's first taste of the bright lights of dramatic arts.

Acting in the play Westwood, an adaptation by Adam Sheppard, Brendan pleased the audience with a small part.

Moore, says his real breakout role came the next year as a key member of a rendition of Hairspray.

Given the choice to either partake in a dramatic composition or a musically based performance, Brendan, three other guys and three girls all chose the musical route.

Brendan was picked to portray John Travolta's character, Edna Turnblad. The American pop culture icon set the bar pretty high for Brendan to reach, especially at such a young age.

The humour in the whole situation, Moore says, was that Brendan didn't really play Travolta since his character was a female—a middle-aged woman at that, one fit with rambunctious hair and a squeaky voice.

"I had him wearing one of my stretchy skirts actually," Moore says, giggling in between words. "He had to wear a dress, a wig. He was larger than life. He actually had to do a lip sync solo."

Overplaying the role was actually beneficial for Brendan in this instance. Edna was a bit of a dramatic being, and the 'hockey guy' fully embraced the character.

In fact, Moore says that particular cast of Hairspray paved the way for the next few years of Grade 8 productions. Future senior level classes put on shows like High School Musical and Fame.

While each actor did its part to trail blaze at Edward T. Crowle, the ringleader was undoubtedly Brendan, Moore says.
"Because Brendan Gaunce stood up and took on a role in a dance scene, I had so many boys come to try out the next year. They weren't dancers, but they knew they could do it because they saw Brendan have so much fun on stage. Kids were looking up to him even before that; he was an all-around athlete, a good kid." – Samantha Moore

A Grade 8 male participating in dramatic arts was nothing ground-breaking at the school. Even playing a woman on stage wasn't that far off base.

The fact that he was doing it without thinking twice, though, that was what made it remarkable, Moore says.

Brendan went from being a role model to the jocks to being a role model to all, appealing to just about everyone in the school. Going out of one's comfort zone is a challenge for most elementary school students.

Then there was his sense of self.

He was the best hockey player in his school, hands down; there was no denying that. He dared elite athletes in the other sports he competed in, putting in valiant efforts and fitting in quite well among those who called basketball, for example, their favourite sport.

It was obvious he didn't need Hairspray to increase his status, or anything along those lines. He did it because he wanted to.

This discreet confidence padded his already sterling reputation as a dependable student.

"He cared about his studies, which actually impressed me quite a bit. A lot of times I'll get kids who believe they're going to make the NHL and their whole life is surrounded by hockey. But he didn't let school go by the wayside. Brendan was never like that. School was as important to him. Or, whether it was important to him or not, he understood the importance of it. He hung in a crowd that valued education and he worked hard to do well in school." – Samantha Moore

Hitting the books was the No. 1 priority for all three Gaunce siblings from the very beginning of their academia-athletics balancing act.

"School has always been the biggest thing in our family. Basically, if you weren't doing well in school then you weren't playing sports. From a young age, it was put in my mind that school was the most important and that you had to finish school work before hockey. Hockey was kind of a side thing, a dessert." – Brendan Gaunce

With the fallback of a middle-class income, Brendan had the luxury of playing a multitude of sports growing up. While hockey was his game of choice—no questions asked—since first coming in contact with the concepts of athleticism and competition, a few other sports still stepped into his wide-eyed realm of curiosity.

In terms of out-of-school sporting, hockey and soccer ruled.

There was a simple formula to follow, one that many Canadian families employ: Soccer in the summer, hockey in the winter.

"If I didn't play any other sports growing up, I think I would be bored of hockey by now," Brendan says. "Playing other sports, you learn things you wouldn't."

Away from school, he strapped on his soccer cleats to play for both Markham Soccer Club and Unionville Soccer Club from the age of four up until high school.

It's a common story for elite athletes, as the dedication required to continue in a chosen sport often diminishes other athletic endeavours.

In Brendan's case, whether he was crossing a ball during soccer practice or practicing his slapshot in hockey practice, being active was a rite.

Even though he grew up during a tremendous couch potato boom, Brendan was drawn to the outdoors. Road hockey over movies, playground soccer over video games.

Then again, kids tend to pinball from activity to activity. This meant video games and movies made their way into Brendan's weekly routine to some degree.

"Basically, my life since I was younger has revolved around sports in some way or fashion," he says. "I didn't mind sitting around, doing nothing, but I'd rather play a game or hang out with my buddies."

9

The same mentality stretched beyond elementary school and into high school. While attending Markham District High School in Grade 9 and 10, he ran track, played football and, of course, suited up for the school hockey team.

Football was, by and large, his strongest sport away from the rinks during high school, as the squad leaned on him for not only offence and defence, but special teams as well. Following Cameron's footsteps, Brendan decided football—his second favourite sport to both watch and play—was a noble choice in Grade 9.

A defensive end, the new kid on the block was not only effective as a big-bodied defender in his first year on the junior team, but as a booter, too. Brendan's soccer background undoubtedly contributed to his secondary roles as the team's kicker and punter.

A year wiser, and with a single football season under his belt as a Grade 10 student, Brendan was given the seemingly improbable to-do list of playing slotback, safety, kicker, and punter for the varsity team.

Opponents were not only three years older (in some cases), but mainly made up of football guys. Brendan, on the other hand, was a hockey guy, meaning it was unchartered territory.

Support from his parents, however, eased the disadvantage.

Especially in terms of silencing any critics that the OHL prospect was making a mistake by risking injury to play a wildly physical game.

For hockey talents, the Grade 10 year is very important. It can make or break your future in the game.

"People would always tell me I could get hurt playing football. But then my Mom used to tell me when I was little that you can get hurt just walking down the street, so I go by that instead," Brendan says, adding his mom has always been a voice of reason.

Once a decision was made by the Gaunce clan—an easy one considering Cameron played two years of high school football—the questions didn't stop.

"Agents said, 'He plays football? You let him?'" Julie says. "And I said, 'Well, yeah.' What if hockey doesn't work out? You miss out on high school. You miss out on so many things."

It turns out the physical rigors did not damage Brendan's health, as he never sustained a major injury pursuing gridiron glory.

It was all worth it.

The extra taxi-cab service stop for mom, the energy spent learning a new sporting craft, the time management adjustment associated with playing on multiple varsity sports teams while keeping afloat in the classroom—it was all worth it.

To boot, Markham District captured the coveted Metro Bowl in his lone year on the Varsity team.

Won by just one secondary school in the entire GTA system each year, it's an absolute honour to be crowned Metro Bowl champions.

By a 19-0 final score, the Markham Marauders took down Scarborough's Birchmount Park Collegiate Institute.

Birchmount is the home of NHLers Wayne Simmonds and Peter Zezel.

On the football field in 2009, however, Brendan and his football comrades had their way with the public school.

***

The minor hockey circle in Canada can be gutless. It can be cruel, obscene, and even downright belligerent.

In some instances, intra-team politics take on lives of their own. They become organisms fuelled by an innate sense of importance by certain individuals.

Aggressive arguments might develop from training camp cuts, ice time, linemate choices, coaching style and, quite simply, anything under the minor hockey sun.

Parents fight for every last inch of exposure, desperately hoping their little Johnny or Suzie makes it to the next level.

Stephen and Julie are more than aware of the parameters associated with the beast that is minor hockey, seeing as they live in one of the nation's hotbeds: The GTA.

Stephen has been heavily involved in the Markham Minor Hockey Association since the early 2000s when he was "roped" into becoming the club's treasurer.

"I sat in at a meeting as the temporary treasurer, and left as the permanent one," he says.

Then, when Brendan was 13, Papa Gaunce became the manager of the Markham Waxers minor bantam AAA team. It was his first foray into the micro-manager's role.

For the 2011-12 season he was the AAA vice-president/convener, despite both of his sons graduating from the system.

It's been a long-lasting ride for Stephen, but he, and Julie, have steered away from any major political discourse along the way.

Hockey is a game for the kids, they say, and the background noise is reserved for elsewhere. In court rooms, office buildings, and the House of Commons.

Julie, a die-hard hockey fan and mom, has always been the transportation engineer—the on-call taxi service—for her children. Though she hasn't stepped behind a Waxers bench, she's knowledgeable enough about the organization—and hockey in general—that she could fill in at a moment's notice.

Julie, a covert contributor to the Waxers' success, and Stephen, an overt one, are supporters for life.

A pair of OHL Cup appearances, one by each son, has something to do with their passion for the grassroots organization.

First there was the 1990-born Markham Waxers minor midget AAA squad, which featured the likes of Cameron Gaunce, Steven Stamkos, and Michael Del Zotto, and won the 2006 OHL Cup.

They are heralded as one of the most talented minor hockey clubs of all-time, seeing seven of 16 players graduate to major junior hockey and go on to play a combined total of 1,372 regular season games in the OHL.

Amazingly, they could have been even better if Cody Hodgson, who played half-dozen years on the '90 team, did not decide to play a year up for the major midget AAA Waxers instead.

Three players—Stamkos (Tampa Bay), Del Zotto (New York Rangers) and Hodgson (Vancouver)—went in the top 20 at the 2008 NHL Entry Draft. Cameron followed shortly after, selected 50th overall by the Colorado Avalanche late in the second round.

Though nostalgia can certainly play an enormous role in creating hyperbole, it's difficult to find many kinks in the '90 team's armour. They were dominant.

At the OHL Cup—debatably the province's most scouted minor hockey tournament—the squad went undefeated. A total of five games resulted in five wins and a plus-15 goal-differential.

In the tournament final against the Toronto Red Wings, the Waxers emerged victorious, 3-2, after nearly coughing up a three-goal lead.

The tournament's MVP was a 6-foot, 165-pound version of Stamkos, a future two-time Maurice 'Rocket' Richard Trophy recipient before hitting the age of 23.
Stamkos' collection of 11 points (four goals, seven assists) was four ahead of the rest of the OHL Cup's pack.

Other notable players from the 15-team showdown include: Toronto Maple Leafs prospect Nazem Kadri (London Junior Knights), New Jersey Devils stud Adam Henrique (Brantford 99ers), and Minnesota Wild up-and-comer Matt Hackett (London Junior Knights).

Looking back, Cameron is still baffled by the talent the Waxers iced from the start of their minor hockey days all the way to the end. "It's crazy we all came from the same hometown and fell into the same team. Obviously, at the time, we didn't realize just how good we were, but now I think about how lucky I was to play with those guys. It makes you better. When you're practicing with them all the time it helps you grow as a player." – Cameron Gaunce

From the Gaunce family's perspective, Cameron's wildly successful squad became a blueprint for Brendan's and, to be frank, every other team within the Waxers umbrella.

The organization didn't know it at the time, but they had unequivocally created an unstoppable force.

"We had so much success with Cameron's team that I honestly felt bad for Brendan," Stephen says.

Stephen didn't feel bad because Brendan was being left in the dust as his brother's team ran away with trophy after trophy. He wasn't being neglected at home, or otherwise.

It was actually quite simple: He was just on a very average hockey team.

And that's where Paul Titanic and Mike Gouglas come into the picture.

Titanic, a celebrity within the Waxers organization as both a coach and father (his son David was on Cameron's OHL Cup-winning team), is not only a dear friend to the entire Gaunce family, but a talking landmark of sorts when referring to Cameron, Allyson and Brendan's childhood.

His influence started with the '90 team, with Titanic bestowing his years as a University of Toronto hockey coach upon the group headed by Gouglas.

For almost a decade, Titanic—the man who learned proper coaching tactics from legendary NHL bench boss Mike Keenan—saw Cameron and his buddies every day at the rink.

"He's always been that voice at the arena," Cameron recalls. "He's such a good hockey mind; really thinks the game well; just knows an abundance of stuff on hockey, and not just the x's and o's."

Interestingly enough, one of the fundamental lessons Cameron learned from Titanic has absolutely nothing to do with the game of hockey.
"Whether you are a student from his school at a game, or someone his wife introduced him to at a party 10 years ago, he's always making the time to come up and say 'hi' to you. That respect for people is something I've definitely taken away from him." – Cameron Gaunce

Gouglas, a disciple of the Titanic regime, having played high school hockey for him at St. Brother Andre Catholic High School in Markham, was handed his first big coaching project.

At the ripe age of 25, he was told to turn around Brendan's team.

With Titanic's guidance in both the first (minor bantam) and third year (minor midget), and Stephen's helping hand as manager for all three seasons, the dedicated Waxer bench boss and his crew of assistants went to work on reconstructing an inadequate team.

"Yeah, OK, Rome wasn't built in a day. There's going to be some struggles but we've got a good core and we'll add on to that each year," Stephen says when asked about the development plan him and Gouglas decided on.

Gouglas, now 30, is the current director of hockey development and coach mentorship for the entire Waxers organization.

Oddly enough, just five years ago, he was the one being mentored.

Not a screamer or yeller, Gouglas used his background as a school teacher as the foundation of his coaching in the early goings. Titanic, a teacher as well, added to the cohesion.

They both knew which buttons to push, the significance of being a leader by example, and possessed a tireless work ethic.

"We really used a lot of the framework from the '90 team in terms of what we were going to talk about, what we were going to focus on," Gouglas says. "I always joke that the '94 team got so sick of losing that once they got confidence they could win and really turned things around."

And they did, indeed, right the ship.

So much so that they actually put together a concrete goal for Brendan and the rest of the 1994-born Markham Waxers AAA contingent.

"It was settled upon that after the minor bantam year that we were going to play in the OHL Cup," Gouglas says with back-handed confidence. "It wasn't to win—it was to get there."

Assembling a staple group of not only skilful and hard-working kids, but a dedicated group of them was at the team's strategic core, Gouglas says.

After establishing the personnel, a certain culture needed to be instilled. Though they were barely teenagers, Brendan's Waxers team had to grow as a collective group. There would be no winning if a succinct message was spewed out by Gouglas a few minutes before game time—discipline and organization had to be thorough and understood.

"When you get to those important games, where you want to get to, the things that are going to make a difference are how hard you compete, how much you'll put in for each other," Gouglas says.

Among the Gouglas-isms was the concept of 'bad fun' versus 'good fun.' Goofing around, socializing to no end (bad fun) was contrasted with working hard and reaping the benefits (good fun).

Following a first round playoff exit in minor bantam to a rival centre team, the Ajax Raiders, the squad's fearless leader knew it was time to push the pendulum to the 'good fun' side.

Brendan, the team's undisputed choice for captaincy, experienced the culture change first-hand, and fondly recalls the transition.

"I don't think we had enough kids that wanted to play with us before. I think our team really developed as people going into our minor bantam year. It was a big character-builder, and that's why we succeeded in later years. It was the first year that it wasn't just about going to the rink and having fun. We went there with a purpose." – Brendan Gaunce

Major bantam, although another quintessential building block for the Waxers core group, was not a tremendously successful season. Despite beating particularly dominant foes like Ajax and the York Simcoe Express in the regular season, Markham was eliminated in the first round of the post-season once again.

This time around, it was the Express disposed of the Waxers, bouncing Brendan and company in six games.

It was back to the drawing board time for Gouglas. But had his finest work been done?

With help from a number of other volunteers, the dedicated 26-year-old constructed a self-styled players guide for each and every kid. It was handed out in major bantam.

Since the team had a year under its belt as a unified group, it was fitting to lay down strict guidelines heading into the middle season of a three-year plan.

Many mature AAA teams believe in a similar system to the one employed by the Waxers.

It wasn't like Gouglas was trying something completely new here. But, at the same time, he was adding a personal touch to it.

Coaches know teenagers are impressionable beings and, if given the right instrument, can string along to a certain chord. Whether that chord is the Markham Waxer way, the Toronto Marlboros manner or the London Junior Knights knowhow, it's like music to a mid-teen's ears.

Equipped with 53 carefully thought-out pages, the Markham-specific guide was, in essence, an all-you-need-to-know booklet on what it takes to be a high performance athlete in a minor hockey setting.

Flip the cover and you'll find a 100-word history on the Markham Waxers. While short—basically just a brief outline of the history of the nickname and a couple side tidbits of information—it's a proper introduction to the next page: The Markham Waxer creed.

Selflessness, preparedness, sacrifice, and respect are some of the values communicated through the straight forward poem-like passage.

Each line of the creed begins with the statement "I am a Markham Waxer," and concludes with a pair of short sentences charting out a given lesson. And in large bold letters near the bottom of the page, an apt closer: "I AM A MARKHAM WAXER."

Throughout the neatly bound guide, from "Waxers History" all the way to an end page roster sheet, there is a common theme expressed: You must have the desire to labour for your teammates at all costs.

Page five is titled "Winners vs. Losers," with "WHICH ONE ARE YOU" closing out a 15-paragraph section of positive against negative discourse.

"A winner makes commitments," it reads, "A loser makes promises."

"A winner listens," it says a few lines later, "A loser just waits until it's his turn to talk."

From pages 20 to 32, the Waxers are given their first taste of the club's off-ice discipline procedures. Although it is a component of the players guide loosely monitored, Markham hopes players abide by the "Nutrition Guide" section.

Finding a home somewhere in between the mini history and what-not-to-eat lessons is one particularly striking page.

The title—"Leadership & Team Play"—is vague but its message is utterly clear.

"Everyone wants to be a leader … in a team game, however, we cannot all be leaders all of the time. Instead, we must sometimes follow the lead of others. For a team to achieve great chemistry and success, everyone needs to accept their own role and make sacrifices for the good of the team." – Markham Waxers Players Guide, Major Bantam AAA, 2008-09 season

An assistant captain for Markham when he suited up alongside players a year older, Brendan was the hands-on favourite to be the 1994-born team's captain from day one of the Gouglas era.

"It was always unanimous Brendan was the captain," Gouglas says.

Like any coach, in any sport, Gouglas values a link.

Brendan was that link and, in turn, the team's foremost opportunist.

"I'm coaching a team now and you sometimes miss coaching a kid like Brendan," he adds. "Not necessarily because of the goals he scored or anything like that, but because of his leadership."

One of the central expectations of a captain, Gouglas continues, is to be a dependable liaison between the coaching staff and the players.

Combining two perspectives can sometimes produce an image equivalent to looking through a pair of glasses when your eyes are perfectly fine. It's a somewhat blurry but you still get the picture.

A captain brings back full vision.

That responsibility, especially from bantam on, is crucial to a club's success on the ice since certain coaching techniques—whether it is in-game strategy or micro-motivation—need an extra push.

In other words, the boys need an almost-man to guide them.

"They would listen to him because they would see him do it. That's why he was our captain. He's as focused off the ice as he is on the ice with hockey," Gouglas adds.

Make tape-to-tape passes during warm-up while others are fooling around. Check.

Go into the corner and knock down the grittiest defenceman on the team in a drill. Check.

Drudge through a bag skate, finishing ahead of everyone else without displaying a hint of irritability afterward. Check.

That was Brendan for the 1994-born Markham Waxers—the heart and soul of a squad that transformed from average to contender over a span of three years.

Granted, Markham's captain didn't develop a selfless presence overnight.

One particular meeting between Gouglas and Brendan, which took place inside the Gaunce's garage, was the tipping point. Or maybe it was just a checkpoint along Brendan's rise to prominence among his peers.

At the practice prior to their encounter, Brendan was showing outward frustration. A mild-mannered teen most of the time, it was out of character for him to display any sort of disbelief or disdain towards the game of hockey or his teammates.

A few misconstrued passes muffed his way, and a handful of other nuisances, set off the faithful captain. Brendan didn't burst out and challenge a teammate to a fight. He didn't he smash his stick in half on the crossbar either.

Instead, he just looked exasperated, lost in himself.

Gouglas knew something was up, and recognized he was obligated to take action. He called up Stephen to notify him he'd be coming over to speak with Brendan.

The two hockey fiends spoke man-to-man. They figured out what was bothering Brendan, pinpointed a solution, and then moved on.

It was subtle, but Gouglas remembers the situation well.

So does Brendan's father.

"It wasn't with the way Brendan was dealing with his buddies," Stephen says, vividly recalling the event. "He could see Brendan getting frustrated and came to deal with it."

There are countless occasions throughout a hockey season where frustration boils over, causing a young player to show signs of weakness.

It's human.

What Gouglas was impressed with most, though, was Brendan's ability to rise above his peers in terms of day-to-day mentality.

"He was always very responsive to what I asked him. I think Brendan did a great job over the years, but I think what I missed most is that he really carried that team on his shoulders. At the same time, he was the ultimate team player. Even then, he showed maturity beyond his years." – Mike Gouglas

It helped the team was winning, and beginning to truly unite as a single entity.

Over this time period, the gap between Brendan and his teammates decreased, as they almost caught up to his superb skill.

But he had a distinct advantage in his back pocket at all time: The influence of the 1990-born Waxers team.

The combination of a positive upbringing and an unparalleled mentor group was starting to work wonders on Brendan, indisputably constructing a leader along the way. By minor midget, he was a purebred horse out there.

"A lot of kids, I think, are happy to just be out there playing high-level hockey, to be in AAA," Gouglas says, adding it's totally fine to have that mindset. "But if your goal is to be in the NHL, it's not easy. It's not easy to even play junior hockey. Brendan wanted it all."

There would be no simple, trouble-free path to greatness in regards to choice of team, either.

The Gaunces were stringent with their boys, turning down offers from illustrious Greater Toronto Hockey League programs to stay put in Markham.

It wasn't that they were snobs, particularly strict, or up-tight— Stephen and Julie just wanted their children to encompass strong values. They didn't want everything to be given to them, especially since the reason for leaving would be to pursue an easier route to their goal.

"That wasn't our belief," Stephen says. "Our belief was to stay home, play with your friends and in the spring and summer we'll let you travel."

Brendan's parents discussed and discussed. They deliberated year after year, without really budging on the situation until his OHL draft year.

"In his minor midget year, we gave him the option. If he wanted to leave, he could; if he wanted to stay, he could," Julie says.

He stayed.

He was a Waxer, Markham born and raised. Plus, there was that whole OHL Cup thing he was aching to score a berth in.

The minor midget season of 2009-10 was a tremendous success for Gouglas, Stephen, Brendan and the entire bunch. It started with a 3-2 win on August 31st over the Toronto Red Wings and ended as they exited the OHL Cup after a 4-2 loss to the Clarington Toros.

A 41-29-11 record was what culminated at the end of the seven-month stretch of hockey, hockey, hockey.

Perhaps more evident than ever before, Brendan was one of the most sought after 1994-born players in the entire province. His playmaking ability, immense size and smarts made him a can't-miss Waxer for any scouts taking in minor midget hockey in Ontario.

"I would say, in terms of recent memories, his ability to dominate a game sticks out," Titanic says. "I remember one Clarington game: He was just dominant. At that point, I realized what potential he had as a player. He pretty much single-handedly carried the team on his shoulders."

One of his best friends growing up, Brandon Pantaleo—another Penny Crescent inhabitant—knows Brendan better than most.

The just-doors-away neighbours were inseparable growing up.

Aside from attending different schools, they hung out non-stop. And, as Ally put it, "They have done everything together. Brendan has kept Brandon out of trouble, and vice-versa."

The familiarity with each other led to some wicked passing plays as two-thirds of the team's top trio. The minute-logging line was spearheaded by none other than Brendan.

Which was perfectly fine in the mind of his favourite winger. "When it comes to hockey, I definitely look up to him. He got me a lot of points. I was never really that talented of a player. He was our best player by far. He was pretty much our whole team, especially when we would lose early in the playoffs as young guys. He did everything back then." – Brandon Pantaleo

Perhaps a little modest, Brandon is no slouch in terms of hockey playing ability. At 19, he'll play for the 2012-13 Markham Waxers Jr. A club. In 2011-12, he was a key contributor for two successful squads, the major midget AAA Waxers and St. Brother Andre Catholic School Cardinals.

Back in their minor hockey days, while the core of the Waxers group grew and eventually became a full-fledged all-for-one squad by minor midget, the reliance on Brendan weakened.

It never left, though. There was an ample supporting cast, but the strong-willed, strong-bodied centreman was a driving force—to say the least.

As stated in the 2010 OHL Priority Selection Preview and Media Guide, Brendan's minor midget year, as a 6-foot-2, 210-pounder, included playing a "very prominent role in his team's success."

A 46-goal, 75-assist performance in a total of 68 games surely deserves such high praise. Throw in 46 penalty minutes and the guy's a 121-point producer who doesn't mind getting his nose dirty.

According to Gouglas, Brendan's superior talent level didn't necessarily put him on a pedestal. He worked as hard, or harder than anyone on that OHL Cup-participating roster.

"Just by having that attitude on the ice, it really pushed the rest of the guys to keep up to Brendan Gaunce," he says. "And when you don't have that, it's tough to motivate your 17 players to work their hardest."

Throughout his minor hockey days, Brendan wore No. 14 in honour of future NHL Hall of Famer Brendan Shanahan, who is now the league's disciplinarian.

In a lot of ways, the forwards from different generations share common traits.

Both go by the name Brendan. Both weigh in the 215-225-pound range. Both are only a tad over 6-feet tall—Brendan 6-foot-2, Shanahan 6-foot-3. Both hail from the GTA.

Plus, it's fair to say that within the next decade or so—pending unforeseen circumstances—both will have played important roles on at least one NHL team.

But Brendan, as a tyke, chose to don the numbers 1 and 4 in concurrence based on much simpler logic: He just liked the Detroit Red Wings as a child.

"When I was growing up, my brother loved Eric Lindros because he was No. 88. Our house number was 88, and he's a great player, so there were two reasons for his choice. I tried to find a player in the NHL I liked, and Shanahan played on my favourite team, which was Detroit. I had one of his jerseys and liked that his name was Brendan, too, and it was intriguing for some reason at such a young age." – Brendan Gaunce

People in the hockey world, even at a young age, expect results.

Brendan, as Cameron's brother and Stephen's son, was presented with an opportunity to slack off here and there. But he refused to.

"He was never, for a second, thinking that because of his name he was going to get a free pass or someone was going to help him out," Gouglas says in dead-pan. "He knew how hard his brother worked, saw how Stamkos worked in practice."

There's absolutely no doubt the fortunate circumstances of Hodgson, Del Zotto, Cameron and Stamkos aligning to play for one minor hockey team made Brendan a better hockey player. Its effect, both short- and long-term, does not have a hint of negative influence.

It very well could have, however.

Brendan could have done what others have before him. He could have concluded that access to resources meant the NHL would be within reach no matter what he did, said, thought.

Instead, he was aware of the resources, but only took advantage of them in a civil manner. There's a difference between being the kid-brother who possesses an ego, and being the kid-brother who is conscious of the harmful development of a large ego.

Considering he was an integral component in securing an OHL Cup berth for the minor midget Waxers, Brendan didn't allow distractions take hold or sidetrack any team goals.

As evidenced by an excerpt from the guide composed by a collection of scouts, the squad's leading scorer was also the ultimate team player. The guide is full of praise for him, reading like more like a recommendation than a description.

"He plays a very effective, smart, offensively productive and honest game while showing that he is willing to do whatever he can to help his team succeed. Gaunce possesses good size, and excellent stick and he has really improved his skating as the season has progressed." – 2010 OHL Priority Selection Preview and Media Guide

The best part about reading that in hindsight?

It appears virtually nothing has changed on a number of fronts, from his ability to provide headship to his hockey club to his love for the game, both on and off the ice.

"We still play road hockey," Pantaleo says in response to a question asking what he and Brendan usually find themselves doing when he's back in Markham. "The only difference is that we're not the younger kids anymore."

Looks like the fortune and fame surrounding him since he was a kid has never gotten the better of Brendan.

***

"He said, 'Ally, can you come home now please.' And that was it. And then he hung up the phone."

Like every weekday afternoon, Ally was making her way home to Aurora after working the day shift at a local fitness centre. It was another Friday in April 2011.

An abrupt phone call from her little brother, Brendan Gaunce, turned an otherwise trivial drive home into one filled to the brim with anxiety and stress.

"A month from now I'm getting married," she assured herself in past days as momentum gathered to her Big Day in May.

All of that was gone now, replaced with utter uncertainty. "Ally, can you come home now, please." She couldn't shake it—that's not something Brendan would say.

Arriving at the Penny Crescent home minutes after Brendan's odd phone call, Ally rushed through the driveway and into the garage.

There, she found her 17-year-old brother—all 6-foot, 200 pounds of him—sobbing, fighting for a simple sentence.

Like a reluctant delinquent pleading his case while dozens of eyes stare his way in a court room, Brendan was able to blurt out a few words.

His head was down. His face was down. He said little. But the impact was huge.

"I tried to ask him what was wrong and all he said was, 'go inside and talk to Mom.' So I did, and I saw my parents there," Ally says. "My Dad said, 'Mom went to the doctor and they found a lump in her breast.'"

Cancer.

One word.

One of the most devastating pieces of information a human being can hear.

It's demeaning and cruel. The word itself doesn't directly translate to 'suffering,' 'agony,' or 'discomfort,' but it might as well. And it's not a particularly dark word, yet, above all, possesses enormous reach.

Doctors don't sit at home praying for a chance to tell a patient they're sick with a possibly fatal disease. They're merely trained to be messengers, bearers of ultimate bad news.

On this occasion, Julie was caught in medical crossfire, assigned the insoluble task of telling her family she had cancer.

Stephen knew first, Brendan shortly after, Ally following work. Cameron was the last to find out because he was out of the country. He would have to hear on the horn.

He remembers the day's proceedings quite well.

"I got a text from my mom after working out. We were talking back-and-forth, just like any other day, and then she told me to give her a call when I get home. I didn't think anything of it but then I got a text from B telling me to hurry up and get home. I knew something was up." – Cameron Gaunce

After arriving home, he booted up his laptop and jumped onto the popular video messenger service, Skpe. Though confused why his mom forgot how to turn on the image portion, Cameron conceded and began listening.

His heart sunk.

It sank more as his mother sobbed. At a loss for words, Cameron could only tell his mother he was there for her and would do anything she needed.

Having broken his finger while playing for the Avalanche at the tailspin of the season, Cameron was back in Cleveland with the American Hockey League's Lake Erie Monsters. They were paired up in the first round of the 2011 Calder Cup Playoffs with the now-defunct Manitoba Moose.

Though he was likely shelved for the remainder of the playoffs, Cameron was enjoying time back with the club he spent the majority of the season with.

After the unexpected Skype revelation, his priorities suddenly changed.

A quick phone call to management and he was back to Ontario as the squad headed westward to Winnipeg for a three-game set.

The days between felt endless, Cameron expresses.

"Me being stuck in Cleveland made me feel helpless," he says. "I couldn't really help her. All I could be was moral support."

When he did arrive home, the eldest son made sure to take care of his ill mother. It came with harsh realities.

Chemo therapy was on the horizon, but it wasn't a day away. This troubled Cameron, as dealing with his mom's state before was already tough enough. The surgery was taking a toll on her. "It was very different. Obviously seeing the effect the surgery had on her and knowing chemo was ahead was the worst part. Just seeing her spirits through it all is what helped me the most. I always knew she was a tough person, but seeing her go through that gave me a whole new perspective on everything. I know I'm better for it, and I think our whole family is." – Cameron Gaunce

"That month was horrible," Ally adds. "We didn't know what to expect, what to do. We didn't know how to talk to her, how to talk to anybody about it."

Instead of putting the finishing touches on Ally's wedding day, the family comforted the house matriarch. The week before the wedding Julie went in for surgery. The week following her daughter's Big Day she went under the knife again.

"I knew something was wrong because he was crying on the phone and Brendan hardly ever cries," Ally explains. "For him to be upset like that, I knew something had to be wrong,"

Like any teenager, he was wrenched by mix emotions and a heavy heart. Brendan was hit hardest by the news.

It took him by the neck—both hands—and threw him against the wall.

This wasn't hockey. He couldn't just fight back. It was his mother's health, something with more weight than any on-ice haymaker.

"It really shook Brendan at the time," Julie says. "Kids hear the word 'cancer' and they think you're going to die."

The sequence of events caught Brendan off-guard.

When he walked into the house after summer school, he was puzzled why his Dad was home at 2:30 on a Friday. The whole 'take a seat, son,' routine usually meant he was in some form of trouble. But there was an eerie tint to it.

"It was kind of surreal. Not in a good way. You always hear about people getting cancer but you never think it'll affect you so closely. When you think of cancer, you think of death; when people have cancer, they die. But, obviously medicine and treatment has improved from years ago. They said she was going to live, 100 per cent. I had to go with the doctor's word because that's the only thing I had." – Brendan Gaunce

Brendan was still a vulnerable 17-year-old. He was faced with the realization that one of his two pillars was bent out of shape. And, at least for a few moments, burdened by the incredibly gloomy emotion of fear. Fear that his Mom could be gone.

"I was looking at it, thinking 'I don't know what I would do without one of them,'" he says after a long pause.

There was really nothing the Gaunce clan could do about cancer. They could yearn for a better god, a better truth, and a better everything —but there was no use.

June came and chemo tagged along. The hair loss and decrease in energy levels came in one foul swoop.

Soon sunny days arrived, as did the family's outlook on the illness. Daily quips about how Mom was suddenly bald began to accompany the usual family chatter.

The boys shaved their heads as they joined Stephen and Ally in a conscious effort to make certain the family's usual bright light didn't watch as her spirits flickered away.

Cancer took the Gaunces a while to adjust to. There's the emotional blow stage after receiving the news, leaving everyone in a state of unreserved and negative amazement.

Then comes the 'Why me? Why her?' stage. Which is followed by the 'OK, let's deal with this,' finale before day-to-day adjustments begin.

As per usual, up next was radiation treatment. It lasted from October to early December.

Only those close to the Gaunces knew of Julie's unfortunate run-in with the infamous disease that kills over a million North Americans annually.

It wasn't necessarily a sense of embarrassment or shame that kept the Gaunces' lips sealed. It was just their modest way of saying to the world that they would be all right.

Comedy became a bit of a haven for the family of five.

"As the treatment started, and my Mom began feeling better, we joked around a bit," Brendan recalls. "It was a relief because there's no point in constantly nagging over something you can't control."

He added it was just a roadblock in Julie's life, merely a stubborn obstacle.

Once 2012 hit, Julie looked like the old Julie. Gone were days of endless bed rest and inactivity. She never lost too much of her daily routine. By January, she was definitely closer to a comfortable state of health.

Giggly, kind-hearted, and energetic, she and Stephen returned to their normal routine.

"Everything's fine now. I just have to get strong again," she says.

Though less serious in nature, a minor heart attack in 2010 was actually the first health scare for the Gaunces in a short span.

Two years removed from the incident, Julie and Stephen can now joke about the serious episode.

"I was having a cigar—it was midnight, the last one of the day—and I thought 'oh gosh, there's pain right here.' I went to bed though, but eventually woke up in the middle of the night. It was really uncomfortable; it felt like indigestion. I drove myself down to the hospital. The nurses and doctor are all looking at me, and the guy says, 'you've had a heart attack.'" – Stephen Gaunce

In trademark fashion, the father of three decided it was best to keep the nagging concern to himself. No phone call, no text, no smoke signal. No communication with his family as he was rushed from nearby Markham Stouffville Hospital to Southlake Regional Health Centre in Newmarket.

A smoker for 30 years, Stephen points to a lack of exercise and a certain soft drink contributed to his health complications.

"Too much Diet Coke," he says.

On the way there, Stephen asked one of the paramedics if he was going to die. The response was a quick 'no.' This meant he would ultimately be fine and, in Stephen's mind, his family didn't need to worry.

Brendan remembers when he heard Stephen was released from hospital and told the family about the episode. Ally and Cameron weren't home, with the latter actually on a bus somewhere in northeastern United States.

"I think I was the luckiest of the three, if you want to call it lucky," Brendan says of being able to see his father alive and well shortly after the heart attack.

Like Julie's run in with cancer, Stephen's heart issue was daunting to the kids.

Most notably, Brendan. Both of his parents—the impenetrable forces who dedicate their lives to taking care of their children—suffered right in front of his eyes.

Protectors are not supposed to feel pain.

"When you're growing up, you don't really notice how fast life passes. But when stuff like that happens to your parents, someone you looked at as invincible when you were younger, it's a shock. With both of them going through something health-related, you start to realize your parents are everything to you, your family is everything to you." – Brendan Gaunce

And the Gaunces trucked on.

Back to work, back to school, back to the hockey rinks. Back to Aurora, back to Belleville, back to Cleveland. Back to normality.

"I think things are probably better now than they were before she was diagnosed with cancer," Ally suggests in January 2012. "It has brought us closer together and made us realize we shouldn't take the little things too seriously."

Case in point, the sister-brother bond between Ally and B is closer than ever.

It's funny what a teenage boy will get up to.

He'll sleep in just for the hell of it on weekends, because he can. He'll avoid going to bed at a reasonable time on a weeknight, instead watching TV until his eyes hurt.

He'll miss the bus because he forgot to pack the project he worked on all night. He'll forget his locker combination repeatedly over a school year, creating a mini crisis.

He'll chase girls, and push curfew as late as his parents will allow so he can keep chasing them.

He'll put his heart and soul into a flag football game during gym class, even though only he and a few others actually care what the score is. He'll walk around school half-wet, and uncomfortable, because he needed to shower after a strenuous gym class game.

He'll also call up his 25-year-old sister for advice, rather than punching in the digits of his NHL-bound brother or trustworthy parents.

"I'll hear about what's going on with Brendan through Ally," Julie says.

Girl problems. Emotional check-ins. Anything, really. Ally never really knows what's coming when her youngest brother calls her up.

She doesn't mind, of course. All along, B has been the baby, and Ally has embraced her self-assigned role as an unofficial caretaker. "I think when I was younger, it was my sister who was more protective of me than Cam, but they were both always very protective of me overall. When Cam left it was different because we always used to see each other every day and talk to each other so I think we got closer as we got older because we knew that we were all moving away." – Brendan Gaunce

It's a part of the Gaunce family dynamic.

She'll be in Aurora—sitting on the couch, making dinner, reading a book—with her husband, Jason, nearby. Brendan will be in Belleville.

Luckily, distance isn't a challenge these days, and all five Gaunce family members are Blackberry devotees.

"Blackberry Messenger has been the greatest invention for us," Julie says, nonchalantly.

For Julie, it's a vehicle to say 'hello' to Cam, a way to let Ally know when she receives mail, and a forum to ask Brendan how school went. The list goes on, but the technological relationships start and end with hockey.

Stephen and Julie make mental notes when watching Brendan and Cameron on TV or in-person. It shows they're focused on their kids' success, and provides them with material for after-game venting sessions. They go hand-in-hand.

Whether they watched Cameron through an AHL-affiliated streaming system online, or viewed Brendan live in Mississauga, there's always an after-game discussion. Since purchasing mobile Internet, they can also watch two games a night—one in-person and the other on the way back from the rink.

When the couple checks out a live game, there's always a small post-game gathering with the son. Mostly hugs and comments. Depending on their performance and mood, Brendan and Cameron might open up and vent about a play or two.

It's the same way when texting, except the warmth and familiarity of having their parents beside them is lost.

Cameron may be on a sweaty bus in the state of Oklahoma, fidgety after another adrenaline-fueled performance in the AHL. Win or lose, he's often eager to chat with his parents about hockey, life, until he finds cosiness in his small space on the team vehicle.

Brendan, though much closer geographically, and in more frequent contact due to his age, is as likely to scroll down to 'Mom' or 'Dad' on his contact list following an on-ice battle.
"There's times where I'm up to 1-2 a.m. after one of Cam or Brendan's games. They'll be heading home from Ottawa or Chicago—wherever—and won't want to stop texting. Stephen goes to bed much earlier because of work, but I'll stay up pretty late. Sometimes I have to say, 'OK, time for bed.'" – Julie Gaunce

It's not particularly unusual for parents to be the sounding board for young adults. In fact, as guardians, it's one of their primary duties.

In the Gaunces' case, it's not merely a 1-on-1 conversation between an adult and their kid.

For Julie and Stephen, taking in their sons' hockey games is equivalent to attending church for an evangelist. The watch and discuss routine is engrained in their everyday lives.

Ally is the same.

"To be honest, I have rarely missed a game," Ally says proudly when asked how often she manages to see Brendan play. "Nowadays, with him in Belleville, I miss a few. But when he was in Markham, I went to literally every single game."

When the Bulls are close by—in Brampton, Oshawa or Mississauga—Ally is the first one to pipe up and make travelling arrangements. She's also less covert than her parents, choosing to show off her pride a tad more.

"I'm into it, but to an extent. I don't want people knowing. I stay to myself but I'll cheer for Brendan or the Bulls when they do something well," she says, adding she'll wear a 'Brendan Gaunce' Belleville Bulls jersey on occasion.

Her house in Aurora with Jason is a bit of a Gaunce hockey museum. Jerseys, newspaper clippings, trophies—they've all found residence in the newlyweds' home.

As the lone girl on a street packed with hockey players growing up, 1987-born Ally was, by nature, a Tomboy. She was surrounded by testosterone, and it wore off.

"I was definitely not a girly-girl, that's for sure," she concludes.

A love for soccer kicked away her hockey passion. Although she played up until the major midget level in Markham, there wasn't much of a future in women's hockey.

And despite not being able to "shoot the puck whatsoever," Ally does have some hockey bragging rights within the close-knit five-pack family.

"She was the best skater out of the three of them," Stephen says, poking fun at the continuous knock on Cameron and Brendan's skating abilities.

He wasn't joking.

Ally takes pride in being the most fundamentally sound Gaunce skater, especially since she was never a figure skater.

"I think I just learned properly. From watching my brothers, I learned what not to do," she says in her dry sense of humour.

After attending Seneca College for early childhood education, the oldest of three siblings met eventual husband Jason. The two dated for a year-and-a-half before Jason, a native of Toronto, proposed.

The engagement passed by like a 108.8 miles per hour Zdeno Chara slapshot. The cancer diagnosis of her mother stunned Ally, but the wedding went on as planned.

Since the family was dragged through the ringer over the past month due to the cancer news, her special day forecasted to be a little less special than imagined.

On May 14, 2011, Jason and Ally tied the knot. Having triumphantly begun a new chapter, Ally was undoubtedly emotional from the moment she woke up.

The day's emotions gulped up every mundane feeling from years past. It was her time to be in the spotlight, her day of complete attention and exuberance.

Like all brides, the Big Day rollercoaster plunged down with a full head of steam towards the final stretch.

Walking up to the altar, with Stephen on her arm and Jason in plain sight straight ahead, she was nervy from head-to-toe. Then, as the about-to-be-wed couple began expressing vows to each other, a pair of teary-eyed young adults gripped Ally's emotion control panel.

"When we were saying our vows, I could see both of my brothers crying," Ally says while describing the scene in distinct detail. "That got me. Everybody else could have been crying and it wouldn't have bothered me, but when I saw my two little brothers start, that was it."

She cried out of pure happiness.

Everything was aligned. She was about to marry the love of her life, the wedding was perfect, and her family was every bit as inspired as she was.

During those intense moments, Brendan and Cameron shared a once-in-a-lifetime moment. They witnessed their sister marry, and shared the same reaction.

While that moment will be frozen in time forever, the boys' similarities are few and far between in the grand scheme of things.

From a distance, when discussing their on-ice attributes, the pair of Gaunce hockey players aren't complete opposites.

Buried below the supposed skating troubles, gritty style of play, resilient work ethic, sizable frames—etcetera—are two rather divergent personalities.

For starters, as Ally states, they have different subconscious approaches to everyday interaction.

"Cameron is extremely stubborn. When he wants something done, and he thinks he's correct, everybody else is wrong. Brendan, on the other hand, tries to please everybody. Brendan's more of a people person who tries to make people happy around him rather than taking care of himself first." – Ally Gaunce

Ask Julie and Stephen to size up their two sons and you'll hear another rendition of B vs. C.

As Stephen notes, Julie is the one to brand most evaluations.

"Mothers can tell that stuff, you know," he says, adding, "I'm in sales, so I'm the type to work the room instead of sitting back. That's like Cameron."

A tell-tale example of Cameron 'working the room' can be found on the Channel 5 News website. The Cleveland TV station gave the Lake Erie defenceman blogging room last season.

His posts usually focused on the past week's battles on the ice, but some Gaunce charm slid its way in. In his April 6, 2011, blog he opens up with quirky humour:

"Hey Monsters fans," the blog reads. "Welcome back my legions of fans (I never learned what 'legions' means, I'm pretty sure it means five or six)."

That Cameron agreed to write the occasional blog for a local media outlet in the first place speaks to his outgoing personality and willingness to throw an opinion out to the world.

"Cameron is very astute," Julie says, "very good at reading things and working the situation. He knows what to say, knows what's expected, and is very good at answering things. He's an amazing speaker."

This type of self-awareness boded well for the oldest Gaunce sibling when it was his turn to experience the draft year buzz. Slotted as a consensus mid-round choice in the 2008 NHL Entry Draft, Cameron's interviews with professional teams boosted his status going into draft day.

To say Brendan does not have an engaging personality as well would be silly. His presence is different than Cameron's, though, as his charm has been built off being an observer.

"He just learned the good traits of everybody and took them on himself," Ally says of Brendan.

And while they may not have noticed it until recently, Cameron was a crucial influence on Brendan's character during childhood.

"He can analyze things much better than Brendan," Julie says of Cameron. "But the thing is that Brendan listens to him. He is a naturally better athlete, but Cameron thinks the game better."

There's no denying that statement, Cameron says, with Brendan's excellence in hockey extending to other sports, such as track and field, volleyball, football and basketball.

"He's been good from the get-go while I've gone a different path," Cameron says, summing the comparison up in a simple sentence.

The Gaunces agonized over Cameron's post-minor midget route. An integral member of the Stamkos-led OHL Cup-winners, there was mounting interest in his services.

NCAA schools—such as Harvard University, University of Vermont, Ohio State University and Michigan State University—as well as OHL teams, put themselves out there for the burly rearguard.

"We weren't sure with Cameron," Stephen says. "We were honestly leaning more towards NCAA."

After tense family conversations and meetings with his agent, the Gaunces decided it was best for Cameron to play Tier-2 Junior A within the Waxers organization. This would let him sit on the OHL or NCAA decision, while wrapping up high school with his friends and still playing competitive hockey.

It's a common avenue for perplexed families. Their concerns mostly revolve around not moving too fast, and allowing the kid to decide for himself.

Although he had opted to play for the local Tier-2 squad, the St. Michael's Majors snapped up Cameron's OHL rights. This left the door open for next year.

"The situation at St. Mike's wasn't one I wanted to put myself into. They were coming off a losing season and were set for another. Plus, it was downtown in that small rink where there are different type of habits that creep into your game. I would have been the seventh or eighth defenceman to start the season, too, which I didn't think would help my development much. So, I thought living at home, continuing to go to the same high school, being comfortable and playing on a good Markham Waxer team was more beneficial." – Cameron Gaunce

Up until about a year ago, Cameron endured constant criticism pertaining to his skating abilities. Scouts and pundits used to hound his awkward technique for both the OHL and NHL drafts.

"Cameron was not a bad skater," his father argues. "Cameron was an awkward skater. He's deceiving. His coach Paul Titanic would get really angry: 'Cameron is fast, he's just not smooth.'"

Having cleaned up and refined his stride, the Colorado prospect is hardly ever condemned for his skating since leaving junior. He's fitting in fine, using his robust intensity and two-way play to climb the organization's depth chart.

Presently at 6-foot-1, 203 pounds, Cameron's frame isn't as bulky as his younger brother's. It never was.

"Brendan's built like my father," Julie says. "Cameron was never the big kid in the crowd. Brendan was always the biggest, always the broadest, and always the strongest."

If you were to plop Grade 5 Brendan next to Grade 5 Cameron, the former would tower over his elder brother.

Having a comparatively wider, more powerful frame didn't get him too far, however.

Brendan says the four-year difference made it tough for him to challenge Cameron because he was just that much more mature. One or two years isn't much in terms of keeping up, but four was insurmountable.

"I always wanted to prove I was better than him but that was only between us, no one else," Brendan says, remembering times of extreme competition in their yard growing up.

One-on-one basketball in the driveway, tennis in the street, soccer at a nearby field—name a sport and venue and they were there, ready to fight to the death.

"We'd get into arguments over this and that," Cameron adds, "mostly because we were somewhat close in age and both boys. There have been many incidents over lost video games over the years."

The feeling is mutual. Brendan knows the competition can evolve into something too heated at times, but they always have each other's backs.

"I think there's no holds bar too because we can be honest with each other. If I had a bad game, they'll let me know. Or, if I'm watching Cam with Ally and he makes a mistake I'll definitely text him after the game about it. But, I think we're just honest with each other and we're probably each other's hardest critics, too. It always helps because after you hear them talk about it—say you don't play as well as you should have—then when you hear other people talk about it's never as bad." – Brendan Gaunce

Aside from natural glitches, the Gaunces are all enjoying life, excelling in their given career paths.

They know right from wrong.

The way in which the kids handle criticism is revealing. They've been raised by top-flight parents who know the difference between humility and arrogance.

Far-flung siblings with similar ages (25, 22 and 18) don't always stay in touch, let alone communicate regularly. Some grow apart after the first one heads off to school, for instance, while others simply don't have an intense connection.

The Gaunces are as normal as any other middle class North American family. But, they tower over most in the loyalty department.

Don't think for a second that Cameron and Ally's evaluations of Brendan's play—their negative and positive one-offs—are ill-intended or cruelly rough. There will be the inevitable petty verbal spars from time to time, but that's about the only time they'll stray away from being a unit.

"I would do anything for Cameron and Ally," Brendan says, bluntly. "And I'm pretty sure they'd say the same thing."

2

BULLISH RISE

Everything is easier the second time around.

That's the way the Gaunce family was looking at a second go-around with the difficult task of deciding where their son should play hockey for the next 2-4 years.

NCAA or OHL?

Even though on the surface it appears to be a 'hockey decision,' parents of elite players know it's a multi-layered, multi-faceted determination that can greatly influence their child's future.

A million questions run through the mind as conversations begin sprouting up. Those same queries stick around, too, until the ultimate choice is made.

Would it be good to move into a dorm, meet new people, and live by themselves? Will they be too far away from home, feel home sick? Is the OHL's pro-like schedule a positive or negative, will he burn out or excel? What if he ends up getting drafted by a team in northern Ontario, so far away from home, and ends up struggling mightily? What if he hates the school or, loves the school life too much, that hockey takes a dip on the priority list?

What about this, what about that. What if, what if, what if.

Finally, a selection must be decided upon.

And, unlike his brother Cameron, weighing the options was never that stressful for Brendan Gaunce and family.

"I did have some interest in the NCAA," he says plainly, however careful to note his minor midget year was much less anxiety-filled than Cameron's. "But, I think, from seeing what Cam went through and how well the OHL accommodates players with schooling, it wasn't a tough decision for me. It was tougher for him."

From Julie and Stephen's perspective, it was the logical choice.

Here they had an ultra talented hockey playing son—second gifted enough son to potentially play the game for a living—who was level-headed enough to essentially decide on his own.

Of course they chimed in by offering conscientious advice, but ultimately they knew he wouldn't fail them. They knew Brendan was an observer of his brother's situation, carefully making mental notes on the pros and cons associated with each route.

Besides, a system was already established in regards to schooling, which let Brendan shift to college without any academic hick-ups.

With Michael Del Zotto as an example, the Gaunces offered Brendan a unique opportunity: You can either go to school in the summers or work in the summers.

In comparison to most of his peers, Brendan was blessed with a nice little advantage—the advantage of choice.

As most would in his situation, the male teen took school over work. His academic path was set.

In his third year with the Bulls in 2012-2013, Brendan plans on attending one of the finest post-secondary institutions in the country, Kingston's Queen's University.

After picking the OHL as his preferred destination, it looked like Brendan's life was fitting into a neat little box, with the overall picture of becoming a professional hockey player appearing more and more realistic. And the 'back-up plan,' one that has an emphasis on post-secondary education, was secured and armed with potential.

On the ice, he was finished putting a definitive stamp on the Markham Waxers minor hockey organization. He was the cornerstone of an OHL Cup-participating squad, guiding them from obscurity to the spotlight.

He grew from a tyke to a minor midget, both mentally and physically.

Zoom. Just like that.

He exhausted his accolades at the minor hockey level, the to-do list was running thin. He was matured past the AAA level in a number of ways—too dominant to strap on the gear, too mature to really find it super challenging.

Simply put, it was time for bigger and better things in Brendan's life.

The OHL awaited.

On May 1st, 2010, the first 'thing' to trump his past experiences was the OHL Priority Selection.

"I knew beforehand I was going to Belleville," Brendan says. "I remember I was in Belleville on the Friday, went out for dinner with the team executives, coaching staff. Then we went to the rink to introduce me to the media."

Suddenly, seemingly overnight, he was an vital member of the Belleville Bulls.

Approximately 190 kilometres east of Markham was his soon-to-be second home. He wouldn't call it home until months later, but the city already felt a breath of fresh air.

He wasn't going to toil with a Junior B, C, or D club, nor play a major midget year. He was selected as a top prospect, not a let's-see-how-he-develops-elsewhere pick.

The Bulls landed Brendan as the second overall choice.

The high selection was unlike all drafts following the 2004's first overall pick of John Hughes, as the Bulls have received nothing but middle-to-late round choices in recent years (eighth in 2005, ninth in 2006, 14th in 2007, 18th in 2009, 19th in 2008).

The organization was tight-lipped about their preferred No. 2 selection, keeping even the team's captain out of the loop until the last minute.

"I don't think I knew Brendan was headed to Belleville until the night before George confirmed it to me. He said Brendan will be our pick. He said he'll be a top line center not too far down the road. The expectations were obviously high as a second overall pick in the OHL, but he's definitely filled all of them, if not exceeded them." – Luke Judson

Brendan was Belleville's first blue-chip prospect in a half-decade. He was a badge of resurgence, a signal to the rest of the OHL that the Bulls could reach prominence sooner rather than later.

He was chosen behind Sarnia Sting forward and fellow 2012 NHL Entry Draft prospect Alex Galchenyuk.

Next in line was one of Brendan's close friends, Scott Laughton of the Toronto Marlboros, the newest Oshawa General.

All three went to rebuilding squads eager for a boost in enthusiasm and talent. Regardless of what was about to transpire in the coming seasons, May 1st was all about optimism, smiles and, most importantly, the players themselves.

Bulls head coach and general manager George Burnett, entering his seventh season at the helm in Belleville, knew what the organization needed, and found it in Brendan.

"Quite simply, we were following him very closely and we knew we were going to pick him at No. 2. We weren't exactly sure what was happening ahead of us, but we had a pretty good idea what Sarnia was going to do. We had a great meeting with the family, a follow-up with Brendan, and we watched him play through his playoff series with Whitby and Clarington, then of course the OHL Cup." – George Burnett

In 2009-10, the Bulls missed the playoffs for the first time on Burnett's watch.

They managed an abysmal 20-40-8 record, placing them last in the Eastern Conference at season's end.

However, in their trusty new forward, the Bulls, in Burnett's words, inherited a "confident," "mature," and "sincere" 16-year-old out of Markham.

Jake Grimes, an assistant coach with Belleville, didn't get out to the minor hockey rinks often over the course of the 2009-10 season. He didn't get the chance to really sink his teeth into the draft crop until the OHL Cup came around.

Going into the star-studded tournament blindly was not necessarily a terrible circumstance for Grimes because it gave certain players a chance to impress him on a fresh slate.

This meant he was able to come back with a different perspective than the dark horses of an OHL organization—the trusty scouts—and perhaps could meet halfway on verdicts.

That was the case with some prospects, but surely not Brendan, as Grimes and his comrades saw eye-to-eye on the prime product.

"At that point," the former Bulls player turned bench boss recalls, "he was the most intelligent player that we had seen."

Before the start of the calendar year of 2010, the Bulls scouting staff and Burnett were enthralled by the highest scoring minor midget player in the province.

While the second half of the season was still to be played, Belleville was already thinking of taking Brendan if the opportunity presented itself.
"I remember—before heading overseas for the world juniors—that I wanted to make it very clear to him that we wanted him. We kept it quite quiet since things can change, but it was very clear in our minds that he was the elite player available in the draft." – George Burnett

The rest of the first round—after Galchenyuk, Brendan, and Laughton—was a mish-mash of youngsters graduating from the Ontario Minor Hockey Association, Alliance Hockey, and Detroit-area teams.

As a 21-man unit, they've been relentless over their relatively short time in the OHL.

In 2010-11, each player's rookie season, they played an average of 55.8 games for their respective squads.

The top five were all left-handed centers and exactly half of the 20-player opening round were forwards.

Following the top three was a slew of players highly touted for the 2012 and 2013 NHL drafts, including the likes of Jarrod Maidens (Owen Sound Attack), Slater Koekkoek (Peterborough Petes), Sean Monahan (Ottawa 67's), and Matthew Finn (Guelph Storm).

Needless to say, the crop consisted of a deep collection of soon-to-be OHL regulars, as well as some high end, NHL-calibre talents.

From Belleville's point of view, Brendan was one of the leaders of 1994-born pack.

Shortly after being drafted, in an office tucked away from any form of chaos, Brendan sat down with an OHL cameraman to answer questions for an introductory video designed to promote the league's incoming elite.

Though understandably nervous, Brendan is genuine and raw in the footage. It's a fitting piece of knowledge for fans, scouts, and pundits.

"My name is Brendan Gaunce, and I am a new member of the Belleville Bulls. I play center," he says, seconds after a fade-into-action shot reveals the second selection of a 300-player draft class.

He's calm, but inwardly excited.

The initial dialogue streaming out of his mouth is descriptive, as if to notify fans of his potential presence on the ice as a newcomer.

About 20 seconds into the video, his trademark smirk emerges, switching his demeanour a the steely stare.

What does Brendan smirk about?

His competitiveness: "I have a will to win, and I do not like losing."

He continues for about three minutes, answering off-camera questions as the shots fade in and out. Among other subjects, he speaks of brother Cameron's role in his hockey life, Belleville's current position in the OHL hierarchy, closeness to friends within the draft class, and a chance at an OHL Cup title.

With 6,517 views on YouTube as of early August 2012, the video has evidently been well-watched.

Only two remarks were left in the comments section before NHL draft talk revved up late in Brendan's sophomore season.

They both remain. One is gibberish, and likely spam. The other, however, is telling. It reads "He's really good at doing interviews."

Seeing as he was a 15-year-old just a month-and-a-half prior to the taping, the commenter was right on target.

Brendan was articulate and mature already, aware that the media plays a considerable role in the machine that is major junior hockey.

Then, as if it never happened, off he went back to Markham for the summer with the anticipation of playing in the OHL stewing in his head over and over again.

***

As a city of around 50,000 people, Belleville is one of the smallest markets in the Ontario Hockey League.

Its club team has yet to win a Memorial Cup in its 20-year existence. They've participated in the tournament on two occasions, first in 1999 in Ottawa, and then nine years later in Kitchener.

The Bulls, coming into the 2011-12 season, were in the middle of a rebuild.

A three-year run from 2006 to 2009, in which they posted combined regular season winning percentage of .657, caught up to them. Like the majority of their OHL counterparts, those few years of glory are always balanced out by disappointment shortly thereafter.

In the early 1980s, the team struggled to keep its head above water, failing to recording an above-.500 regular season record until its fourth year as a member.

As the decade wore on, the cycle started up once again.

Marquee talents left the city for new adventures, hockey-related and otherwise, while the team swayed between second and sixth place in the east's Leyden Division.

The 1985-86 season was a beauty, however, as the 37-27-2 Bulls made their first trip to the league finals. They were downed by the Guelph Platers, eight points to four, in the finale series.

It was an end result that undoubtedly throbbed, but a remarkable feat for the young franchise nonetheless.

The next decade was one giant build-up, with their record—aside from a poor .386 winning percentage in 1996-97—improving from year to year.

They hit the 40-win mark for the second time in franchise history in a resurgent 1997-98 campaign. With a goal differential of plus-76, they were masterful in pursuing a first OHL title.

That dream turned into a nightmare when the underdog Plymouth Whalers upset Belleville in six games in the second round of the playoffs.

With the squad's core not getting younger, momentum reached a tipping point for the Lou Crawford-led Bulls. Entering the 1998-99 season, anything less than the J. Ross Robertson Cup—or an appearance in the OHL final—was considered a bust for Belleville's coach.

Only one other team in the entire league, the 104-point Barrie Colts, scored more goals than the Bulls in the regular season.

Leading scorer Justin Papineau, a Los Angeles Kings pick in the 1998 NHL draft, notched 99 points in 68 games to rank ninth amongst point producing peers. Calgary Flames draft selection Ryan Ready (92 points), current NHLer Jonathan Cheechoo (82), and another Kings draft pick, Kevin Baker (81), all recorded breakout numbers, too.

En route to a date with the London Knights in the OHL final, the Bulls, who claimed the No. 3 seed at season's end, swept the Sudbury Wolves, took down a dominant Ottawa 67's squad in five games, and finished off the Oshawa Generals in five.

In the final, history was made.

The Bulls were crowned OHL champions on the shoulders of playoff MVP Papineau (51 points in 21 playoff matches), and goaltender Cory Campbell, yet another Bulls player who became Kings property through the draft.

Off to the Ottawa-hosted Memorial Cup they went, ironically falling to the 67's—a team they disposed of in the OHL playoffs—in the tournament's semi-final.

Until the 2007-08 season, almost 10 years later, the Belleville fan base did not see action past the conference finals. It wasn't a massive stretch of time by any means, but long enough to worry some die-hard supporters.

Armed with a roster heavy on 19 year olds in 2007-08, the Bulls appeared to be a team of destiny yet again.

Present coach Burnett was in his fourth year as leader; P.K. Subban and Shawn Matthias looked primed to crack an NHL lineup before hitting overage status; netminder Mike Murphy collected his first of two OHL Goaltender of the Year honours; and trade deadline acquisitions added considerable depth for a long playoff run.

It was time to attack the OHL's elite, and perhaps run up the ranks.

They claimed the East Division banner for a second time in a string of three years. That year was their most impressive, however, registering a franchise record 102 points.

Like in 1999, Belleville demolished whoever stepped in their way en route the OHL final. It took only two games over the minimum to meet the Memorial Cup hosts, the Kitchener Rangers.

But, the Rangers weren't going to let the eastern victors roam free. Not only did Kitchener take the OHL championship in seven games, but they also finished ahead of Belleville in the Memorial Cup round-robin, then smashed them by a score of 9-0 in the semi-final.

Belleville made the national tournament an impressive two times in a nine-season span.

However, they only have one claim to fame to date: A 1998 OHL title.

When things are good in Belleville, more eyes than usual are drawn to the centre of the Bay of Quinte Region. When things aren't running so smoothly, it's easy for an at-large OHL fan to pay little attention to the Bulls.

It's a market that does not garner elaboration, unless prompted by a big time event or particularly strong squad.

For that reason, a player can get lost in the sort of 'anti-hoopla' associated with the eastern Ontario hockey town often overshadowed by sexier nearby OHL centres such as Oshawa and Ottawa.

The relative mediocrity of the franchise's on-ice product since their last real kick at the can in 2008-09 doesn't help a player get noticed by the mainstream like someone residing in Windsor may, for instance.

This under-the-radar type of situation in Belleville has likely never burdened Brendan from a scouting perspective but, as a whole, probably hasn't helped raise his overall profile either.

The list of Belleville Bulls who have made it to the National Hockey League is not as expansive as some of the league's prospect factories—the Kitcheners, Londons, Peterboroughs, etc.—of the province's major junior loop.

In terms of reaching higher ground, about 60 Bulls alumni have made it to The Show, which is impressive for an organization established two decades ago.

Each has etched their way there in a different way. Still, the end-goal remains the same no matter who is strapping on black and yellow. There's a handful of present NHLers—David Clarkson, Kyle Wellwood, Daniel Cleary, P.K. Subban, Jonathan Cheechoo, a few others—who breathe hope into the brethren that currently man the franchise's roster spots.

They represent the what could be and the what I ultimately want to be even though their playing styles, hometowns, and ethnicity vary.

Playing in the NHL is a privilege, and most 16-20-year-old's know that. Including the Belleville Bulls.

They're keen on taking that next step in their hockey career, but also know the guy next to them wants to accelerate just as much—and maybe even more—than they do. So, it's a constant battle.

They're itching for ice time but ready to show their character, their sacrifice for the greater good, if ice doesn't come their way on a given evening.

At the same time, the maturity level of a high school undergraduate, or recent grad in some cases, is not picture perfect for certain situations. There's a vast array of personality profiles on a hockey team, and this dynamic creates an environment prone to dissipation or prosperity.

The key for OHL general managers and coaches is to create balance within the locker room. Personalities need to be kept in line at all times, ensuring the overall product dressed each night is concentrated on the task at hand.

And while there is an endless list of potential profiles to thumb through, some prominent ones emerge on almost every single team.

There's the quiet guy: The lead-by-example phenom whose hockey instincts and gentle charisma blend well. He's the one who everybody likes because he doesn't step on anyone's toes.

Or, the upbeat, raw-raw type: The in-your-face veteran that seemingly pounds back a Red Bull energy drink prior to every pre-game pep talk. He steps on a toe, figuratively and literally, from time to time.

Others, they're 'wise beyond their years,' as the saying goes. Instead of following, they take it upon themselves to do the opposite, which is lead. Forget the nagging, the complaining—they're here to play. They're focused, and know what it takes to be successful on both an individual level and as a collective.

Each OHL roster can be picked apart and analyzed for hours on end. The 2011-12 Bulls are no exception.

Which brings us to Brendan Gaunce: A teenager who is tough to strictly categorize.

From the etched out profiles described above, some would slot Brendan in the 'quiet guy' position, which is a fair assessment. Then again, he's not withdrawn or anything along those lines.

He's a warrior in-play, but a soft-spoken, kind individual away from the rink. He's aware of the above-average skills he possess on offence, yet is just as mindful of the defensive end.

He's a prospect NHL teams were torn on all year.

Not because he was inconsistent, but because it's difficult to really pin-point what his true potential is as a forward.

The character is there, and there's little resistance to that notion. People tend to enjoy his presence, whether it's laid back Brendan or a more outgoing, get-up-and-go Brendan.

The volatility of his personality and playing ability is downright intriguing.

What most agree on, though, is that the guy is ahead of the learning curve in terms of mental maturity, physical size, defensive awareness, and shooting.

That's the consensus.

And Belleville, as an organization, hopes of the above qualities —and more—continue to impress.

Before the first game of the 2011-12 regular season, a September 23rd road contest versus the Ottawa 67's, Brendan weighed in at 6-foot-2, 212 pounds as a 17-year-old.

A rookie the year prior, he had just come off intense off-season workouts with former NHLer Gary Roberts, and participated in the Ivan Hlinka.

A few exhibition games set the table for the determined, bullish centre.

Unbeknownst to Brendan, it was time to press a letter upon his chest, time to acknowledge the organization's trust in the potential first round pick in the upcoming draft.

They needed to recognize his absolute importance to the rebuild following their last Memorial Cup run, and emphasize his responsibilities moving forward.

"Before our first league game, coach brought in four sweaters with letters on them. He had them wrapped up and then gave them out one-by-one. He started with our captain, which we all knew would be Luke Judson, then he went with Stephen Silas, our assistant captain last year, then he handed out Brady Austin's, and mine last. It was a pretty cool feeling, just to get it in front of everyone who picked it. Obviously I feel it's a great honour and I'm going to try my best to lead them." – Brendan Gaunce

There he was, sitting there with a brand new Brendan Gaunce Bulls sweater customized for the upcoming season. It was the very first moment he was recognized as a true leader of the squad.

But wait.

Was he ready for the challenge? Could he channel his inner Mark Messier?

In his freshmen season, Gaunce would have been overwhelmed by the assignment of being one of four captains on the squad. It would have been like a bolder weighing on his shoulders.

Stitch a letter on a rookie's sweater? Forget it.

At the start of his sophomore training camp, though, he was mentally prepared to counter the boulder.

He was a year wiser and a whole lot more comfortable as a Bull. "Before I got the 'A', one of my goals this year was to be a better leader. As a rookie you can kind of say stuff but you could be stepping on guys' toes because you're only 16 while some guys are 20 years old. And, if you're trying to give them advice, it's a little awkward on your end, just because you don't know how they're going to take it. It's kind of like your younger brother giving you advice, which no one likes. I was planning on being a better leader this year. The letter on my jersey just adds some motivation." – Brendan Gaunce

Leaders serve a monumental purpose on a hockey team.

Through jubilant, mediocre, average, and trying times, a leader is always cautious, constantly aware of the situation's true relevance.

Instead of getting caught up in a longer-than-expected winning streak—putting in a lacklustre effort in practice, for example—a leader trains harder than ever before. Most times, they don't feel highs or lows because their emotions remain stagnant from start to finish.

For Bulls assistant coach Grimes, there's a sparkling moment when Brendan showed his worth as one of the emerging leaders within the organization, and the league.

"I remember towards the end of that span, Burnett called for somebody to step up." he says of the awful hockey Belleville displayed from a period starting in early December 2011 and finally ending in late January 2012. "And he did. He stepped up and had an incredible third period. He kept it going for a couple of games after, too, because he's the type of guy who can do that."

The 'incredible third period' Grimes is referring to occurred on home ice against the Sarnia Sting on January 28th.

The inter-conference foes met only once prior—a 4-3 shootout win for Belleville in which Brendan scored in the shootout and picked up a pair of assists—to the winter match-up.

After six straight defeats and only one win in their last 12 contests, the Bulls were absolutely desperate for a victory. It didn't matter how it came, they would be happy with two in any fashion.

Trailing by a goal heading into the final frame, Brendan took matters into his own hands. A mere 32 seconds in, he fired a laser beam of a shot from just inside the Sting blueline. It handcuffed Sarnia goaltender J.P. Anderson, clanking a post before hitting mesh.

The teams traded markers to make it 4-4 at the end of regulation. Brendan pitched in defensively down the stretch, as per usual, and led the charge in the physicality department.

Overtime solved nothing, so a shootout finish was in line.

Jordan Mayer biffed on Belleville's first shot at glory, while Craig Hottot made no mistake for the visitors. Sting forward Nail Yakupov was then denied by Belleville's Charlie Graham.

Brendan was up next.

Exerting a certain quiet confidence, he came in on Anderson right down the middle of the ice with little speed. At the hash marks, without a hint of trickery or flare, Brendan sniped top corner.

A Joseph Cramarossa goal later, the Bulls were victorious. The two Markham natives stole the win right out from underneath the Sting's nose.

It effectively marked the end of a terrible, terrible losing skid for Belleville, and Brendan was an instrumental component in the halting process.

Grimes was pleased with more than pleased with the performance. He was truly coming into his own as a principal piece of the Bulls puzzle.

"I think he's definitely a role model for a lot of guys—young and old—based on the fact that ever since we met him he's carried himself without being cocky in any way. He's carried himself as a player, through thick and thin, who will play in the National Hockey League. And, you just know it. He knows he is, but he doesn't act like he is. He just persists in a way that no matter how hard things get he never gets down." – Jake Grimes

Theodore M. Hesburgh, the infamous past president of the University of Notre Dame, once said, "The very essence of leadership is that you have to have vision. You can't blow an uncertain trumpet."

Generally speaking, there's nothing really offsetting about Brendan. He rarely exerts form of nervousness, fear, or hesitation.

If his demeanour were a heartbeat, it wouldn't jolt high in pressure situations or dip low in relaxation.

He's a rock, for the most part. In a good way, of course.

It's part of the reason why, from his minor hockey days onwards, Brendan has been leaned upon in the leadership department. There hasn't been a single season when his coach doesn't consider him one of the squad's integral constituents, on the ice and in the dressing room.

Although the majority of his OHL peers can hold the same claim up until hitting the major junior ranks, only a select few can proudly say they walked into the dressing room of a team in of the best developmental leagues in the world for the first time and was welcomed as a leader already.

The assemblage of Bulls veterans have embraced the second overall choice in the 2010 OHL draft since his arrival in Belleville.

"First things first, he brings leadership. He has since Day 1. And even though he's a second-year guy now, he acts like a fourth-year guy. Not in terms of talking to us, more so in leading-by-example. When something needs to be said he'll say it but other than that it's his performance on the ice. He already acts so professional. We're still teenagers and joke around, but he's mature and always doing something that will make him better." – Luke Judson

The intangible attributes have always been there, right next to the tangible ones. While Brendan ripped up the province's best defences as a kid, he still paid attention to what was happening around him. He didn't zone into his own success.

There was a sense of pride building inside him that would eventually become second nature.

He consciously decided that being there for his teammates was just as important as excelling on an individual level.

Childhood best friend Pantaleo, for example, might not possess the same innate hockey playing abilities, but there was no way Brendan could accomplish anything on his own

"I think most guys like to have the pressure on them, although they might not all admit it," Brendan says. "That's how you become a leader and I think this year the bounces seem to be going my way and the confidence seems to be going up with it."

When Brendan glides up to the faceoff circle, with his torso and head hunched over—ready for an all-important draw with 30 seconds left in the game—there's nothing that can breach his attentiveness.

When he steps onto the ice for the first time in a few days, an immediate feeling of concentration overcomes everything else. He doesn't like missing a beat, at any time.

As a team-sport athlete, it's extremely comforting to look across the dressing room and see a guy who is so in tune with the task at hand that it instantly has a positive effect on your own ability to focus.

You know that leader sitting 10 feet away isn't worried about what happened at school earlier in the day. He also isn't concerned with other problems in his life, relationship issues and whatnot.

There's only one thing on his mind: Hockey.

"He knows when it's time to get down to business and when it's time to joke around," Judson says of Brendan.

A further area of expertise for most successful leaders is how they act away from all of the chaos.

It's one thing to stand up in front of a group of your peers and perform an uplifting speech or score when it counts. It's another to be parallel—the same guy everyone looks up to—away from tense moments.

"He sets the tone all the time," Judson continues. "He knows that on the bus after a loss if we're talking too loud or having too much fun that we need to settle down."

On February 29th, 2012, after a 4-1 victory, Brendan displayed a hint of that tone-setting quality.

At 30-29-1-0, and with a crucial contest versus Mississauga two days away, Belleville was in an interesting position. They hadn't played as many games as the majority of the Eastern Conference, which gave them a slight edge down the stretch.

"There's two ways you can look at having games in hand," Brendan says, "you waste them, or take advantage of the opportunity. We're going in with the mentality that we have the upper hand right now, because it's really in our hands."

It turns out they decided to choose option B, taking down the Majors 4-2. Fittingly, Brendan contributed by assisting on Zharkov's goal, the first of the game. He finished a plus-2 in the vital late-season tilt.

The relatively young leader that he is, Brendan knows he isn't leaned on to carry the entire load. His comrades—Judson, Payerl, Silas—were all considered valiant officers to the Bulls group of foot soldiers.

"Luke, being our captain, is definitely the main leader-by-example. He probably works harder than anyone on our team, maybe in the league," Brendan notes.

From brushes with greatness (2007-08) to knee scrapes from nearly hitting rock bottom (2011), the pride of Emo, Ontario, saw it all in a Bulls uniform. His versatility as a hard-nosed yet skilled player worked wonders for his ability to lead.

Whispers out of Belleville suggest Brendan is next in line to the throne as Judson enters the post-OHL life. He may be the one receiving the torch in the fall.

Questions will inevitably be raised if Brendan is indeed appointed captain of the Bulls. They won't necessarily come because he doesn't deserve it—more so because he'll have large skates to fill.

Judson is a bit of a god in Bulls country, so the next captain's credentials will be questioned regardless.

In training camp, Brendan will have played total of 133 regular season and 10 playoff games in the OHL.

Over that time, he has accumulated 107 points, which averages out to recording about a point in every three out of four games.

Of his 40 total snipes, four have been game-winners while 30 per cent have come on special teams.

But those are just numbers, right?

A leader has to have balls—they have to be stern and willing to ruffle a few feathers. They can't be passive or cute, seeing as no true leader cares more about impressing an audience than performing for the greater good.

A leader also buys in 100 per cent—no ifs, ands, or buts. They don't debate the coaching staff's strategies unless its merited.

A leader is, by and large, Mr. Respect.

They absolutely have to possess a strong sense of respect for not only the game of hockey, but themselves, their teammates, fans, and staff.

They can be flashy or of the no-frills variety—it doesn't make a difference. Appearance isn't really a topic of conversation in the leadership think pool. Especially at the major junior level.

What matters is what's between the ears.

The brain of a leader must be fully functioning, completely aware, and unwilling to roll over when told to sit.

Leaders usually exert a distinct sense of quality, in really being a cut above the rest. They're not arrogant, but they're also far from unconfident.

"If you want to be a leader, you can't be afraid to say something. We're not 10 years old anymore. If it's in the hockey rink, I think guys understand that you have a certain competitiveness to win. What's said in the dressing room has nothing to do with how you act outside of the rink. If you get called out, guys are just trying to get more out of you." – Brendan Gaunce

***

The typical athletic male teenager living in Canada fawns over the notion of being able to participate in a sport at such a high level as the OHL.

While the 68-game schedule can take its toll on players—emotionally, mentally, and physically—the trade-off is pretty unbelievable.

Certain markets, such as Kitchener, Ottawa, and London, draw more than 6,000 spectators to the rink to the majority of their 34 home games throughout a campaign.

It's big business.

Having the opportunity to be the center of attention in front of thousands of patrons is unquestionably special. The brand of the CHL has grown exponentially, and the youngsters lacing up each night are the ones to thank.

They're also the ones to be thankful.

Former OHLers are often quoted in media saying things like, 'It all passes in a blink of the eye. I tell guys playing in the league now to cherish it.'

Four years can feel like a lifetime when you're 16-20 years old. But when that time has passed, most reflect on their time in a positive light.

Whether aspirations of making the NHL are realistic or not, the battles on the ice and the thrills off it are pretty unforgettable.

Even after Brendan Gaunce's freshman season in major junior hockey, he was grateful for the desirable situation he found himself in. "There were mixed emotions last year. We obviously wanted to make the playoffs, but we were facing Mississauga. It was good to make the playoffs, tough to go home, but there was always that thing in the back of your mind. Most of the guys don't admit to it, but you go home and the lifestyle is a lot different. You realize that being in Belleville and being able to play hockey every day is a lot better than what normal kids do. You take it for granted when you're here." – Brendan Gaunce

Despite admitting it was nice to get some extra rest before really digging into his summer workout routine, there's no chance in hell Brendan would have preferred to be in Markham if it meant the Bulls were booted from the playoffs so quickly.

The Bulls really didn't deserve to make the post-season in the first place, as they finished the regular season with a .338 winning percentage. They weren't the most deserving No. 8 seed in OHL history, that's for sure.

Since the Mississauga St. Michael's Majors were hosting the 2011 Memorial Cup, their ticket in the national championship was already punched. This gave Belleville a slight edge.

It was better to face-off against a team that knew their destiny than one fighting for its life.

On paper, the Bulls didn't look on par with the Majors—up front, on the blueline, or in net.

The only real advantage was that the Bulls weren't supposed to be where they were—in the playoffs—and Mississauga was forced to fight off the temptation of looking ahead.

Alas, nothing came of it.

The 108-point Majors allowed just a single goal in a four-game sweep.

Mississauga goaltender J.P. Anderson stopped 17, 21, 19, and 21 shots, respectively. With the low shot totals, the San Jose Sharks prospect wasn't tested much but he still pulled off three straight shutouts.

Austen Brassard was the lone Belleville player to solve right-hand catching Anderson, scoring a second period goal in Game 1.

Brendan was held off the scoresheet altogether, unable to contribute when his team needed him the most.

Keep in mind his role as a 1994-born rookie was fairly limited. He didn't get the power-play, penalty kill, and dying minutes ice that he would become accustomed to as a sophomore in the 2011-12 season.

When you dissect Brendan's first season, there's one portion of his debut that can be circled in red.

It's not his bullet of a shot over the shoulder of Kingston Frontenacs goaltender Philipp Grubauer for his first OHL goal. It's not the four-assist outburst in Game 2 of the regular season either.

It's what followed. Brendan went pointless for most of October.

Aside from a two-point effort on the 1st, and a three points in two games blip before the first full month of OHL action concluded, he was virtually invisible in the box scores.

In the 11 other games in October, the prominent point producer in minor midget was silenced. He recorded zero points, eight penalty minutes, and a minus-6 rating.

"Last year, I think he had to deal with a lot of adversity. I don't think he had the start to the season he wanted but he's been able to battle through it and work hard. A lot of people would have shied away from the situation, but he didn't. I think that showed his character a little bit." – Cameron Gaunce

The 6-foot-2, 207-pounder was the size of a man who owned an impressive tool belt of skills. But, that didn't mean major junior hockey was going to be a breeze.

He didn't enter the OHL as a long shot or a gamble by Belleville. The leading scorer in minor midget the year prior was supposed to be there.

However, the growing pains were evident, especially in the offensive end. The transition from being a dominant first line centre in the OMHA to a top six pivot in the OHL was gigantic.

Unsurprisingly, as the 2010-11 regular season wore on, Brendan's confidence and contributions to the beleaguered club rose substantially.

The first few months were spent in the trenches, battling for every square inch of ice as a 16-year-old in a 19-year-old's league. The adjustment period is necessary to most.

Sarnia Sting playmaker Alex Galchenyuk was one of a select few from the 2010 OHL Priority Selection class to come flying out of the gate. The crafty Russian-American notched 17 points to Brendan's nine by the end of October.

"Brendan had a very solid year, most of the time playing against the team's top line," Bellville's general manager and head coach George Burnett says of his rookie season, in hindsight. "A lot of times 16's come in and play on the third or fourth line. He was thrown into the fire."

It's not great for the confidence when your teammates are struggling, too.

The Bulls were downright awful at points during their 30th season in franchise history, losing 8-0 to the Kitchener Rangers on November 5th; 6-0 to the Erie Otters on November 25th; 10-2 to the Windsor Spitfires on January 15th; and then 7-0 to the Sault Ste. Marie Greyhounds on January 29th.

The common denominator in all of those lopsided affairs was a lack of offensive punch.

At the end of the regular season, Brendan and his teammates endured 25 losses in which they scored just a single goal or less. They were shutout eight of those times.

Prior to the 2010-11 season, the Bulls didn't appear to have what it took hang out with the best in the Eastern Conference. And they didn't surprise anyone.

In terms of the rebuilding year's affect on Brendan, it was probably a more beneficial environment than most would think.

Here he was, a young buck on the OHL scene. Playing on a struggling, middling team like Belleville allowed him to work out the kinks without getting tangled up in the numbers game.

If he were on a team of greater quality and saw his ice time reduced to a fourth line role, the Brendan of today might be slightly different.

The reality of the situation was that the franchise who drafted him really needed his help and, fortunately for Brendan, also had some help to provide as well.

Burnett, assistant general manager Barclay Branch, as well as assistant coaches Jake Grimes and Jason Supryka, comprise a commendable staff in which Brendan can seek advice from.

After some seasoning to begin the year, Brendan harnessed an assigned role as one of the squad's go-to penalty killers. Although they finished 16th in a 20-team league with a 76.7 percent kill rate, the Bulls still made strides when a man-down.

Like the vast majority of his rookie peers, the initial fine-tuning eventually transformed into real results.

In the second half of his 65-game debut, Brendan registered 19 points. It trumped his first half by just a pair of points, but there was far more consistency towards the end.

For instance, following Christmas break he held down a five-game point streak, when his longest beforehand was two.

After the Majors—the eventual Memorial Cup finalists—swept the significantly below-.500 Bulls, Brendan and his teammates were left with only a few more team events before summer vacation.

One in particular, their annual awards banquet, emphasized the well-rounded value Brendan brought to the organization.

He was honoured with the co-Rookie of the Year award (shared with Subban) and Bobby Smith Award for on-ice and classroom performance. In addition, Brendan made the All-Academic Team along with Michael Curtis, Alex Basso, Dylan Corson, Adam Bignell, Scott Simmonds, and Braeden Corbeth.

Captain Luke Judson, naturally, cleaned up in the hardware department, taking home the Don Foster Award for MVP, George MacIntyre Memorial Trophy for outstanding forward, and Jake Gilmour Award for fan favourite.

It was a benchmark year for Judson, one he couldn't duplicate in 2011-12. In the same amount of games but with a weaker supporting cast, the 1991-born Bull potted a career-high 56 points.

He led the team in a number of offensive categories, yet didn't have an innate knack for the net like an elite scorer does.

It was either a demonstration of Judson breaking out and showing his true colours, or a sign of the times in Belleville. Whatever the reason, the team's captain didn't produce at the same rate in 2011-12.

Brendan, who would indubitably shoulder more of the load in the subsequent season, knew the pressure was on him to produce more than 11 goals and 25 assists for 36 points in 65 games.

And with a bit of a revamped roster, he expected improvements from the entire team.

"This year, we have a lot more depth. And the confidence in ourselves is the big thing, having an extra year under our belt. Last year we thought, 'Oh, if we keep it close, or if we lose by one, then we're happy,' but it's not like that this year." – Brendan Gaunce

Even though they started the regular season off with a 2-1 defeat at the hands of the Ottawa 67's, little to no optimism was lost inside the dressing room.

Last year's Bulls might have rolled over and allowed Ottawa to trample over them like a dead carcass. The loss was, in an odd way, reassuring, Brendan said.

One important moment absent from Brendan's first year as a Bull was scoring a game-winning goal. Capturing the game-winner token early on in his second season would truly set the tone, he thought.

A 4-3 win over the Sault Ste. Marie Greyhounds in the home opener was a splendid way to recover.

The next weekend the squad saw almost identical results.

One-goal loss Friday, one-goal win Saturday. The only difference this time was that both took place inside Yardmen Arena.

"At home, I think I was more excited than anything because our fans hadn't seen our team yet this year and I knew this year we were going to be improved. I think we showed it, beating Oshawa at home. It was a great feeling." – Brendan Gaunce

The 2011-12 season was on. A solid crowd of 2,684 attended the kick-off at home.

There were 66 games to be played, though—a long season on the horizon.

The Lion's share of the matches remaining in Belleville's season were spent teeter tottering between being an average or subpar squad.

But, how about the ups, the times when the Bulls looked like a legitimate contender? Or, when Brendan appeared to be an unstoppable force?

How were they achieved? What did they feel like? Were they more impactful on him than the low points? What stuck out about particularly successful games? What made Brendan tick, make it through the season without any dramatic drop offs?

Let's let Brendan's own words answer those questions.

— Date of conversation: October 29th
— Team record: 7 wins-7 losses-0 overtime losses
— Brendan's statistics: 4 goals-4 assists-8 points
  o <u>5-3 win over Barrie on Oct. 26th</u>
    "With Subban going down, Chartrand has really stepped up his
    game and Wednesday night was no different. He's showing why
    he should be a starter in this league. We're working well as a
    team right now, too. We scored five goals and kept them to three
    so we're pretty happy about that."
  o <u>Game-winning goal in same game</u>
    "I went to the front of the net, a rebound came out and I batted it
    in. I guess I was in the right spot at the right time."
  o <u>Facing the Petes on Oct. 29 for the second time in young season</u>
    "I don't think there's been any extra fuel to the fire yet when
    playing the Petes. But, we play each other eight times a year and
    they're big divisional rivals. We're both improving teams so I
    think the first two games have been pretty good and tonight I'm
    expecting the same."

— Date: November 6th
— Record: 10-7-0
— Stats: 7-5-12
  o <u>1-0 loss to Mississauga on Nov. 6th</u>
    "We're not scoring as many goals as we want to, but our defence
    and Malcolm Subban are playing so well right now. We played
    more defensively-minded tonight because of the 3-in-3 this
    week. We still got 30 shots. J.P. (Anderson) played well, he stole
    the show."
  o <u>Riding the Bulls bus</u>
    "This weekend was a bit different with the bus. There were less
    guys on it because some went home with their families. When
    we're altogether though, and winning, the lights are on, guys are
    jumping from seat to seat. It's an awesome feeling."
  o <u>Overall thoughts 17 games in</u>
    "Right now, if we were to look back on the season, we'd be
    pretty happy with ourselves. The early games hurt us but we're
    pretty happy with the standings, being third or fourth in the
    conference."

— Date: Nov. 13th
— Record: 12-7-0
— Stats: 8-6-14
  o <u>2-1 win over Oshawa on Nov. 13th</u>

"The atmosphere on the bus right now is pretty cool. They said we haven't won five in a row in three years. It's what you dream of as a hockey player, being on the bus with the guys after, looking back on the game after winning another in a row."

o   Shootout miss in same game

"I'm pretty confident in myself in shootouts just because I know I do have a good enough shot to fool the goalie, and you have to come into the shootout being confident in yourself. If you come in with a little bit of doubt, I don't think you're going to be able to score because the goalies are always coming out, really challenging you. Today, I should have scored. I missed the net but luckily Malcolm played a great game and Shawzie—local Belleville guy Jason Shaw—got the winner. He's pretty excited right now."

o   Taking care of their own end

"I think our defensive play has really stepped up this year. And obviously our goaltending, with Subban and Chartrand, is one of the best tandems in the league. We really look at our defence and goaltending as big factors in our wins because we aren't scoring as many goals as other teams. We're getting those wins at 2-0 and 2-1, and I think we're putting a lot of pressure on our defence but they stepped up these past five games."

o   Making some noise in the east

"We came in this year knowing we had the talent to be at the top of our division and we're showing people now. We've heard many things from the media that our team is not good enough this year and that it is another rebuilding year, but we have the confidence and optimism in our room to show people who we really are and we're doing that right now."

— Date: Nov. 20th
— Record: 13-9-0
— Stats: 9-8-17

   o   6-3 win over Peterborough on Nov. 16th

"Wednesday was a big game for our team. Mainly because Peterborough is so close to us in the standings. Being able to contribute in such a big way in that game is good for my confidence and for the team in general."

— Date: Nov. 27th
— Record: 16-9-0
— Stats: 14-9-23

   o   Getting into a groove as a team

"We're showing everyone that we can be one of the better teams in our conference, in the OHL. And I think I'm just a beneficiary of our team's success right now."

- o Injury bug staying away
  "We set goals for our whole team that we wanted to be in the top four, top five by the end of the season. At the start of the year we were having our problems, a lot of injuries and weren't really clicking that well. We have had our full roster lately, though—knock on wood—and I think our team is coming together pretty well right now."

— Date: December 4th
— Record: 19-9-0
— Stats: 15-13-28

- o 8-1 win over Kingston on Dec. 2nd
  "That game was pretty big for our organization because it was our coach's 500th win and our team's 1000th win so it was kind of ironic. As of late, I think we've found our scoring touch. People were saying that coming into the season, that we couldn't score. I think we're kind of showing everyone that we know how to score. Before we were playing more of defensive system."

- o Battling the tolls of a three-in-three
  "I don't think it's hard to get up for them, but by the third game you're definitely feeling the effects of the first two. It's a lot harder on the road. You have to kind of get into the mentality that you have to get to bed on time when you're on the road and plan your day as you would when you're at home and in your own bed. You have to go in there with the same focus as a home game."

— Date: January 15th
— Record: 22-29-1
— Stats: 21-23-44

- o Team picks up familiar face at trade deadline
  "Joseph played with my brother in Mississauga, and he's from Markham. Before coming to Belleville I knew him to say 'hi,' but not on a personal level. He's obviously a highly skilled player. I think he has transitioned his game a lot since joining the league. He's worked on all facets of his game, become more physical. He can play the skilled game and the power forward game."

— Date: February 6th
— Record: 24-24-1

— Stats: 22-25-47
  o 6-3 win over Kitchener on Feb. 3rd
    "That was one of our best games since Christmas break. I don't
    know if Malcolm was necessarily the reason, but he came back
    and the confidence we have in him gave us a big boost. I think I
    played one of my better games. I thought I played really well."
  o Playing on the small surface
    "When we go into small rinks, we don't adjust fast enough to the
    different style of play. As the game progressed, we got better and
    better but didn't start soon enough. For us, I think we have the
    most difficult time out of anyone in the league coming into
    smaller rinks. We practice in a big rink, and the whole game is
    based around it. The rinks like Peterborough, Niagara, Owen
    Sound. are so condensed that everything has to be a lot quicker."
  o Special teams out of sync
    "I think our penalty kill is one of the better ones in the league,
    we take pride in both of our special teams. Right now, we're not
    finding chemistry on the power-play. Nothing seems to be
    working at all. It's not even that we need a ton of goals on the
    power-play, we just need game-changing goals. I think the
    power-play is one thing I need to work on. It's such a huge
    momentum shift when you can get one."
  o Ready for what's next
    "We have the mentality right now that the Feb. 10/11 weekend is
    the biggest of the year. If we win three games this weekend, we
    could be up to fifth or sixth in the conference. We're going to
    come in with the mentality that we can win all three games, and
    that we will win all three games."

— Date: Feb. 14th
— Record: 26-25-1
— Stats: 24-27-51
  o Remembering short-handed goal on Feb. 14th
    "I was in on a breakaway against Igor Bobkov. We were told he
    is really good high, so I shot low-pad. He stopped that then I had
    a rebound, and he stopped that, too. I was behind the net and
    pissed off I hadn't scored so I just shot it on net. It hit off his butt
    when he was sitting down and it went in."

— Date: Feb. 29th
— Record: 30-29-1
— Stats: 27-35-62
  o 4-3 loss to Peterborough on Feb. 26th

"We were obviously happy we won those games, but our attitude going into Peterborough was the same way as always. They play well in their own rink and it's a big difference from ours. We went in and figured it's basically a pinball arena. I don't think we played as well as a team as we should have."

o Reliving 25th goal of season in same game
"It was a relief to score it at a good time, too. I think it was 1-0, and I've hit about 8-10 posts in the last 5-6 games. It was good to get one in the net when I actually fanned on it. I came down before and tried to go blocker side but I missed the net. I went blocker side again. I don't know if I actually fanned on it, but it stayed on the ground and the goalie didn't see it."

— Date: March 5th
— Record: 31-30-1
— Stats: 27-37-64

o Reflecting on the positives
"I think we showed how good our team is in November when we went on that 12-2 run. We do have all the tools to go far in the playoffs and upset someone. Especially with Malcolm in net. Even though he's had a couple of rough weeks, he's still one of the best goalies in the OHL. We can upset any team, and I think that's how we're all looking at it in our room. We can't let outside negativity affect us, especially this late in the season."

o Hoping to carry February vibes into March
"I don't know if I'm coming in more prepared or anything. I think we've just gotten off to solid starts. We were hitting posts early on before, but they're going in now. It's not just us, it's our team in general. We're feeding off hot starts."

— Date: Mar. 21st
— Record: 35-32-1
— Stats: 28-40-68

o Showing his feet can move
"I was racing against Christian Thomas short-handed. He and the goalie were giving mixed signals as to who would get the puck, so I just hustled and put it short side high. I came down and didn't see much to shoot for, so I went five-hole. The puck slide through his legs but hit the post. It was a really weird thing. I could see it sliding by him and he didn't even notice. I was so mad, it was going so slow. I wish I could have went and hit it."

o Capping the regular season off right

"I thought I had a good last three games. Sudbury was one of my better games of the year. My legs felt good, and overall it was a good time to spurt. I had that little dry streak but everything seems to be working for us right now."

***

If Brendan Gaunce has a soft spot for anything, it's probably the sport of football.

During its season, Sundays without hockey and mounds of homework are wholeheartedly reserved for the gridiron game.

Sit back, relax, forget about the world. Don't worry about all that other stuff—it's for later.

In the National Football League, the Baltimore Ravens are his club.

Ray Lewis, and all the junkyard dog defender that he is, sticks out to the former high school player. He's Brendan's Brendan Shanahan of football, his go-to guy.

As a youngster, Brendan not only pretended he was a street hockey version of former NHL netminder John Vanbiesbrouck. In games involving the pigskin, the kid they called 'B' wore a Lewis jersey with pride.

One thing Brendan admires about No. 52 for the Ravens is his durability.

Lewis, a future Hall of Famer, has only sustained two major injuries over his 222-game career. That's an admirable feat when you consider how many blowing hits a linebacker gives and receives over the course of a season, let alone a 16-year career.

In the 2011-12 campaign, Brendan did not miss a single contest.

He played all 68 games of the regular season and an additional six in the playoffs. As a player who doesn't shy away from physical contact, that's quite remarkable.

You could say it's Lewis-like, even.

"Right now, I have a hurt wrist. I don't know when I did it, but it hurts a lot to shoot pucks. I haven't had anything major, but a few small things this year. At one point, my neck was really sore. At one point last week, my lower back was really bad." – Brendan Gaunce

He said that in late February, which means the "hurt" wrist, "really sore" neck, and "really bad" back never caught up to him.

Brendan battled. He pushed through the pain.

Another minor ailment at the time, which went unlisted by Brendan, was a black eye, suffered in his fourth and final tilt of the season on February 17th, 2012.

Oshawa Generals grinder Scott Sabourin, who tallied 19 points and 111 penalty minutes in his third season in the OHL, was Brendan's opponent.

After being taken into the sideboards with ample force, Brendan dropped his mitts at centre. Sabourin followed his lead.

Even though he's about 20 pounds lighter, Sabourin took it to the Bulls assistant captain. After a few seconds of grappling, his left hand freed up long enough to jab Brendan right in the mug.

Brendan remained in good spirits when recalling the foggy sequence of events, despite being the fight's uncontested loser.
"I had a really nice black eye. That's about as well as it went. No, no it was good until the end. My helmet fell off, then he put my jersey over my head. The ref came in, but he threw a hard one, right in the eye. We were getting absolutely dominated that game. We were losing 8-1, and I was just really angry." – Brendan Gaunce

It was the third fight of five in a blowout victory for Oshawa on home ice.

Fortuitously for the Bulls, a serious injury was not inflicted upon their star.

A knock on some NHL prospects is their inability to stay healthy through the rigors of a pro schedule.

As Belleville's roster as a convenient example, there were only two other players—Garrett Hooey and Brady Austin—that can proudly say they suited up for every game of the regular season.

After another trio of 67-gamers, the team's stock of stable players dwindles.

What makes Brendan's full attendance impressive is the noticeable consistency. In his rookie season, the new kid on the Bulls was fifth in games played with 65, only missing three matches.

All of this would be pretty ordinary if playing a power forward game wasn't Brendan's bread and butter. But that's obviously not the case.

The extreme measures of participating in off-season training at the Gary Roberts High Performance Centre apparently pays off. So does eating well and developing proper sleep patterns. Luck plays a major factor as well.

It all adds up to Brendan being seen as a dependable asset who not only has the aptitude to compete neck-and-neck with the best in the OHL and beyond, but the stamina and robustness to battle all season long.

Brother Cameron's stint in the league, from 2007-2010, yielded three sturdy seasons, too, playing 63, 67, and 55 games, respectively.

"He's making strides to become the player he can be at the next level, and I just think he needs to keep doing it," Cameron says, when asked if Brendan should alter his style of play to stay healthy in the long run.

Longevity is a virtue in the game of hockey.

Being able to withstand the countless puck battles in the corner, hundreds of position driven tussles in front of the end, over the course of a career, is an added bonus to any NHL-calibre talent.

Cameron doesn't think the moderate crash and bang game his younger brother employs will bring him down over time.

When you question Brendan about it—fighting, in particular— the concept of honour seems to overpowers any sort of fear of injury.

He's a team-guy first and foremost.

"I don't have a problem with fighting at all. I think it shows unity and how guys stick up for each other. Without fighting, I don't think games would be as intense, and I don't think teams would be as close. You wouldn't think guys had your back. I really don't mind it. After a big hit, if there's a fight, it's about sticking up for your team." – Brendan Gaunce

After two OHL seasons, it's clear Brendan isn't afraid to engage in the odd tussle, accumulating a total of six fighting majors—a pair in his rookie season, four in his second.

His very first fight was against Windsor Spitfires forward Brady Vail on January 15th, 2011.

The short-lived tango wasn't anything to write home about, but a win for Brendan nonetheless.

As the combatants skated off the ice, the colour commentator told TV viewers they shouldn't be surprised Brendan won, referencing his performance at the under-17 tournament where he was considered a "man amongst boys."

And although he refrains from using his "man" strength to punch opponents on a regular basis, Brendan's 68 penalty minutes in the 2011-12 indicate he's no pushover.

"Trust me," Cameron explains, "my brother does have that same kind of temper and emotional involvement that I do. I just think he has a better handle on being composed, which can come off as him not being as physically involved in games as he should be."

Generally speaking, he's known as one of the OHL's fiercest competitors.

On occasion, the inner fire will get the better of him (e.g. fight against Sabourin), but the rest of the time he tends to keep an even-keel. The leader inside speaks up.

And, as John F. Kennedy was famously quoted, "leadership and learning are indispensable to each other."

You don't wake up one day and suddenly become a mature leader. It's engrained over years of understanding right from wrong;

knowing when to speak up and shut up; and figuring out those little details that make a leader so vibrant.

Integrity is a trait linked to virtually all leaders, in all walks of life, and Brendan appears to have that characteristic under wraps.

"The thing about Brendan is that he doesn't let all of the attention get to him. He doesn't look as it as an ego-boosting thing. He's a really modest kid, has a lot of character. He's the same kid I grew up with. If he wasn't going to the NHL and doing something different, I know he'd act the same." – Brandon Pantaleo

After skipping town for the OHL, it's commonplace for a player of Brendan's ilk to lose touch with buddies from back home.

There's various reasons why it happens, ranging from a natural disconnection due to the distance to an artificial drop-off in contact for no good reason.

In Brendan's eyes, keeping the line of communication open is imperative. It was especially important in his rookie season.

"You always hear stories of guys going away not talking to their friends at home and they go back and things have changed. That's definitely an aspect I've tried to keep up. I talk to my good buddies a couple of times a week. Sometimes through Skype, or maybe Call of Duty. One of my best friends, Erick Delaurentis, plays for the Wellington Dukes, which is 15 minutes down the road from us in Belleville. Seeing him throughout the week is nice. It's kind of a change of scenery from always seeing the guys on the team." – Brendan Gaunce

Realizing the importance of not getting completely caught up with his 'new life' in Belleville went a long way once Brendan began transitioning into a larger role with the Bulls.

"Most of the guys, when they come in at 16, are hard to crack," Judson says. "You try to get to know them but they don't say much. Brendan is an easy guy to talk to, though, and is very down-to-earth. I was excited to get on the ice with him the first time."

Finding the perfect balance between "being a goof off the ice" and "getting down to business on the ice," as Bulls broadcaster David Foot puts it, allowed Brendan to effortlessly transition into the OHL.

Grimes tends to agree.

"He's serious at all times, but he's much more relaxed off the ice. He can keep the room light when it needs to be," he says. "When guys need a laugh, he can do it. On the ice, he's dead serious—he's watching like a hawk."

***

Hockey players are a habitual bunch.

Meticulous stick taping, putting one's equipment on in the exact same order each time, listening to the same pump-up tunes over and over —these are all fairly common pre-game rituals.

Sometimes a little tweak can make the word of a difference.

What was Brendan Gaunce's secret to success during the 2011-12 campaign?

A longer pre-game nap.

"Last year I only slept an hour," he says, adding he wanted to "try something new."

Considering Brendan thoroughly enjoys sleeping as it is, the added shuteye was a natural fit.

At 1:30 p.m. on game days, he slips under the covers, setting his alarm for 4 p.m. Then, after a meal and shower, it's off to the rink.

That's the bullet point version of his early game day customs. It's an important component of his lifestyle, as most hockey players can attest to.

Brendan must have nailed the 2.5-hour sleep to the second for the week ending on November 27th, as he was named OHL Player of the Week.

"At the time, you don't really notice how big the award is. But, when you look back on it, there's probably 400-500 players in the OHL, so it's a big honour," he says a week later.

A first-star selection in a 3-1 victory over the Erie Otters on Thursday night, in which he picked up a pair of markers, started the week off with a bang.

Brendan kept the momentum going the next evening— duplicating his performance with two more goals and finishing plus-3— in a 6-0 romp over the Guelph Storm.

The week's final contest, a Sunday afternoon meet-up with the Oshawa Generals, brought his point total to six over a three-game span, collecting a goal and an assist in a 4-1 win.

When asked what the difference between his award-winning week and the others, Brendan pointed towards the Bulls' performance as a unit, noting he couldn't have captured the honour without help on the power-play.

Belleville fired at a 25 percent rate, scoring three goals on 12 opportunities.

"If you ask most hockey players, they'll say they feel best on the power-play instead of the penalty-kill or even-strength. Mostly because you're a man-up on the other team and can show more creativity. Our power-play right now has been improving." – Brendan Gaunce

At season's end, Brendan ended up scoring in 24 of Belleville's regular season games.

The team lost only six of those contests, which, when you do the math, equals 25 percent.

If he continues to produce in a timely fashion in the future, there's no reason to believe the Bulls' 75 percent win rate won't stay the same or increase.

Production from your big guns is a hallmark of most successful sports teams.

"There's moments now when I watch OHL games and I'm thinking, 'Wow, that's the same Brendan out there, he's taking over.' When he was in the offensive zone, there's really no stopping him. In minor hockey, he just had the power to take over the game." – Brandon Pantaleo

While attending a game in Belleville on February 11th, the ex-linemate saw glimpses of the old Brendan.

"Last night he scored a wrap-around goal in Guelph and I started thinking, 'I've seen that before,'" Pantaleo says.

The rangy centre is fond of the tricky manoeuvre, occasionally capitalizing on a goaltender caught out of position. Overall, he scores a fair amount of his goals around the crease area.

"There's probably a couple," Brendan says, pondering his favourite offensive move, "but they all have to do with wrap-arounds. Yeah, I'd say they are probably my favourite play to try. I've noticed my strength is definitely not toe-dragging at the blueline."

When attacking, Brendan isn't necessarily an easy target to slow down. His stick-handling skills aren't out of this world, but he's more than capable of protecting the puck on the outside, for instance.

Once the play develops in the opponent's end, a knack for incredible positioning takes over.

"He's always in the right spot," Foot says of Brendan, "very rarely in the wrong position. He has great eyes, hands, shot."

Playing with Brassard and Zharkov for the majority of the 2011-12 season—with Payerl stepping in as one of his wingers towards the end—Brendan displayed his distribution skills from start to finish.

In an end-of-season coaches poll, he was chosen as the third best playmaker in the Eastern Conference.

This tag cemented his significance to the Bulls offence, and as a centrepiece to their entire strategy.

The minor midget point producing machine may not have taken the OHL by storm via a league-leading point tally. However, you'd be hard pressed to find more than a dozen players with a more complete package.

Score. Assist.

Hit. Backcheck.

Win faceoffs. Rally the boys.

Repeat.

3

SPENT

He was embarrassed.

Not the kind where you lock yourself in your room to hide from the world, but still embarrassed.

He was embarrassed enough to get red in the face. Yet, he was still able to be a good sport about it.

"I won't say who I got the gift from," Brendan Gaunce says, telling the story shortly after the Christmas break away from OHL hockey, "but I got a letter from Team Canada as to why I didn't make the selection camp."

The letter clearly did not come from Hockey Canada's office, nor did it come from a family member playing a practical joke. It didn't fall from the sky and into his locker at school. A rival fan didn't send it to his billet's house to provide false thrill.

No, it was from a teammate looking to score a laugh or two at the expense of Brendan during the Bulls' holiday party.

"I didn't mind it too much," he enforces, with an overtone of disenchantment in his voice.

Of course, the letter was embarrassing; he had to read it in front of his peers. He had to wing a speech made by someone else.

Unlike gag gift receivers around the world, he wasn't given the Twilight series on DVD, a Snuggie blanket-sweater or a personalized hammock. His gift wasn't generic or thoughtless in any way. Instead, it was something that poked at his ego, a piece of paper that represented an unexploited chance.

There was no other way to take it. Just shake it off, and move on. He's one of the assistant captains and thus should know better to not take it personally.

Besides, it was a gag gift, and humiliation is one of the key ingredients. Could he blame the unnamed teammate? Never.

Let it be, he thought, it's actually kind of clever.

Belleville's captain, Luke Judson—a five-year veteran of 299 OHL games—has witnessed his fair share of gag gift receiving and giving. He remembers past presents such as the classic bench warmer seat (given to a fourth-line player) and a flashlight used to find a player in the shadow of someone else (given to a brother of a pro hockey player).

Judson sees the entire gag gift experience like the majority—a team-bonding event with some ill-advised laughs.

"At Secret Santa, I don't think anyone gets too upset over anything," he says. "If they do, they haven't showed it yet. Brendan took it well. He had a smile on his face. It's all in good fun—we have a tight group here."

With the letter-reading scenario re-playing in his head, Brendan digresses over the Alberta-based 2012 World Junior Hockey Championships.

Held in the mountainous part of the prairies, with the entire hockey world watching, it would have been an invaluable experience for the then-17-year-old. It's not exactly a once-in-a-lifetime opportunity, but close enough to leave a stinging feeling when left out of the fold.

"I wouldn't say it was shocking," Brendan says of being excluded, "because of the age and the calibre of players in the 1993-born age group. However, it was definitely disappointing. It was a goal of mine at the start of the year. But, it was nothing I lost sleep over."

Michael Bournival; Brett Connolly; Brendan Gallagher; Freddie Hamilton; Quinton Howden; Jonathan Huberdeau; Boone Jenner; Mark Scheifele; Jaden Schwartz; Devante Smith-Pelley; Mark Stone; Ryan Strome. All forwards for Team Canada at the world juniors, all drafted in either 2010 or 2011 to NHL teams, and all born before September 12, 1993.

Brendan?

A forward, yes; drafted, no; and born about six months later than those listed above. If selected, he would have been the so-called baby, the youngest forward to represent.

Would he of slid into the baby role? Probably not. OK, would he of fit into the team's dynamic? One would think so. How about being a positive influence on the dressing room? Most certainly. Does he offer a one-dimensional game—is that it? No. No, definitely not.

Something has to give.

Bulls head coach and general manager, George Burnett, was an assistant coach for Canada out west. Under Vancouver Giants bench boss Don Hay, Burnett, Ryan Huska of the Kelowna Rockets, and Pascal Vincent of the Montreal Juniors, made up the supporting cast chosen to guide the squad to glory.

"It's traditionally a 19-year-old's tournament. There are some 18's playing in it, and an occasional 17-year-old. I think that Brendan will be a part of that process next year. If he's playing in the CHL, I don't think there's any question his successes at the provincial and national levels will allow him the opportunity to come in, participate, and be considered." – George Burnett

The only player from Brendan's draft year that ended up making the final cut for the squad was defenceman Ryan Murray from the Everett Silvertips. Regarded by many scouting services, independent and otherwise, as a top five prospect in the draft at the time—and also having an extra year of major junior experience on Brendan as a 1993-born player—Murray's selection was in no way a surprise.

Barrie Colts forward Tanner Pearson, though born in 1992, was the only other undrafted player to don Canada's red and white against the top under-20 squads in the world. Coming into the tournament, he recorded an astounding 66 points in 30 games in the 2011-12 season.

His relative anonymity before the season began—selected 266th by Barrie in the 14th round of the 2008 draft and recording 42 points in 66 games in 2010-11—surely helped the Kitchener native stand out as the slots were debated. His accumulation of points in the current season looked ever so impressive.

The main difference between Pearson and Brendan is age. While the Markham product may act like a man and look like a man, he was still perceived as a boy because he was 17 until March 25, 2012.

Nevertheless, losing out on representing Canada for a second time in his young career—the other at the Ivan Hlinka Memorial Tournament in August 2011—was nothing for Brendan to hang his head about. There were dozens of fellow CHL players in his position— expecting the best but fearing the worst.

Nowadays, aside from the Winter Classic and Stanley Cup playoffs, the world juniors is arguably the hockey event of the season. It has become an entity in and of its own, a seemingly unbreakable ritual for Canadians.

The Gaunces are no different than their fellow countrymen.

"I can't remember not watching it," Brendan says.

To be a part of the spectacle, he says, would have been a tremendous honour.

***

Teams struggle, there's no hiding that.

At all levels of hockey—of basketball, of football, of rugby, of cricket, of whatever—they all face adversity. 'They're in a bind' is one of the truisms of sport for a reason.

Throughout a given season, teams are susceptible to a mixed bag of slumps, hot streaks, inconsistent periods, and downright average flashes.

But it seems that, in comparison to other developmental hockey leagues in North American, the ebbs and flows of a CHL season are unmatched. The United States Hockey League and British Columbia Hockey League are not as prominent, and the National Collegiate Athletic Association simply has fewer games.

Because of the CHL's pro-style schedule and solid educational standards, stress can pile up on the league's 16-20 year old players.

In some cases, a week straight of failure on the ice in the CHL expands past dropping couple of games. Many times it means a team is on a dreadful four-game losing streak and, suddenly, the bus ride from Sault Ste. Marie to Ottawa is much longer than expected—and quieter than imagined.

In other words, certain low points are conceivably lower in the CHL because of its all-in nature.

Teens are dedicating nearly full-time hours to a sport, when mathematically-speaking only a per cent of a per cent will play a regular shift in the NHL. It's a relentless, head down grind that—for more than half of the league—leads to the exit sign after a maximum of 75 games.

Over the OHL's nearly 40 seasons of operation as a 'Major Junior A' loop, there have been some unpleasant team lows.

A squad that comes to mind immediately is the Guelph Platers. They lost a whopping 25 games in a row in the 1982-83 season. It stood as the longest drought for five seasons, until the Kingston Canadiens dropped an absurd 28 straight contests in the 1987-88 campaign.

Of course, those are extreme, isolated examples of team futility, but it drives home the notion that even though it's an elite development league, the OHL has its fair share of god-awful records.

Now, although a team's final placing in the standings is usually the only thing remembered years down the road, a season's story cannot be told without an in-depth evaluation.

A club's regular season, at virtually all levels of hockey, consists of numerous intervals and roadblocks, segments and triumphs, chapters and disappointing times.

There's no need to look any further back than the 2005-06 Belleville Bulls to find an above-average squad that struggled at times throughout the regular season.

While they finished at a respectable 32-28-5-3, securing third in the East Division, the season was not as unswerving as their record might suggest.

After starting the campaign 1-6-0-0, the Bulls—equipped with the likes of current NHLers P.K. Subban and Shawn Matthias—looked like a basement dwelling crew, one sprinkled with talent but destined to falter from start to finish.

They began their 68-game trek with a pair of losses to the Brampton Battalion, as well as singles to two divisional rivals—the Kingston Frontenacs and Peterborough Petes—all within the first seven contests.

The defeats were close, but not all edge-of-your-seat, one-goal games. This mediocrity didn't produce what was expected: Wins.

In essence, they were in a slump right off the hop.

They went on to recover quite nicely, winning four straight after the 1-6-0-0 start, including three away from home, to bring their confidence up. The team's collective flow had been given a slight push upwards.

It would be brought down, though, as the squad returned back to a below-.500 (5-9-1) record by the end of October. Then back up again thanks to a mid-season stretch where they came out on top in 11 out of 16 consecutive games.

Such is life in the OHL.

Every team, except for a select few in the history of the league (see: London Knights, 2004-05) hits rough patches through the 68-game schedule.

Looking to desperately improve on a woeful 2010-11 record of 21-43-0-4—which, more by default than anything else, granted them a first round date with the powerhouse Mississauga St. Michael's Majors—the 2011-12 version of the Belleville Bulls appeared to be prepared.

A fresh start, and some new faces fuelled training camp and the first string of regular season battles.

The year-older crew came out of the gate with a sufficient 4-3-0-0 record.

Each notch in the loss column by Game 7 on the schedule was by two goals or less (2-1, 5-4, 5-3), indicating the club would likely challenge the majority of teams in the league. They were nearly perfect at home as well, dropping just a single game out of four.

By the time they packed up their belongings after their eighth game of season—a 5-0 loss to the Niagara IceDogs on the road on October 13th—the word slump wasn't uttered by the Belleville media, the club's personnel, and surely not its players.

Things were glossy for the most part, with a few tweaks needed here and there in order to keep those smiling faces around Belleville in an upright position.

Skip ahead to mid-November.

The Bulls are in the middle of a mini two-game skid. The first half of the slide included three unanswered goals to begin an eventual 4-1 loss at the Peterborough Memorial Centre to the Petes. The other was a 3-2 defeat to the Ottawa 67's on home ice.

Special teams killed the Bulls in the former, as the Petes scored both a short-handed marker and power-play goal to top off a 2-0 lead. John Chartrand of Barrie, Ontario, the Bulls back-up goaltender, was between the pipes. He was solid, turning away 31 in the defeat.

Despite having their No. 1 man, Malcolm Subban, back in goal for a date with Ottawa, the 67's simply found a way to win. Belleville outshot Ottawa, 42-28, but couldn't recover from a two-goal deficit.

Understandably, losing crucial games following a pretty strong run—having won eight of their last 10 games—did not sit well.

November 20th, a day after the defeat to Ottawa, Brendan Gaunce reflected on the Peterborough contest, calling it the "worst game we've played all season."

The Ottawa game wasn't the oft-reliable centre's greatest performance from an individual standout, as he took a hooking penalty halfway through the middle frame. Nine seconds into his sentence inside the penalty box, the 67's tallied their second of the game.

Head coach and general manager George Burnett agreed with Brendan, to some extent at least, as he laid the hammer down in practice.

A 45-minute bag skate ensued, leaving the Bulls roster exhaustedly lunging for a shot at ending the two-game slide they had thrust upon themselves.

"It was probably one of the hardest ones of my life. Coach is trying to get it into our minds that we have to get out of this losing streak quick. We have a pretty big road trip coming up, so today was a hard work day and I think guys got those two losses out of their minds." – Brendan Gaunce

Using his power as the club's fearless leader, Burnett sent a firm message to his group of combatants: Losing will not be taken lightly.

Evidently, he went further into that train of thought, essentially saying practice will not be taken lightly either.

Most of the players on the Bulls roster—if not all—had experienced a dreaded bag skate first-hand before. They're not uncommon by any stretch.

The one enforced by Burnett was a serious calorie-burner, though.

"We didn't have pucks at all. We did this one drill where we would go down-and-back, one at a time. We did that for about 15 minutes. Guys were gassed. And then coach said, 'OK, warm-up is over.' Then one line was at one end of the ice, one line was at the other, one at the sideboards, and we each had to do 45 seconds of stops and starts. We had to do three periods of that and an overtime period." – Brendan Gaunce

Ah, the bag skate.

It was brought to the mainstream by the Hollywood motion picture Miracle, the one about the supposed miracle on ice the United States national team pulled off at the 1980 Olympics.

Herb Brooks' infamous after-game antics—dragging his players out onto the chopped up ice surface for some extracurricular skating with no pucks allowed—were not original by any means. But, it was indubitably made popular through the movie, as it displayed a form of punishment towards players that is not necessarily typical.

In a lot of ways, bag skates are about mental toughness and stamina rather than any sort of physical testing. The 'suicide' pattern is not implemented to inflict physical anguish, rather than remind players their duty to the greater good—to the team.

In Belleville's case, a temporary lapse in group dedication had swept through the otherwise tight-knit, got-your-back-at-all-costs crew.

It was just a two-game losing streak, and there was over 60 per cent of their regular season schedule remaining. The actual bereavement —the four points missed out on—wasn't the issue. The effort and mindset, however, was.

"I don't think we were working as a group and I think guys kind of put themselves before the team. And I'm not singling anyone out, just in general. You could tell guys were just thinking of themselves. I was a part of the problem, too." – Brendan Gaunce

Brendan was held scoreless during the aforementioned losses to Peterborough and Ottawa, though he managed to remain even in the plus-minus category.

During the six previous games in November, the dependable centreman notched nine points. A game-winning snipe against Owen Sound on home ice on November 5th was the sterling highlight.

All was forgotten by the time the bag skate came around, however.

Temporarily replaced by sorrow, the self-inflicted skating-only practice acted as a sure-fire wakeup call for the Bulls, who were 13-9-0-0 with 46 games left.

There was still a ton of hockey ahead and, with an overall impressive start to build off of, plenty of promise hidden under the shaky back-to-back games.

From November 24th to December 3rd, the Bulls gave the phrase 'bounce back' new meaning.

Draft eligible goaltender Malcolm Subban stood on his head, allowing just six goals in as many games. The offence flexed its muscles, too, winning convincingly, 6-0 (Guelph Storm) and 8-1 (Kingston Frontenacs), during the six-game streak.

The squad was back to their pre-bag skate shape, fighting and clawing for every inch of ice with a stern attitude in tow.

The margin of victory during this six-game span was much larger, too.

Case in point, instead of having to deliver under pressure in a 2-1 shootout win over the Oshawa Generals on November 13th, the Bulls took down the same East Division opponent early on in a 4-1 win on November 27th.

Then, just five days after disposing of the same Windsor Spitfires, 4-1, in front of 2,632 Belleville supporters at the Yardmen Arena, the Bulls ran into a determined goaltender.

An ordinary 2-1 loss on December 8th marked the beginning of a vile period in Belleville's rickety season.

Spitfires netminder Jaroslav Pavelka turned away 42 of the 43 shots to outduel Subban's respectable 29-for-30 night. Failing to notch more than one goal for the first in almost a month, the well-oiled machine's wheels stopped turning.

The Bulls offence was beginning to illustrate tell-tale signs of its 2010-11 self, where it scored a league-low 175 goals in 68 games. Their top scorer in Brendan's rookie season, Luke Judson, was a veteran who figured out the league's intricacies. He scored 28 to lead the woeful charge.

Nevertheless, a reality perhaps more concerning than the lack of offence versus the Spitfires was that it was the Bulls' opener in a three-in-three weekend trip, with stops in both Plymouth and Saginaw, Michigan, on Friday and Saturday, respectively.

Aside from Games 3-5 back in late September and early October, this was the team's first three-in-three set.

It would be a test of their road warrior value, and a first real encounter with the Western Conference's talented assets. By season's end, all three squads ranked in the top eight in the west, including No. 2 Plymouth, who garnered 97 points and the second most goals for.

The Whalers burst out to a 4-1 lead after the opening 20 minutes of Friday's contest—an insurmountable lead for most offence-driven clubs, let alone the Bulls. Two late markers, counting a power-play tally from Brendan, weren't enough, as Plymouth held on for a 4-3 victory.

Efforts against the Spirit provided much of the same, except with the score tight in the early goings as opposed to late in the match. Four third period goals, including an empty-netter that made it 6-4, sealed the deal for Saginaw.

The Spirit's four-pronged deadly attack—Josh Shalla, Michael Fine, Brandon Saad and Vincent Trocheck—combined for an average of two points a piece.

Another tight game where Belleville could not conjure up a full-game performance. In this case, the old adage of having to 'play a full 60 minutes' out there, in order to emerge victorious, seemed to fit perfectly.

After the visitor's dressing room was cleared out, it was time to begin the healing process following an unsuccessful road trip.

Even though it felt like their offence was going, the Bulls averaged only 2.7 goals per game, which will never amount to a tick in the win ledger against quality opponents.

Cue the seven-hour bus ride home from eastern Michigan to eastern Ontario.

Thoughts of regret fermented in each player's head, as they wondered if every ounce of effort was expensed for the all-for-nothing road trip.

The bright side?

Three losses to Western Conference teams was a helluva lot better than to the Ottawas and Peterboroughs back east. Six points were claimed by the home teams they danced with, but it could have been worse.

Following a three-day lull between Saturday night's disappointment in Saginaw and a Wednesday evening game at home versus the Kingston Frontenacs, players rested their minds and bodies.

The home atmosphere will groom their conscious' well, and they'll be able to get back on their feet, Brendan said.

The roar of cheers from the hometown fans were all for nothing, however. Scoring, or a lack thereof, was detrimental.

On just seven shots in the final frame, Kingston banged in a pair to pull away from the Bulls, 3-1. Brendan snuck the lone puck past the Frontenacs' wall in net, Igor Bobkov. It was his 19th marker of the season in just 32 games, a team-high and already eight more than last year's final total.

The 35-shot effort represented a fourth consecutive defeat for the squad, their longest stretch without a win.

Regrettably, previous skids were topped by this one.

There was only a single match left prior to Christmas break, a home contest versus arguably the best offence in the OHL, the Whalers.

It was an opportunity to create a joyful atmosphere in the dressing room before parting for the holidays. Winning against the best brings out the best emotions.

And Belleville took full advantage, pulling off a comfortable 5-1 victory over one of the league's darlings. An unassisted tally from Daniil Zharkov, 7:29 into the middle period, proved to be the difference.

Brendan was held off the scoresheet, but his teammates picked up the slack. Three forwards—Michael Curtis, Adam Payerl, and Brady Austin—pitched in with multi-point efforts.

Off to their hometowns for holiday cheer, the Bulls parted ways on a hopeful note. For good reason, too, as their 20-13-0-0 record slotted them in fourth position on the Eastern Conference standings board.

When they boarded the team bus after a gutsy 6-5 victory in northern Ontario over the Sault Ste. Marie Greyhounds on December 29th, the 2011-12 Belleville Bulls officially hit the halfway point.

Thirty-four games behind them, thirty-four ahead.

Then eight games above-.500, sitting cozy in a playoff spot with first round home ice advantage privileges, the gang was on a bit of a high.

To a degree, they were exceeding expectations; they weren't blowing the top off the probability jar, yet they were pushing the boundaries and searching for their true potential.

That identity search began a day before New Year's Eve.

And it didn't exactly quickly.

Up north once again, this time to the nickel factory town of Sudbury, an eager Bulls squad was sure they could tame the average Wolves.

The home team's sophomore centreman, Andrey Kuchin, decided to play hero, however, potting the overtime winner with a mere 31 clicks left in extra time.

For Belleville, the 4-3 defeat was far from a blowout, far from a worrisome affair.

Nevertheless, it nudged the dominoes enough to kick-start a far-reaching tumble down the standings.

It wasn't predictable, per se, but overachieving teams always tend to walk on cracked ice until the inevitable happens. A turn of fortunes was in line.

With the Battalion, Generals and 67's (twice) on their radar following the Sudbury setback, the team knew there would be no gimmies to begin 2012.

An awareness of what's ahead only goes so far. Execution is what truly matters.

Boom. Boom. Boom.

Loss. Loss. Loss.

Three games and three lacklustre results: 4-2, 4-1, and 7-2.

The New Year's Day match against the Battalion saw Matt MacLeod—who finished the season with a dull nine goals in 56 games—score a pair en route to a two-goal win for Brampton. The Bulls were outshot once again, 37-24, and lacked a finishing touch by getting outscored 2-0 in the third period.

It only got worse for Belleville three days later, as a 1-1 game turned into a 4-1 loss after an ugly showing in the final 20 minutes of regulation. In the first five minutes of the third, Lucas Lessio notched his second of the game while his teammates killed off a crucial minor penalty to secure the victory for Oshawa.

Then there was the five-goal thumping at the hands of divisional foe Ottawa, a bi-product of a lopsided 45-26 shot total. A terrible start—four goals for the 67's in the first 19:50—proved to be an uncultivable mountain.

Belleville was unmistakably losing focus, having trouble with their confidence and work ethic.

"We hadn't had a real cold streak yet this year, and we knew it was going to come sooner or later because every team has one. Ours is right now but our coach is trying to prompt us to start working a lot harder in practice so we can get out of this faster than others would." – Brendan Gaunce

Those words came after the Bulls were handed their fifth consecutive loss, a heartbreaking 3-2 decision to the 67's. It was the second half of a double-whammy—they lost both in a home-and-home series with Ottawa, a team ahead in the standings.

Brendan insisted the results of the previous five games weren't rooted in a lack of collective effort.

Other than the 7-2 shellacking, the Bulls competed hard, kept up with the other squads, he said. He argued the colossal mishap—which, at the time, tied an October 13th loss to the Niagara Ice Dogs as the worst of the season—was closer than the final score indicated.

"After the first period, it was 4-0 and we were trying to turn it around. It's one of the toughest buildings to play in. We won the second period but then we came out into the third and the game was just over after they got three quick ones. They had better jump to their game." – Brendan Gaunce

At the same time, he was realistic. They weren't exactly playing high-end hockey out there.

There was a passionate fan base to please—even their own careers to extend—and this was no other way of going about it.

Star goaltender Subban was on the shelf since pulling his groin in a practice shortly after returning to Belleville after Christmas. The ailment forced him to miss 15 straight games from December 29th to February 3rd.

Despite the substantial forfeiture, Belleville still faced with pulling out wins, and Brendan knew that.

"I'm not going to make any excuses. We weren't very good. But, we were also missing the top rated goaltender in the league most of the time. I think we can make some adjustments and will start to see the wins return a little bit. It helped we had a big six-game winning streak earlier this year because we know we can do it. Our spirits are a lot better than last year since a year ago we knew we didn't have the talent then to win six in a row and get back on track. But, this year we know we have the talent and work ethic." – Brendan Gaunce

Indeed, they did boast a more complete lineup in the 2011-12 campaign.

He was also spot-on in stating every team gets themselves into at least one mess over the course of a season.

But would they be able to shimmy out of the mammoth hole?

Five days following a January 7th loss to Ottawa, they looked like they were boosting themselves up, at least for a moment, by yanking out a 3-2 win in Brampton versus the Stan Butler-led Battalion. Though the Powerade Centre-hosted game was a bit of a yawner for those in attendance, the game sheet provided evidence that Belleville snapped a five-game losing streak.

Like the spring breeze after spending a full day indoors, the two points reinvigorated the Bulls. There was reason to believe again.

On January 14th, having already dropped nine of their past 15 games, a Saturday night face-off against the upstart Wolves didn't look particuarly imposing to the Bulls.

The absence of their starting crease protector was as blatant as ever before, however, as Sudbury managed to post a pair on Chartrand before the first period horn sounded. The veteran of 60-plus OHL games let in another in the opening half of the second period before being replaced by call-up Charlie Graham.

The Wolves were relentless, poking another two past the youngster on just nine remaining shots.

Brendan, who scored the Bulls' second marker of the evening, ended up minus-2 in the 5-3 loss.

"I just think we're going through a slump right now as any team does, but it's a bit longer than usual," he says, with a small sense of worry lingering in his voice.

With two points in their back pocket, the Wolves bolted to fourth place in the Eastern Conference, while Belleville slid to seventh.

Were things on a rapid down slope because their mid-season MVP was out nursing a groin injury?

Brendan didn't think so.

At the same time, he was fully aware of the difference between playing in front of Goalie X and playing in front of Subban.
"We do have two capable goaltenders, and they wouldn't be in the OHL if they weren't good enough to be on any team in the league. Malcolm's confidence in the net helps a lot, though. He's one of the best goalies in the league, if not the best. Whenever you have a goalie of that calibre,

games seem to swing in your favour even if you're not playing as well."
– Brendan Gaunce

Subban, who was drafted 24th overall by the Boston Bruins in June, posted a .923 save percentage in 39 games at season's end. His three shutouts complemented a nifty 2.50 goals-against average and 25-14-0 record.

The kid was a stud from the start to finish. But he was tugged down on multiple occasions due to health problems.

Alas, even if the Bulls' main guy in between the pipes was healthy, it's tough to imagine the next 11 days wouldn't have been the same painful ride.

In their rear-view mirror was a 1-5 slide. In the short-term future were meetings with Ottawa, the Majors, the Kitchener Rangers, Kingston, and Niagara.

"I think we can easily get back on track with one big win," Brendan says on Sunday, January 15th, hours after losing 6-1 to the 67's in the nation's city. "We're hoping that'll happen on Wednesday."

The beginning of the 11-day plunge obviously didn't go as planned. Another defeat to the most eastern OHL club hurt.

But, Mississauga was next on the docket and they played a similar brand of hockey to Belleville's. Their 201 goals in the 2011-12 regular season eclipsed the Bulls tally by just a single marker. They allowed two fewer goals as well, making the comparison even closer.

The lone penalty called in the second period, a two-minute slashing minor assessed to Zharkov, was the tipping point that gave the rivals the big win instead of the Bulls.

Stay-at-home defenceman Alex Cord notched the power-play marker—his first of the year—with roughly four minutes to play in the middle frame. A 14-4 shot differential in favour of Belleville in the final 20 minutes did not produce any celebrations, leading to a 3-2 defeat.

It brought their record in 2012 to a meagre 1-7-0-0.

Yikes.

In games following their victory over Brampton, Belleville stayed out of the penalty box quite well. That didn't mean they weren't being scored on at a high rate during those man-down situations, though. In five penalty kills, they were scored on twice, both game-winners.

Double yikes.

Starved for more offence, having averaged goals 2.4 per game since returning from Christmas break, a bitter Bulls team was in need of a high-scoring tilt versus the Rangers at home.

The match-up presented an interesting viewing for various NHL-affiliated and independent scouts.

Brendan and Radek Faksa, also a draft eligible forward, are considered very similar prospects in terms of how each player's long-term development correlates with current attributes.

Faksa, a Czech Republican scooped up by the Rangers in the 2011 CHL Import Draft at the 22nd overall position, plays a game well-known to Brendan.

The two are tall and wide, with the 1994-born Faksa standing at 6-foot-3 and weighing 202 pounds. Additionally, they both employ a two-way game as defensive forwards with ample scoring touch. They finished with similar statistical lines at the end of the regular season, too —the Ranger with six less games played and two less points recorded.

And, of course, both were eligible for the 2012 NHL Draft and went in the opening round of 30. Faksa was chosen 13th by the Dallas Stars.

So, the table was set for an epic war of the 2012 draft eligible power forward titans, right?

Nope. Brendan was held off the scoresheet while Faksa managed a single assist.

Someone else stole the show instead.

Those gathered at the Yardmen Arena to watch their Bulls take on the Rangers were presumably fixated—like most fans in the league—on the offensive prowess of Ryan Murphy, a Carolina Hurricanes prospect and Kitchener's top defenceman.

His presence on the rush is unmatched by his rearguard peers, side-stepping and stickhandling around opponents with incredible ease. Murphy's upside is often clashed by poor own-end skills—except sometimes it just doesn't matter.

With less than four minutes remaining in regulation, one of those 'doesn't matter' times was created. The 5-foot-11, 176-pounder capped off a four-point night by scoring the game-winner. At the time, it was his finest performance of the season and effectively began an eight-game, 19-point hot streak.

Murphy's unassisted winner came on a Kitchener power-play, which ran at a 50 per cent success rate versus Belleville.

Back to the drawing board the Bulls went, attempting to figure out exactly what was stalling their development.

They were in a major funk, dropping four in a row and 13 of their last 16.

It wasn't a slump. It was a season-ruining disaster.

Something had to be done. The tide had to be turned, or the season would plummet to a non-playoff end or an extremely difficult first round date like last year.

In trying times, a hockey club's blood flows directly through its liaisons, its on-ice leaders.

Brendan, Judson, Austin, and Stephen Silas, were the captains.

With a 'C' on his sweater, Judson took great pride in being the lead-by-example soldier on and off the ice.

They weren't hanging their heads in public, but surely there were some sleepless nights amongst the core of the Bulls.

Even Judson began doubting his abilities during the drawn out losing streak.

"Me and Brendan, as both leaders on the team, started to question ourselves. We questioned our own play, and how it was contributing to what was going wrong. I think we knew it would come around eventually, though. The work ethic was there, the attitude was there; it was just mistakes that always seemed to end up in our net." – Luke Judson

The imperative phrase in his passage—"how it was contributing to what was going wrong"—really displays how sunken the team's ego was.

At this point, the Bulls hit rot bottom, and let their surroundings cave in.

Before the avalanche of losses could suffocate their confidence, they set out to finish the month of January on a positive note.

Three games stood in their way: A Sunday matinee in Kingston on the 22nd; then two games in three days, first westward to Niagara to face the Ice Dogs on Thursday and a Saturday night home game against the Sarnia Sting to close out the month.

The Frontenacs, led by one of Brendan's childhood idols—Doug Gilmour, at the general manager's helm—were rebuilding. They didn't look too dangerous in the Eastern Conference, but weren't pushovers, either.

A bit of a wild first period told the bulk of the game story, as all five goals in the 3-2 Kingston win were netted before the opening frame's final buzzer rang.

Belleville, winners of the first three games of the season series—by a combined score of 15-3, including an 8-1 thumping of the Frontenacs on Friday, December 2nd in Kingston—somehow lost consecutive matches to the Limestone City club.

What happened to their mojo—where did it go?—the Bulls leadership group pondered.

"I've told every reporter the same thing: I think every team, at some point in the year, is going to have a lull like that. January's skid went a lot longer than we would have liked—obviously, it was a whole month, basically. It seemed to never end. There were games where we were in disarray. We thought we could have won them but it just didn't happen." – Luke Judson

The month of horror concluded on a high note, fortunately, as Belleville took a 5-4 decision at home versus the Sarnia Sting.

Two days earlier, at the ancient Jack Gatecliff Arena in St. Catharines, the Ice Dogs filled the Bulls in yet again. This time it was a 6-0 shellacking.

In two trips to the small ice surface in Niagara, Belleville was absolutely dominated.

Two games, 11 goals for the powerhouse Ice Dogs. Two games and zero goals for the underachieving Bulls.

Whether the remarkably smaller ice sheet, in comparison to Belleville's large surface, played a factor or not, those scoring numbers are staggering.

It's funny how seemingly irrelevant things make a world of a difference when you're in need of a little buoyancy. For Belleville, that came with the simple flip of the calendar.

After the one-goal victory over a highly skilled Sting squad, they were able to mentally regroup, reshape their collective mindset.

That horrendous showing in January—two wins in 12 games— could be left in the dust because it was now a new 30-day cycle.

Nothing drastic happened between the month closer on January 28th and the month opener February 3rd.

There wasn't a sudden injection into the lineup since the trade deadline was in early January. The team was in relative good health as well, and didn't switch on or off ice strategies.

The Bulls, simply put, could literally turn the page on an awful stretch in the season.

"We want to turn things around here in February and really surprise people down the stretch," Burnett says.

And they did, with a vengeance.

At least for a little bit.

From the game in Kitchener versus the Rangers on the 3rd, a 6-3 victory, to a 3-1 win over the Guelph Storm on the road, things were dandy.

The squad pulled off a respectable three-wins-in-four-meetings stretch.

But then it all came tumbling down.

It hit harder than the January slump. It stung more than the 6-0 loss to Niagara, the finale defeat in the dreadful first month of 2012 for the Bulls. It bit them in the behind.

"It was the worst game I've been a part of in the OHL," Brendan says, each word trickling out of his mouth slowly. "It was like, 'Oh my gosh, when is this going to end?' It was not a game anyone wanted to be involved in."

Their arch rivals handed them an embarrassing three periods.

Nine for the 67's, zero for Belleville.

"After the game," Brendan continues, "we all kind of looked at each other and said, 'We just lost 9-0 in the OHL.'"

That type of asymmetrical final score does not come around too often in an OHL season. To be on the wrong end of it feels utterly unpleasant.

Calling the dreadful experience an "eye-opener," Brendan was about as shocked as the 9,411 assembled in Ottawa's Civic Centre. Except the energy moving through his body did not have a hint of positivity—it was completely harmful and off-putting.

The worst part was that they were walloped away from home.

Or, was that a blessing? Would the Yardmen Arena faithful have put up with such a miserable scoreboard reading?

When you examine the game summary, two things come to mind: How could Brendan possibly escape with a minus-1 rating, and how on earth did Belleville outshoot Ottawa 35-33 in a 9-0 loss?

On the whole, the old-fashioned Capital City Beat Down represented the sum of all that had gone wrong for the Bulls in January.

The built up turmoil was inevitably going to explode once a talented team penetrated wonder goalie Subban.

"We came in wanting to get four points over the weekend and we had already done that. Obviously that's not the right attitude. We were too complacent," Brendan concludes.

The weird thing is that a section at the end and into February—four wins in five games—decided to plop itself right in the middle of two desolate patches of play, as if to taunt the young players' minds.

The next week, packed full with four games over six calendar days, presented a brand spanking new low.

After a relatively tight 6-3 loss to the 67's on Wednesday, February 15th, and another laugher versus an out-of-division opponent—this time the Generals—Friday, the Bulls' confidence was absolutely shot.

In that two-game sample, they dropped a couple of important matches by a combined score of 14-4.

To say the Generals had their way with Belleville would be an understatement, as they quietly inflicted an 8-1 blow. The game was ugly, with a grand total of 76 penalty minutes assessed, in large part due to five fighting majors per side.

But, that was just the tip of the iceberg.

Sensing a team under distress, Oshawa capitalized on the Bulls' unadvisable state. They notched two tallies in the first, and then three each in the middle and final frames. It was a slaughter from beginning to end.

Luckily, with the tilt being the Friday night road game in a two-game weekend, the Bulls were able to strap on their short memory caps and ride obliviously into a home match versus Mississauga.

Clearly playing with a chip on their shoulders, the down-but-not-out warriors lambasted the Majors. They racked up the same total as the Generals accumulated the night before, winning forcefully by a score of 8-3.

The win ended a nasty trio of losses in which the opposition kicked the Bulls when they were down—way down.

Their patience with mediocrity was unmistakably wearing thin.

It was now February 18th, and the Bulls record was 27-27-1-0. They were amazingly one game below-.500 and tied with the Majors for eighth in the Eastern Conference.

It felt good, Brendan explained, to feel invigorated again. Belleville could see an exit, a way out of the tunnel of doom.

"This is one we had marked down as a must-win for us," Brendan confesses, talking about the Feb. 20th home game versus the basement dwelling Erie Otters. "We got back on track yesterday, and tomorrow will hopefully be a nice checkmark after the week."

Or so he thought.

Again, in blatant defeat, the Bulls managed to outshoot the enemy. Erie sent 33 on target in this case, while Belleville put 42 pucks on net. A 3-0 lead after one period, however—no matter what OHL team has the advantage—is difficult to overcome.

Despite their best efforts, the Bulls were downed 4-1.

They lost to a team who only won a handful of games the entire year.

"I think you can call it inconsistency. We've been trying to take that out of our game, but as of late we haven't been able to hide it. I don't know if it's that guys aren't ready to play on the road, or we psyche ourselves out—I really don't know what's going on—but we have to snap out of it as we head down the stretch and hopefully into the playoffs." – Brendan Gaunce

Win one, lose one, win two, lose three, win one, lose one.

That was how their February was unravelling.

Out of those five defeats, a pair—a 6-4 loss to Ottawa and the recent 4-1 loss to Erie—were in front of their hometown fans.

The Yardmen patrons were far from pleased with the subpar efforts. And understandably so, seeing as the Bulls left a crucial set of points on the table thanks to a loss at the hands of the worst club in the league. With no more than 15 games remaining in the season, no less.

The playoffs, at least for the few days between the Erie loss and the team's trip to Brampton to face the Battalion on February 24th, seemed like an afterthought.

Belleville needed to get their act together for the long run first and foremost. They couldn't wrap their heads around a post-season berth at that point.

"I guess we looked at Erie and thought it was going to be easier than the night before," Brendan says, uncertain, really, of what to say. "But, they're one of the hardest working teams in the league since they're so young, so they took it to us."

With making the top eight in the east on their minds, the Bulls scribbled down some 'must-win' dates.

The Eries, the Kingstons—those types of teams—should be a cinch, right?

If they faltered to produce in said games, more formidable tasks would take its place. It was of utmost importance to capitalize on softer opponents.

"We were playing at home, and we came in with the mentality that we were going to win the game. But, you can't do that against any team, no matter who it is, in the OHL. We knew we had to get the two points we lost to Erie back against London." – Brendan Gaunce

On they marched.

The Bay of Quinte Region's major junior team realigned themselves before the weekend, managing to salvage the three-game week of February 20th.

They took down Brampton (2-1) and the London Knights (3-2) in low-scoring affairs on Friday and Saturday, respectively.

The ebbs of the Bulls 2011-12 season were gradually activating, slowly creating some constant flow. They looked saved, and the season looked salvageable.

And it certainly was.

Although, there was one more meeting with their most dreaded opponent, the IceDogs. They met for a fourth and final time on March 3rd. This time around it was Belleville's turn to play host, to entertain the former Mississauga-based franchise in what was a severe mismatch on paper.

One of Canada's world junior hockey goaltenders, Mark Visentin, didn't show up—he allowed three goals on 17 shots—yet talent-heavy Niagara thumped Belleville by a score of 10-3.

"I think we kind of went in scared, just because of how good they are. It never turns out well if you're scared. And we were timid. It was just a bad night, in general. It was 2-1 after the first period. Then we got a couple of penalties and they capitalized. They have the best power-play in the league, and after that they had wind in their sails while we had none." – Brendan Gaunce

The victory saw seven IceDogs register at least two points. League veterans Steven Shipley and Freddie Hamilton left Belleville with smiles on their faces, each netting the uncommon road hat-trick.

The unpleasant statistics usually associated with losing such a one-sided affair wasn't that terrible after all. While five Bulls players, including Brendan, finished the game minus-3, it's a miracle no one was minus-5 or worse.

Statistics aside, the crushing blow was the fact that they were 1-11 in meetings versus the east's two juggernauts—Ottawa and Niagara —and were in line to draw one of them in the first round.

Not only were they ripped apart in the win-loss column by the top two seeds in their conference, but they were competitive in only a couple of the games. It wasn't a matter of some unlucky bounces. Belleville had their work cut out for them, to say the least.

As spring approached and the regular season's end was in sight, the Bulls could smell a first round date with either the 'Dogs or 67's.

They knew it was unavoidable, considering the circumstances. Their only chance was to slip into sixth place, which was an unlikely scenario.

Only seven games stood between the 10-3 loss to Niagara and the end of Belleville's required schedule. With opponents as tough as the Barrie Colts (eventual No. 3 seed in the east) and as weak as the Frontenacs (last place) on their plate, there was a realistic opportunity for the Bulls to choose their own destiny.

"Nobody on our team wants to come eighth," Brendan pleads as the team prepares for the March 7th tilt versus the Petes. "We're going to have to play the IceDogs if we want to make it to the OHL finals, though, because they are the best team in the east."

In speaking about Ottawa, the assistant captain presented a slightly more optimistic outlook.

In fact, he believed there was something to prove to the 67's before packing up for summer.

"It's definitely a team we want to play because the games we've lost badly are big shots to our pride. We want to win games, and when you're losing 9-0 to a rival like Ottawa, it's never something you want to happen as a hockey player," Brendan says.

After an unsuccessful road trip northwest, to Sudbury then Barrie, the Bulls rolled into Belleville without a playoff spot clinched.

A spot was within their grasp, but they let it slip away by scoring just a single goal in 120 minutes of hockey.

However, a 3-2 triumph over the Generals on the 14th of March, their 66th game of the season, finally secured a playoff spot.

The zig-zag season was about to culminate with an opening round date with either Niagara, Ottawa, or Barrie.

"I don't think we have any other options right now," Brendan states dryly. "At the start of the year, our goal was to be pretty much where we are now. If we finish sixth that'll be right on."

It was a realistic benchmark for a rebuilding franchise that struggled mightily to put pucks in the opposing team's net during the 2010-11 campaign.

At the conclusion of the 680th and final game of the OHL regular season on March 18th, the scene was finally set.

In the Eastern Conference, Niagara (No. 1 seed) drew Oshawa (8), Barrie (3) got Mississauga (6), while Brampton (4) and Sudbury (5) were set to duel.
And Belleville (7) would face—gulp—the relentless Bull-killing machine that is the 67's (2).

They just missed their mark of finishing sixth in the east, as their 71 points was only behind the Majors' final tally.

The outlook looked daunting.
How would they please the patrons of the Yardmen Arena? Please their parents? Their coaches? Themselves?

But, after all—as the saying goes—that's why the games are played. No one is guaranteed the satisfaction of winning a playoff series until four victories have been collected.

After four hours of homework on Monday, March 19th, an eager Brendan joined players and staff for a team dinner the following night.

The annual supper occurs right before the playoffs, a sort of 'hooray!' and 'see 'ya later' to the regular season—a transition point if you will.

"After our last weekend, the guys are really happy," Brendan says Wednesday night, hours before leaving to Ottawa for Game 1. "Playing Niagara, for us at least, is a lot more daunting. We're looking forward to the playoffs, and we feel we have a good chance against Ottawa."

The firepower of Tyler Toffoli (100 points in 65 games to lead all OHLers not named Michael Sgarbossa), Shane Prince (team-high plus-34), and Brendan's buddy, Sean Monahan (10 power-play goals), comprised just the first layer of talent on a well-groomed 67's squad.

They were furnished with fully capable trigger men as well as a solid defence corps led by the likes of captain Mark Zanetti and ultra impressive Cody Ceci. Petr Mrazek, of World Junior Hockey Championship fame, was also their crease protector.

On paper, the comparison was nearly laughable.

And not because Ottawa possessed super-human skill or Belleville was a complete mess, but since the 67's demolished their opening round foes in the regular season.

Nevertheless, the post-season is almost always a different monster.

Just like they accomplished earlier in the season, as the end of January transitioned into the start of February, the Bulls needed to turn the page.

If they stood a chance of surviving the opening round of the OHL playoffs as a No. 7 seed, the cliché of 'leaving it in the past where it belongs' needed to be fulfilled. Then again, that's purely mental.

Strategically, altering a team's outset this far into the season would be disadvantageous.

"Nothing will be tried that's new," Brendan says. "We're not going to change our game. We're going to play it the way we can."

In spurts, Belleville displayed an above-average team game. Their goaltending was virtually impenetrable, and they found a way to snipe in a timely fashion. For moments in time, they made their case to be included in the conference's top four or five teams.

For the bulk of the season though, the Bulls were a team on a month-by-month search for a concrete identity.

They were an enigmatic squad, defeating first place London but looking abysmal versus last place Erie, and struggling to sink their teeth into a prolonged stride of excellence.

An overall record of 35-32-1-0 didn't provide basis for substantial faith.

The top three franchises in the east looked light-years ahead of their lesser peers.

***

It was time to rumble.

Thursday, March 22nd, marked the start of Round 1. It was second season time, the launch into a new chapter of Bulls vs. 67's.

A power-play marker from Toffoli in the dying minutes of the opening period brought those in attendance to their feet, but not for too long. A deflection off Judson's stick tied things up before the teams headed to their dressing rooms.
The second period looked similar, with the two squads trading goals. Belleville's came off a nice heads-up pass by Brendan Gaunce, who fed Payerl on his off-wing. Subban managed to stop a Taylor Fielding penalty shot, too, a sure game-saver.

The third period proved to be goalless, and the opening game of the Bulls' 2012 playoff headed to overtime.

The fight Belleville fought for 60 minutes was punched right in the noggin.

The OHL's 52-goal man in the regular season and Los Angeles Kings draft pick, Toffoli, slid one past Subban on a breakaway early in the first overtime period.

In his 20th straight start, Subban turned aside 40 saves. He wasn't the reason the Bulls lost. That unwanted crown went to Ottawa, who simply capitalized when it mattered most.

"We outplayed them the first game, I thought," Brendan says a day after the loss. "We came out on the wrong end, but we had the confidence and the momentum afterwards. It was the first close game against them in a couple of years."

As much as the extra time defeat gave the underdogs some street credit, it didn't change the fact they still had to win four games before the other team.

The next game, again in the nation's capital, was scheduled for Friday evening. This meant the image of the 67's jumping on top of hero Toffoli would be rather temporary.

Game 2 of the Eastern Conference quarter-final was incredibly heated, even before the puck dropped. Ottawa captain Zanetti was assessed a five-minute major for spearing Belleville's Zharkov in the warm-ups.

Cooler heads prevailed as the game progressed, but the intensity between the two teams—who were meeting for the 10th meaningful game against each other of the season—was at its peak.

Trade deadline acquisition Joseph Cramarossa factored in on both Belleville goals, yet the home team busted out a 4-2 victory. Belleville's gem in net, Subban, saw 46 pucks come his way in the loss.

Monahan, picked up the eventual game-winner—his first of two on the night—10 minutes into action.

"He's been playing really well, especially in the games in Ottawa," Brendan says after the series. "In our building, I think I've had some pretty good games, too, though."

The competition between the two 1994-born teens, which had its highs and lows from Brendan's perspective, was magnified in the playoffs because of the importance of each shift.

It was the do-or-die playoffs, not the regular season anymore. "I think our regular season numbers don't really show how good of a team we are. One thing coach showed us is that if we didn't play Ottawa at all, we would have finished in third or fourth. But, obviously, going 1-7 against our division rival doesn't help at all." — Brendan Gaunce

The rationalization of their futility versus the 67's in the 2011-12 season was healthy.

It helped them accept the underdog role without hesitation. If they were to deny what happened in games past, who knows what would have transpired in games three and four.

The Bulls knew they were heading home with a mammoth task —a 2-0 deficit. Their passes needed to be crisper, checks needed to be harder, and hands needed to be softer.

Exactly a minute into the second period of Game 3, Zharkov blew the top off of Yardman Arena. An unassisted marker amplified the positive energy already created by over 2,500 screaming Bulls supporters.

It was all for not about four minutes later though, as Ottawa big-man Tyler Graovac put one home to tie the match up. The 67's added another two to close out the middle frame with a comfortable 3-1 lead.

A short-handed breakaway goal by Curtis lifted the Bulls spirits. Then puck-moving defenceman Jake Worrad, who played one of his best matches of the year in Game 3, eventually scored the game-tying goal about six minutes into the third period.

The score was knotted with little time left in regulation. The Bulls had their nemesis right where they wanted them. They didn't want to run-and-gun against one of the most talented squads in the country.

Down the stretch, Subban slammed the door shut.

So off to overtime they went, with the home team holding the bulk of the momentum in the palms of their hands.

Wily veteran Jordan Mayer sniped the winner for Belleville 14 seconds into extra time. After going upstairs on Mrazek, the Kingston native slid across the neutral zone on his knees in celebration, channelling his inner Theoren Fleury.

"We haven't had the best luck this year in terms of coming back in games, but playoffs is a whole different story," Brendan says following the uplifting victory.

The Bulls solved those tricky Ottawa folks for the first time in ages. They snuck out a win from a 3-1 deficit, willing their way to glory.

"We finished Game 3 with a strong effort and brought that momentum into Game 4," he adds.

Game 4 could be massive, Brendan confidently thought. A series-tying win would be huge.

The pressure was on for Belleville to perform once again. And they didn't disappoint.

A pair of goals in the opening frame—one from Curtis, another via Brendan on the power-play—set the tone. The Bulls needed just 40 more minutes of shutdown hockey to tie the second best team in the east, 2-2, in the first round.

They kept the relentless 67's forwards at bay in the first half of the task. The third was another story, however, as three different Ottawa players scored over a seven-minute span.

Heading into the first overtime, Game 4 projected to be the opposite of Game 3's collapse by Ottawa. The Bulls appeared cooked, out of their comfort zone as the club was forced to pick up the pieces after a terrible third period.

Who would be the hero this time around? Maybe Monahan, maybe Brendan, maybe Toffoli, maybe Judson.

It turned out to be Austin.

He notched his lone goal of the playoffs and seventh of the year for Belleville. None before the post-season marker were even in the same galaxy in terms of importance. The far-side wrister was a keeper for Austin, a story for the grandkids.

"Those were two pretty neat games to play in," Brendan says, completely undermining the fact they proved to critics that they belonged in the series.

If you tally up what transpired over the first four games of the Eastern Conference quarter-finals, it was really rather remarkable what Belleville accomplished considering their awful record versus Ottawa in the regular season.

Three out of four games went to overtime, with the Bulls coming out on top twice. The other was a 4-2 loss, which included an empty-netter. In all, the four-game combined score was 13-12 in favour of the No. 2 seed.

Both teams hadn't found their groove on the power-play, as the 67's went 2-for-15 and Belleville 1-for-20. The poor showing was expected from Belleville, who were dead last in man-advantage success rate in the regular season, but not sixth best Ottawa.

"Both crowds have been great so far," Brendan says when asked about the playoff atmosphere created by the two passionate major junior hockey cities. "Obviously Ottawa has triple the amount of people we have in Belleville, but it's been crazy-loud here with the cowbells. Both teams have fed off the hometown crowd, that's for sure."

More fuel for the fire.

The series shifted back to the Ottawa Civic Centre for Game 5.

The nation looked on, watching through their television sets via Sportsnet Friday Night Hockey.

Nearly 7,000 fans packed the barn.

They went home happy, as the Bulls allowed a trio of goals in the third period en route to a 5-2 loss. Payerl, Mayer, Austin, and Worrad, saw the worst of it, ending up with, at best, a minus-3 evening.

Ottawa's breadwinners took care of business in the offensive end. Prince collected a hat-trick after an empty-netter, while Toffoli and Monahan contributed a pair of points each. Netminder Mrazek came through when called upon, too, turning away 32 of 34.

With the season teetering in the wrong direction following the game, Brendan digressed and vented about his subpar performance.

"I really don't think I played well in Game 5. That was probably my worst game of the series," he says. "I don't know, I just didn't like how I felt after the game. I didn't do enough to help our team."

Did the national audience get to him? Get to his teammates? "It should have been more motivation, but it certainly didn't look like it in the way we played. I don't think the TV coverage was really a big deal," Brendan pleads. "We really just wanted to steal one in their barn, whether it was Game 1, Game 2, Game 5, or Game 7."

At 2-2 in a best-of-seven, a player of Brendan's quality couldn't afford to not do enough to help his team. They were a single defeat away from turning their backs on the 2011-12 hockey season.

It wasn't quite the end, but winning two in a row twice against the 67's was a steep challenge.

Unsurprisingly, the goalies stole the show in the pivotal Game 6. Subban and Mrazek traded saves in front of a boisterous Belleville crowd that could feel the season slipping away.

Garrett Hooey, the pride of Hampton, Ontario, drew first blood at 3:22 of the middle frame when Mrazek improperly handled a shot from Payerl.

The 67's answered by throwing a flurry of pucks at Belleville's cage. Eventually, thanks to some poor defensive coverage by the Bulls, Toffoli pounced and made no mistake. He was alone at the side of the net, easily able to pot his fifth of the series.

The superstar continued to buzz the net with his teammates. Just five minutes into the third, the hard work paid off.

Toffoli stuck the dagger into the heart of Belleville with his second of the game.

Players, coaches, and fans, all knew it was over.

As the seconds ticked off towards the final buzzer, the favourites rejoiced while the home team looked dejected.

The 31st season in the club's history was officially history.

Asked about that last game, it seemed as though Brendan was still stuck on Game 5, digging deep for answers to why it didn't work out.

"The first couple of games we were hitting the posts," he says, "we had tons of shots on the power-play. In Game 5 though, we had absolutely nothing to show for our power-plays. Ottawa plays you so tight when you're on the power-play. Everywhere you turn they're right there."

The Bulls just lost Game 6, but he was choosing to dwell on the game prior.

More than ever, his fiery spirit was interfering with what mattered most.

Unlike the other leaders on the team, there was definitely a next year for Brendan, and maybe the year after that, and maybe another after that. The others were either gone, or probably gone, or would only have a single season remaining in their OHL careers.

"I think it was mixed emotions at the end of the year. I think some guys were happy with their performances as a whole. The overagers weren't as happy since their OHL career is done. I don't think anyone was 'happy' with getting kicked out of the first round, but I think on an individual level most were happy." – Brendan Gaunce

It's an intriguing mechanism when you take a step back and think about how the major junior hockey world functions.

Together virtually every day for months on end, players pound and seethe for each other. They bear their fangs in unison.

Then, suddenly, part ways, off to various summer activities before returning or, for the older guys, gone entirely.

"I said bye to them all," Brendan says of his beloved teammates, "but we have a banquet in the summer so I'll get to them again then, too."

Less than a week later, he was back in the Toronto suburb he calls home in the summer months. Markham was unchanged.

But the switch from Belleville to the GTA, especially in terms of routine, always takes some adjusting.

"It's a completely different lifestyle coming home. Being away from hockey for a bit is actually quite nice right away. You know, it's good to see my family and stuff like that. Then again, you don't get to go to the rink, don't get to see the guys every day. It's hard to explain, but I'd say there's definitely some mixed feelings." – Brendan Gaunce

With the OHL draft just around the corner, a first round exit doesn't necessarily mean the coaching staff has a vacation after the on-ice play stops.

As a player, the transition to next season is not as immediate. At the same time, the lure of a fresh start stirs inside each player's brain. For those heading back into the fold, it's never really that far away.

Premature predictions and instant prognostications are rarely accurate down the road. They do, however, offer interesting insight into how a player evaluates what's in front of him at that very moment.

When assessing his team's chances in 2012-13, after barely finishing unpacking for the summer, the operative phrase used by Brendan was we'll be "one year older."

"I don't think any team would go into a new season thinking they're aiming to be a lower seeded playoff team. We have the tools and the necessities to be a good team in not only our conference, but in the league as a whole. I think everyone has a positive mindset at this point. We're going to be one year older." – Brendan Gaunce

As for the near future, the big-bodied centreman planned to relax for a short two-week stint before starting back up at the Gary Roberts school for hard-knocks.

This would give him plenty of time to watch the rest of the OHL playoffs, right?

"No, I hate it," he says, with no explanation until further prodding.

Not even the Western Conference, teams the Bulls play only a couple of times a year?

"I don't like watching the Eastern Conference at all," he enforces. "I guess I don't mind the west when you put it that way."

Are you rooting for any team left in the playoffs?

"Nope. I have friends on the teams but I'm not rooting for anyone."

Told you he was competitive.

***

Brendan Gaunce's sophomore season is only a few games past the halfway point.

The Christmas break is a thing of the past, with the January blues piling up so rapidly that it plants a sizable heap of frustration and angst on his lap.

The power forward's body is well rested, thankfully. He had plenty of time to bond with the family dog, siblings Cam and Ally, parents Julie and Stephen, as well as a few high school buddies.

Plus, Santa was good to him.

Jolly holiday traditions of relaxing with the family don't come around again until next year, a whole 12 months down the road.

But, time to get back to the grind for the highly touted NHL prospect.

His second home, Belleville, doesn't exactly exert fervour, however. The town is a relatively tame place in comparison to the major suburban centre he's accustomed to, Markham.

His billets are "great." They do what surrogate parents are supposed to do, and he couldn't ask for much more.

Outside, the trees are bare. Snow hasn't formed a crisp layer on the ground yet. It's as if the flakes are waiting in the wing of frigid temperatures, ready to pounce at the right opportunity.

Like most Ontarians, Brendan knows the enormous snowfalls are predestined, inching closer with each passing winter day. Global warming exists, of course, but it can't keep snow off the ground the entire season.

On January 13th, a headline on a local web-based news service named QNetNews reads 'Winter delivers first true taste.'

Over 10 centimetres of precipitation was left at Brendan's doorstop in Belleville that day. It was the first real snowfall of the winter.

Considering their luck, the Bulls should have seen it coming from miles away.

They ended a five-game losing streak the night before the great storm, narrowly escaping a road match in Brampton, 3-2.

Momentarily, the future looked sundrenched and fresh. The weather gods felt it was time to go against the grain, however—they had other plans.

Ironically, the Wolves, accustomed to flurries and storms up in northern Ontario, trotted into Belleville on the 14th.

They shook off their snow-filled boots, netting two goals in the first period—one from Andrey Kuchin with less than a minute to play—to ambush the Bulls.

Brendan, particularly rattled by his personal performance of minus-2—despite scoring his team's second goal in a 5-3 loss—let it all out after the game.

"I think whenever I'm not producing at the standard that I want to produce, but the team is winning, I'm happy. However, I get very frustrated with myself when I'm not helping my team and we're not doing well. I'm obviously gripping my stick too tight because I should have had about four or five goals in my last eight games. Instead, I have two. I think frustration is one thing I need to overcome if I want to play hockey at the next level." – Brendan Gaunce

For one of the only times between the beginning of the season in late September to the Sudbury game—technically Game 41 in mid-January—Brendan's guard came crumbling down.

The pressures associated with his draft year appeared to be gaining an unhealthy head of steam.

Because of some poor play to start the calendar year, much of the hoopla that hovered around the nameplate on the back of his sweater since joining the OHL was dissipating.

The honeymoon was over. The burdens, the demands, the strains were getting to him. His body was in tip-top shape, but his brain was scrambled.

When a player admits to gripping their stick too tight, you not only know there's an obvious on-ice problem at hand, but you also know his/her head is not in right place.

Players at the major junior level have taken shifts in thousands of games already in their careers, lacing up for 50-plus-game seasons since they were 10.

Everything on the ice comes relatively easy over time. It's their natural environment for growing as a person.

When a slump surfaces, however, bad habits emerge.

They sometimes translate into poor in-game play that isn't noticeable to the regular fan, but still harmful to their production as a member of the team.

In Brendan's case, water was being tossed on his ferocity streak. There was something remarkably off about his performance as a member of the league's elite forward fraternity.

Sure, he'd get an assist here, a pair there. Maybe a power-play goal in a 5-3 loss. The point production well wasn't running dry or anything.

Instead, it was his overall presence on the ice that was being affected. It was buried somewhere between the categories 'trying too hard' and 'it's just not working right now.'

If a player's instinctive concentration is off due to an increased desire to help their team in the offensive end, nothing first-rate will happen.

In the 5-3 loss, Brendan potted his 21st goal of the year. But, it didn't have enough oomph to vanish the mental wall that had been built over a six-game goalless drought beforehand.

It didn't register as an accomplishment in the bowels of his mind. Rather, he was consumed by the pitfalls.

"I think the first four or five games of the new year was my worst segment of the season," he says of his point-per-game performance that was stalled by an inability to contribute elsewhere. "I wasn't scoring when I had to, I wasn't playing as defensively minded as I should have been. Yeah, it's probably the worst string of games I've had this year."

The logical follow-up question: Is anything bothering you, Brendan?

"I don't think there's anything, anybody, but myself to blame for that. There were no glaring problems, distractions or injuries. I just don't think I was ready to play yet and it showed, obviously. I didn't come back from the break with the best head on my shoulders, if you know what I mean." – Brendan Gaunce

He's human.

Brendan was bound to go through a personal lull.

All of his draft eligible peers experienced the same at points in their seasons as well—whether that was in the form of a long-term injury or some on-ice struggles.

Being a fraction of that unfortunate community was an undeniable fact. That didn't mean it sat well in Brendan's head, though.

The bottom line was that he wasn't being himself. The consummate power forward, the lead-by-example assistant captain, the win-at-all-costs teammate was aloof.

The posts didn't help, either.

It's no secret goal scorers prefer to not hit the post at all. The sound of rubber against metal pierces the ears. The imagery of seeing a black object bounce off a red bar produces a cringe.

'Just go in!!!' they holler under their breath.

Perhaps the worst part of being in a slump is the requisite after-game talks. You know they're coming from your parents, your friends, the media, and on occasion fans expressing their displeasure on Twitter.

'Good job out there, but…' is a frequent slump conversation starter. 'There was this one play where you could have done this, instead of…' is another.

For the most part, the commentary is well-mannered and positive. Other times, it may come out wrong and ignite a heated conversation. In both cases, it simply sucks because it shows you've played poorly that night.

The Gaunces would habitually make the short trip to a nearby Tim Horton's after the bulk of Brendan's home games during the 2011-12 season. Depending on what had transpired inside Yardmen Arena that night, the conversation floated from hockey to school to general life topics.

When Brendan was dissatisfied, however, it was time for Mom and Dad to sit back and take it all in.

Might as well order an extra large beverage, their youngest son needed someone to vent to.

Sometimes barely left room for air in between monologues. Which was fine because the makeshift therapy sessions were designed for babble.

Julie and Stephen weren't expecting Brendan's mile-a-minute verbal notes to make much sense. They just wanted to be there for him.

In the end, though, it was Brendan who needed to make a change. The talking was nice, but it didn't resolve anything in the long run.

He needed to prove his worth, start displaying his aptitude against OHL defenders once again. Most importantly, he had to regain his role on a middling team and lift them through an incredibly bleak month.

"Frustrated isn't even close to describing what we're all feeling," Brendan says after the Bulls lost 6-0 to Niagara, their 11th defeat in 12 tries dating back to December 30th. "Especially some of us that feel it's our fault that our team isn't winning."

The frustration was at a boiling point in Brendan's mind, both as an individual player chasing a dream of playing in the NHL and as a leader on an OHL hockey club.

"I don't think I've ever felt this bad about hockey, about losing, over the past two weeks," he expresses.

Those words hold a lot of weight, and can be perceived in countless ways.

One may observe that Brendan is giving up, throwing in the towel. Another may think he's simply just stuck in a rut. A third may attach his words to a lack of confidence. And so on.

Above all, past all of the possible scenarios and opinions, was the context that surrounded such a bold statement.

Plain and simple, the team's play was mirroring their snake bitten spirits.

They needed to turn things around fast, and Brendan's skills would have to run the table in order to have that happen.

"I don't know if it's anything in particular that's bringing us so far down. I think teams are coming out more hungry, more aggressive than us. They're getting the bounces because they want to win more than us. I don't think it's anything glaring, of our skill, or what they've been watching. If you want to make a playoff push, we have to beat the teams above us." – Brendan Gaunce

With those remarks, he's reflective and intellectual in his speech.

But, it's blatantly obvious Brendan is worried about the self-inflicted ruin the Bulls were in by late January.

A will to win was missing in the Bulls lineup, and a will to be the guy who steps up—whether by-example on the ice or through a motivational speech in the dressing room—appeared to be lost within their 17-year-old assistant captain.

Coach Burnett, ever-optimistic about his team's fortunes and individual abilities, felt Brendan always placed a certain onus on himself.

In his eyes, this massive slide was no different than the rest of the season in terms of where Brendan fit in.

"Brendan has remained pretty strong throughout and I think he's a winner. He wants to lead the way in important situations and he wants to be the go-to guy and accept that responsibility. I think that he's made it clear on a number of occasions, whether it's in the media or otherwise, that he expects a lot of himself. He's one of our alternate captains and clearly a guy that we look to when we need a push." – George Burnett

One of Brendan's mentors, fitness guru Roberts, made the trip to see the Bulls play at home against Mississauga on January 18th.

There, as an eye-in-the-sky type, he immediately noticed a serious problem in Brendan's approach to the game.

He believed one of his summer workhorses was playing far too defensively. It was as if his pupil was overcompensating for his team's lack of scoring touch by making sure nothing got to the net.

"Truthfully, he didn't have a great game. And he knows it. I talked to him after the game and I said, 'B, you've got to move your feet.' I said, 'You're standing still way too much on the ice.' He's such a responsible player defensively, and his team is struggling right now so he's really focusing on his own end. But the problem is that he's a centreman who is standing still all night, and not creating any offence at all." – Gary Roberts

The OHL is by-and-large a meteoric learning process, Roberts emphasized, and it's better to work out the kinks in major junior than in the pro ranks.

He's absolutely right.

At the same time, it doesn't feel that way for a blue-chip prospect like Brendan. Especially since he's one of his toughest critics.

"The way my game translates is that I need to be thinking when I'm playing because if I'm not then my best skills won't be used properly. If I'm frustrated going in to make a play, I obviously won't make the play I want to, which just adds to my frustration. A calm mind coming into the game is the key to my success." – Brendan Gaunce

Would he reach out to his brother Cameron?

Surely he's gone through a very similar experience as a hockey player. Certainly there are a handful of examples the older Gaunce brother could draw from.

That's what is so advantageous about having a sibling follow the same career path as you—the answers are an honest phone call away.

However, Brendan didn't feel there was a need to touch base with the Colorado pipeline rearguard.

Which didn't exactly shock Cameron. The second overall pick in the 2010 OHL draft is self-sustainable, he said.

"I talk to B, but he doesn't usually reach out. If he has an issue that he feels can be corrected, he has enough people around him to tell him what he should be doing. I think he likes to experience things on his own. A lot of things he's going through I didn't go through, anyway. He's very self-motivated so I feel like sometimes he doesn't come to me. I watch a lot of his games so I have a pretty good idea of what's going on." – Cameron Gaunce

As a male teenager, it would almost have been more surprising if Brendan had reached out to Cameron regularly.

Hockey or not, those of his age and gender don't typically spill their feelings out for the world to see.

Just like when he was the kid-brother in net during hockey games, Brendan was by himself. He had to blaze his own path.

4

ON DISPLAY

It's October 6th, the first day of the 2011-12 National Hockey League regular season. A wildly popular Toronto sports radio show is salivating over the prospect of having one of the city's most famed sports icons on the air for a chat.

Another failed Maple Leafs season is not the topic of conversation, however.

Gary Roberts High Performance Training, and its steamrolling success, is the reason Gary himself is a part of the schedule.

Since his 2009 retirement from 23 years of service in the NHL, the fitness guru has built one of the most talked about summer training programs for elite hockey players.

Tampa Bay's Steven Stamkos, Philadelphia's Luke Schenn, Phoenix's Paul Bissonnette, Boston's Tyler Seguin, Anaheim's Andrew Cogliano, Pittsburgh's James Neal, Montreal's PK Subban, Nashville's Ryan Ellis, and Calgary's Mike Cammalleri, are all proud graduates of the Gary Roberts school of working out.

After dabbling into questions about the nuts and bolts of Roberts' program, the show's co-host punctually asks him what the core differences are between training a 17-year-old and a player in his mid-20s.

First, Roberts touches on developing a heightened work ethic for the younger guys in order to instil a culture of determination for years to come. Then, he mentions it's crucial to harness a certain consistency into their training.

Without interjection from the other side, Roberts decides to take it upon himself to center in on one kid, in particular.

"He's a man already," Roberts starts. "This kid is a machine, an absolute machine off the ice. He's already at the level of a 21-year-old that's training in the National Hockey League right now."

That 'kid' is Brendan Gaunce.

About three months prior, Brendan had dusted himself off after a mini two-week break following the hockey season to become one of Roberts' devoted summertime pupils for a second straight year.

His introduction to the boot camp, now held at the Fitness Institute in North York, came when workouts were held in the former NHLer's basement.

The Gaunce family was originally connected to Roberts through Greg Roberts, Gary's brother, who used to coach within the Markham Waxers organization.

Since Cameron had already christened the program a year prior, Stephen and Julie thought it would be a great opportunity for Brendan. He was venturing into pretty important training years leading up to the 2012 NHL Entry Draft, so they thought, 'Why not?'

"For Cameron—the way it switched his body type around—it was unbelievable," Julie raves. "When you're with guys who have made it, like Stephen Weiss for example, every day, you can't have an ego."

Cameron was always the heavier one growing up.

Roberts' program, and its concentration on various aspects of conditioning, transformed the Colorado Avalanche draft choice into a prototypical NHL-ready defenceman. His frame is now solid, yet lean.

Weighing in at 200-plus pounds as a 16-year-old, Brendan wasn't too far behind in the lumpy body type department.

While he was blessed with substantial height to balance things out a little bit, there was some serious work to do if he was going to impress the scouting fraternity down the road.

"My first impression was that he was a really good kid who came from a good family," Roberts says. "As for his body, he was shaped more like a pear than anything else. He was a little chubby, but not much different than a lot of kids that age."

In short, the chiselled frame every hockey player yearns for was indeed there, its framework intact. It just needed to be filled in with strength.

During the three-plus months under Roberts' regime in the summer of 2010, Brendan's sister Ally was around on a regular basis. She hadn't moved in with Jason yet, so she was home most times Brendan walked through the front doors after his work out.

"I would see him after, and he would be dead," she recalls. "But he would love it—he would always have a smile on his face."

In bed by 10 p.m. each night, Brendan woke up bright and early to trek over to the Roberts home with Cameron. They endured day after day with 'Gary, the hard ass,' as Stephen calls him.

A good hard ass at that, Stephen enforces, knowing the program has—and will continue to—pay off for both sons.

One point Roberts always drives home during media interviews is that the combination of ample rest and proper nutrition is just as important than what's done inside the gym.

A multi-hour lift session is not on the work out menu, as Roberts limits his athletes to less than two hours a day. Instead, organic food and various naps act as substitutes.

Mondays, Tuesdays, Thursdays and Fridays are stamped as weight lifting days. Mondays and Thursdays usually focus on lower body strength, while the other days highlight the upper body.

On Wednesdays and Saturdays, the athletes take to the running track, chugging along to enhance their stamina. Sunday is reserved for rest.

The whole reason Roberts developed the program in the first place was to present future NHL stars with an all-encompassing platform where they're able to get the most out of their bodies over the long-term.

Anyone who knows Roberts' history with hockey-related injuries, as well as his improbable performances in the post-season after the age of 30, is also aware of the type of seesaw battle he endured to close out his career.

"I'm not one guy sitting here saying I know it all," Roberts admits. "I just know from experience what I would change if I had an opportunity to do it all over again."

He was always one of the fittest on the team, yet the end crept closer and closer, ahead of the pace, because of the ignorant approach he showed towards health early on in his career.

Look no further than his all-time gutsy performance in the Maple Leafs 2002 playoff dash.

Most NHLers at Roberts' age would have been running on empty from the opening puck-drop for Game 1 of the first round, but the 36-year-old power forward was just getting started.

Nineteen points in 19 games was an incredible production rate for one of the eldest Leafs at the time.

However, following the deep post-season push, Roberts underwent double shoulder surgery.

"What I try to emphasize to these guys is that it doesn't happen over one summer. My mission statement is that I had longevity through a lot of challenges. My goal is to hopefully help these young players avoid the challenges I had, but still have that ability to have longevity. For me, being an ex-player and understanding the type of player these guys have to be to be successful, it allows me to assess their needs more specifically." – Gary Roberts

By snagging Brendan as a client at such an impressionable age, Roberts was presented with a gold field to mine. The second Gaunce boy was one of his new projects.

The grunts, moans, aches, pains and buckets of accumulated sweat during the off-season are instrumental to improving a hockey player.

Long gone are the days of smoking cigarettes in between periods. Drinks named Bio Steel run the roost now. The modern era of the sport demands continuous focus.

Brendan's minor hockey coach, Mike Gouglas, has witnessed first-hand what it takes to accelerate your on-ice growth as a player by committing to an off-season work out bible.

"I tell people this: You can almost hear a pin drop because the guys are there to work," he says with a deep stare. "They're there to get better. They come in, do what they have to do and then they're out, home, recovering."

It's a 365 days a year occupation, with some vacationing sprinkled on top for good measure.

In the summer of 2011, Brendan's fitness crew consisted of brother Cameron, University of Alabama-Huntsville freshman Jeff Vanderlugt, New York Rangers prospect Ethan Werek, Florida Panther Stephen Weiss, Anaheim Ducks prospect Peter Holland, Chicago Blackhawks prospect Brandon Pirri, and Washington Capital Wojtek Wolski.

That's decent company, to say the absolute least.

One thing differentiated him and Vanderlugt from the rest: They were the only undrafted members.

This seems like a major disadvantage, especially since NHL teams keep a close eye on a player's off-season training and, thus, require their players to be in tip-top shape.

According to Roberts, though, Brendan's relative inexperience— in hockey and life, in general—didn't affect his performance at the gym, or on the running track.

Cameron, one of Brendan's toughest critics on and off the ice, has trouble finding anything negative to say about his younger brother in terms of fitness arena presence.

"He most definitely keeps up. In our group we had a couple NHLers, and a couple guys who were top-tier prospects for their NHL teams, and he more than kept up. In the running, he was usually one of the fastest guys there, and in the gym he was lifting just as much, if not more, in all the exercises. When it comes to anything physical or anything athletic, Brendan is definitely way beyond his years." – Cameron Gaunce

Gouglas approved of Cameron's praise for his kid-brother.

"You wouldn't know he was the 17-year-old of the group if no one told you," he says. "He's doing the right thing. He's taking advantage of what he has access to, who he gets to learn from."

With a poster boy of Stamkos' stature—both physique-wise and in regards to natural goal-scoring ability—it doesn't get much better.

Another benefit to Brendan was the non-athletic experiences.

Roberts' prestige in the GTA, coupled with a lack of hockey-related stories out there in the summer, opens up a ton of media opportunities for Gary Roberts High Performance Training.

As the program picked up some major fame in '11, cameras frequented the centre. The Toronto media hype machine was in full effect.

A recurrent news hook in the stories was that these players—the highly touted prospects and all-world talents—are absolute monsters away from the rink.

They don't sit back and count their millions under the Tuscan sun. They count the number of bench presses and wind sprints, instead.

"In terms of the exercises, they're basically the same," Gouglas says of the program and others like it. "No one is re-inventing the wheel at this point. What Gary offers, though, is an attention to detail."

The nutrition, the concentration on rest, and the all-in attitude, Gouglas added, is what makes the Fitness Institute's main spectacle such a hit.

The whole perception of 'living the dream' as a filthy rich professional athlete is skewed anyhow.

Because the trade takes such an immense toll on your mind and body throughout the season, an after-season vacation is almost necessary. After that, it's back to business.

Living the dream is actually more about 'invigorating the dream' than anything else.

"Where you get to sleep in, wake up, play video games, have a Subway sandwich at 3 p.m., and then go to the rink," Gouglas says, rhyming off what some believe takes up a professional hockey player's day. "That is so far from the truth. You see those guys with Gary and they're waking up at 5:30-6 a.m. They're at the gym working out, they're focused, and they're wide awake."

The guys who chose to live the so-called dream are also the ones gassed in the third period of an OHL playoff game in their draft year, most definitely regretting the extra time they took off prior to the season's puck drop.

A select few can get by on mere talent. The rest aren't so fortunate and, oddly enough, probably prefer it to be that way. The challenge keeps the adrenaline pumping from Game 1 of the regular season to the very end.

When you factor in that there are only about 800 NHL player jobs up for grabs each year, the intensity seems even more extraordinary.

Like many professional routes—whether it be related to law, science, academia or electronics—athletic endeavours cannot be obtained without a relentless pursuit behind the scenes.

The most prolific lawyer, for instance, does his best work away from the spotlight of a high stakes court room.

That's the mentality, the lifestyle, Roberts drives into his eager apprentices.

Brendan noted the early morning dedication that he, Stamkos, and the others employ, is a bi-product of witnessing Roberts in his true element.

Perhaps predictably, he's the hardest worker out of all of them. "It's crazy the motivation you get from him, just because of how hard he is working at 45. We were the earliest group at 7:30 a.m. and he was always there before us and had finished his work dout. He must have been getting there at 5:30 a.m. and working out harder than we were just to stay in shape. I heard Stamkos say that because of him he's a better player and I can second that because he is an unbelievable role model." – Brendan Gaunce

Give the Belleville Bulls assistant captain a few moments to speak his mind about summer conditioning, and Roberts' name will come flying out of his mouth a dozen times.

Twenty-eight years separate the two. That's nearly three decades.

Does the age difference matter when it comes to bonding and landing on a mutual respect for each other, though? One would think so, but it turns out that's really not the case.

"He is probably the most intimidating guy I have ever met. I mean, he's a great guy; unbelievably nice and kind to everyone but when he's in the gym that's his second home. His eyes are just straight glass—you can never get an expression out of him. That's the best part of going there, though, as weird as it sounds. It's just so easy to find motivation when you're around a guy like Gary." – Brendan Gaunce

Stating he "better be" back for a few more summers, Roberts said Brendan will be a "beast" once he hits the age of 20.

"It's incredible to see him run on the track, or lift weights at the gym, with guys older than he is," he adds. "He keeps up, it's pretty impressive."

Roberts—citing a conversation with Stamkos following a mild-mannered race around the track—said that by the end of the 2011 summer, Brendan was one of the quickest guys in the entire program.

If there's one thing that counteracts development for aspiring and current professional hockey players, it's that the dog days of the off-season don't include many cheers, hoots, and hollers.

In-game recognition is easy to come by for the stars during the season, but not necessarily in the summertime.

Although the Fitness Institute gets more fanfare than your regular gym thanks to its reputation of pumping out and luring in quality athletes, there's no equivalent to thousands upon thousands cheering for your benefit.

Meeting or exceeding a goal during a workout session may garner a high-five or two, at most.

However, Roberts recalls a certain situation when Brendan received an unexpected compliment for a job well done.

"One of the biggest thrills for me since I've been doing this is Brendan coming up to me after year one and telling me his confidence changed. He walked by a girl and she said 'nice body' to him and he literally had to take a second look because he didn't think she was talking to him." – Gary Roberts

The always modest but rarely taken aloof Gaunce kid obviously made some strides since stepping foot inside the Roberts realm of supreme conditioning. And someone of the opposite sex noticed.

It didn't come with the flick of a switch. The fat loss and muscle gain process is a formidable task for anyone.

He wasn't stuffing his face with meals from McDonald's, Wendy's, or other fast food joints, either, instead pledging his life to the game of hockey. Brendan was about two years into a strict eating regiment.

If he wanted to be a professional, he had to walk, talk, train, eat, and act like one.

For Brendan, fast food is long off the radar. Pita Pit and Quiznos serve as his 'guilty pleasures' in Belleville when mates at school sprint off-campus for a bite to eat.

Bulls employee Josh Sweetland, who takes care of media relations, was one of the first people to meet Brendan when he joined the organization.

Since Sweetland interacts with players on a daily basis during the season, him and Brendan have developed a respectful, reciprocated relationship.

He's even seen him grow up a little.

"The changes I've seen in him, just even physically, is enormous. He's gotten into a lot better shape. Coming into the 2011-12 season, after the summer he had, he shaved off some of the baby fat a 16-year-old usually comes into the league with. He's grown into his frame more." – Josh Sweetland

When asked about his body type in May 2012, Brendan was pretty realistic.

He insisted he has never had a problem putting on weight in the summers. Unlike some of his peers, his diet and training patterns are designed to lean him out.

After only a week or two of lounging around his place in Markham after the season ended in utter disappointment thanks to a six-game Round 1 loss to the Ottawa 67's, he started doing half-days with Roberts and the crew on April 30.

An early playoff exit meant he was in good shape time-wise as he prepared for the fitness tests at the highly anticipated 2012 NHL Combine.

"I'm getting bored around the house," Brendan says on April 28, "but working out is not my top pick right now."

Luckily, it didn't take long for his mind and body to adjust.

Although the day-by-day order of muscle focus was altered from the 2010 and 2011 summers, no striking changes needed to be made. He was able to pick up where he left off.

By the time the Combine rolled around—taking place from May 28 to June 2 in Toronto—Brendan believed he was in the best shape possible.

In the days leading up to the mighty fitness showdown, Brendan didn't feel any unusual pressure or discomfort.

Once it was his turn to be tested, however, an uneasy mood drifted into his system. He knew immediately something was off, that he wasn't completely in control of himself.

"I thought I did pretty well. Obviously the results kind of go with that," he says of his initial thoughts. "After the Combine, though, I was really mad at myself. I didn't think I did as well as I could have. That whole day I was kind of pissed off."

Basically, he emerged from his day at the training centre pleased with how he looked in front of scouts, as a whole, but also felt he left something to be desired on a personal level.

Brendan said he let himself down in events such as the 'Standing Long Jump' and 'Jump (Mat) Mode – Ground Time.'

Displeased or not, the power forward was one of the superior athletes on hand at the Combine. If he left his tank empty upon exiting the fitness training centre, he might have walked away with a few more top 10 finishes.

The results tell the story well: First in 'Vertical Leg Power Pause Average (Lewis)'; second in 'Vertek Leg Power No Pause Average (Lewis)'; second in 'Upper Body Power 4 kg Ball'; fourth in 'Vertek Leg Power Peak No Pause (Sayers)'; fourth in 'Right Hand Grip'; fifth in 'Vertek Leg Power Peak Pause (Sayers)'; fifth in 'Pull Strength'; sixth in

'Left Hand Grip'; seventh in 'Push-ups x Body Weight'; tied for ninth in 'Vertical Jump No Pause'; tied for 10th in 'Vertek Vertical Jump Pause.'

Clearly, he did just fine in the leg exercises—a first, second, fourth, fifth, ninth, and 10th place, ranked him amongst the best in lower body strength and conditioning.

The type of exercises in which he missed out on the top 10 include 'Fatigue Index,' 'v02 Max,' and 'Standing Long Jump.' He was also off the board in physique-focused tests like 'Sum Of Six Skin folds,' 'Wing Span,' and 'Body Fat.'

As for what he figures went wrong, the usually calm-cool-collected Brendan noted a sudden brush with the nervous bug.
"It's just a different atmosphere than going to the gym. Obviously I hadn't gone to the gym for a few days because of the interviews and other commitments before the fitness testing. That's not excuse since everyone went through the same thing. But, I don't know, it just felt weird." – Brendan Gaunce

The jury is out on whether or not the scouting world takes results from the Combine into account when ranking players. Either way, it's a subjective topic with a subjective undertone.

What the public and players do know for sure is that a strong showing at the Combine cannot damage a prospect's reputation. A team may have their doubts about a particular player, and the Combine helps them either move on from the obstacle or move on from the player entirely.

Perhaps the most intriguing part of the whole process occurs outside the testing center's walls.

The convenience of having over 100 draft eligible kids in one facility at one time is a heavenly notion to NHL teams.

Picking their brains, digging deep into the seriousness of a nagging injury, asking about family matters—these are all reasons why the interview aspect of the Combine is believed to be more valuable than the fitness spectacle.

***

When a man gently guides his sailboat through the ocean's waves, there's a certain purpose to every sudden switch of momentum, every flinch of steering.

His left wrist acts on the same impulse as his right, one habitually snapping at each approaching wake.

The calmness—the absolute bliss—of floating across acres upon acres of open water allows for sufficient rest, a welcomed intermission for the hard-working sailing man.

Conversely, when currents from weather patterns and vessels approach, a strong sense of valour takes over the man.

Naturally, the backlash from the water comes and goes, with the former most prevalent. The sailing man revels in the furious competition of wrestling with the waves. It is his responsibility.

He has become accustomed to the unrelenting rigors of the constant fight. He knows the fight is a damn good fight. It's one he wouldn't trade for the world, or the sea.

The immediate moments following brushes with danger allow the sailing man to collect himself later, and reflect on what's important. His goals remain the same as ever: Personal triumph.

In many ways, a modern day hockey player's voyage to the game's highest peaks is much the same.

An elite sailor, in this case, is no different than an elite hockey player.

Nothing happens overnight. Substantial development never occurs over a year's time. There's an all-encompassing process that every ride of the wake—every goal—contributes to.

Honing one's craft is a passage, a sailing journey that has wavy stops in dungy small town arenas, highway coffee shops, crowded airports, and—of all things—gigantic malls.

Brendan Gaunce's first step out of the GTA hockey waters began when he was seven years old.

Brendan was already a stand-out amongst local peers back then.

Julie drove her youngest offspring westward to London throughout the spring and summer months so that he could practice with his Pro Hockey Development teammates. Following in Cameron and Stamkos' footsteps, Brendan stayed put in Markham during the winter but ventured off to the Forest City over the course of the summer.

World-class talents such as the Anaheim Ducks' Corey Perry and Columbus Blue Jackets' Rick Nash slipped on the Pro Hockey Development jersey during their childhoods as well.

The likes of London Knights forwards Ryan and Matt Rupert and Brett Welychka, as well as Windsor Spitfires forwards Michael Clarke and Chris Marchese—to name just a few OHLers alongside Brendan— were all members of the 1994-born squad.

The team was constructed solely for tournament play, a format common for pick-and-choose summer clubs. Its purpose was to pool together the finest Ontario-based players in order to bring home some hardware.

And although OHL scouts don't exactly frequent games played by 10 year olds, the high-end exposure never hurts.

"It's amazing how many kids you see drafted that played in the Brick's Super Novice Hockey Tournament," Julie says, noting the life experiences Brendan faced at such a young age were an added bonus.

The furniture store's showcase tournament, which takes place in Alberta's overzealous West Edmonton Mall each summer, is on par with a Star Trek convention in terms of popularity within its target market.

Brendan, ahead of the curve in terms of hockey sense and defensive awareness, took home Most Valuable Player honours.

His coach at the tournament, Lindsay Hofford, who is the current director of scouting for the Knights and CEO of Pro Hockey Development, saw a bit into the future back then. He witnessed a glimpse of the type of player Brendan would become when he was ready to compete in the OHL.

"A lot of the kids don't understand that the rink is 200-feet long. Brendan was always a kid that understood you could sacrifice a bit of offence to play defence. He was always reliable in defensive situations. That always set him apart from the other kids at that age. He was really able to play the complete game." – Lindsay Hofford

Continuing on until his Bulls responsibilities took precedent 12 months of the year, Brendan was a Pro Hockey Development player for a full decade.

Washington, D.C., Boston, Massachusetts, Los Angeles, California, were all places Pro Hockey Development tournaments took Brendan and his buddies.

One particular trip, all the way to Sweden, presented an interesting match-up in hindsight: Brendan versus Filip Forsberg.

In Scandinavia, half way across the globe, two highly touted NHL prospects jockeyed for ice at a tender age.

It brings new meaning to the phrase, 'what a small world.'

Those summers with Hofford and the bunch were extremely beneficial to the Gaunce family.

It allowed them to get away from the busyness that is the GTA, for one. It also opened up new doors, relieving potential pressures down the road.

Because of Pro Hockey Development, Brendan became comfortable with competing against the best 1994-born players on the continent, and sometimes in the world.

He also learned how to pack a travel bag, a duty he grew accustomed to shortly after joining the OHL.

Those Pro Hockey Development days are so far in the past that Brendan barely remembers the specifics.

Since, he's played in a few specialty tournaments and showcases, which may or not have something to do with the lack of retained memories. They've been trumped by an ever-growing international resume that began when he got the call half way through his rookie year as a major junior hockey player.

The first star-studded event he participated in was the 2011 World Under-17 Hockey Challenge, as a member of Team Ontario.

Accompanying him at the one-week event held in Winnipeg, Manitoba, were a few recognizable names to Brendan: Good friends Sean Monahan (Ottawa 67's) and Scott Laughton (Oshawa Generals); and a number of familiar foes, such as Jarrod Maidens (Owen Sound Attack) and Andreas Athanasiou (London Knights).

After a 20-6 combined score over a four-game round-robin in which Ontario finished unbeaten, they squeaked past Team Quebec in the semi-final before winning 5-3 over the United States in the final.

Just like that, Brendan was a gold medal winner.

It wasn't his first tournament win, by any stretch, but it was different than the previous ones: A gold medal that truly meant something.

One of Brendan's assistant coaches in Belleville, Jake Grimes, who headed Ontario's coaching staff, hammers home the point that the U-17 experience is a godsend for players like Brendan.
"The OHL rookie season, as a 16-year-old, is always tough. They go from being the best player on the team their whole life to, in most cases, getting limited minutes in the OHL. So, halfway through that year, they get a little bit of good news if they make our Under-17 team in November. Then when they go back into the environment with their own team they're more confident." – Jake Grimes

Amazingly, the champs did not have a single player in the top 10 in tournament scoring. There were no Ontario-born skaters who notched anything close to Matt Dumba's tournament-leading 12 points Canada Pacific.

Ontario's goaltender, Daniel Altshuller, and one of its top forwards, Athanasiou, picked up all-star nods, but the team's first place honours weren't earned via superb individual efforts.

After a gold medal was placed on each player's neck and the winning dressing room was turned into a temporary party area, each Ontario member went a separate route. Back to their respective OHL teams they went, all with a renewed sense of optimism and hope for the second half of their rookie seasons.

Looking back, Brendan remembers one particular aspect of the entire event. Yes, the gold medallion in his bedroom is a constant reminder of the on-ice success, but there's a sentimental attachment to the U-17's that he'll likely never forget.

With the tournament final just hours away, Ontario's equipment and training staff decided to elevate the significance of meeting the United States in the final. Though they could have rolled in a TV displaying highlights from the 2010 Vancouver Olympics' heart stopping finale between Canada and the US, they opted to offer motivation in a more discreet way.

"When we went into the dressing room," Brendan says, "there was a sign on the door that read 'Team Canada.' Then, when we went inside, the Ontario flag had been replaced by a Canadian one."

The pack of 16-year-old hockey players were obviously aware they weren't technically playing as Team Canada.

The gesture still hit home. It provided that extra push, that extra 'hey, let's go' dialogue needed to come out on top in such a crucial game.

Although Brendan isn't necessarily close with each and every member of that team now, there are a few U-17 teammates he still considers close friends.

The whole dynamic of separating on-ice feuds from positive off-ice relationships is all a part of becoming a professional athlete, Brendan insisted.

The mindset of distinguishing between friend and foe is tough to grasp at first, though.
"We played Scott Laughton of the Oshawa Generals eight times in my first year in the OHL. So, the first time I saw him at the tournament it was kind of weird. Guys like that; we usually leave those emotions on the ice. We're all friends and buddies when we come together for specialty events. I don't think it was ever that bad, but we've gotten older and we've learned that hockey is just a game. I think when you're younger and you hate a guy on the ice, it kind of translates to hating him off the ice, too." – Brendan Gaunce

In some instances, the relationships have blossomed beyond what Brendan expected.

For instance, Windsor Spitfires forward Kerby Rychel—son of former NHLer, Warren—is someone Brendan has known since the Pro Hockey Development days.

Talking virtually every day, the two 1994-born males have become closer since entering the OHL together. While playing nice off the ice during the regular season is gratifying, fun, and just an interesting element, there's nothing like pulling the exact same sweater over their heads.

That feeling from the U-17 tournament was resurrected when Brendan was chosen to don Canadian red and white for the first time in his career.

The annual Ivan Hlinka Tournament, which took place about a month-and-a-half prior to the start of the 2011-12 OHL regular season, was new territory for the young buck from Markham.

He would be on display for scouting pleasure once again, but this time with heightened pressure and a lust for a more important gold medal in the grand scheme of things.

Plus, it meant he would venture to Europe again—just like during his Pro Hockey Development days—to play fellow 2012 draft eligibles.

It was also an opportunity to build up a reputation within the national program's brethren. Playing for Ontario is one thing, but Canada is a completely new level.

Brendan, forever thankful for the privilege, shined as bright as a transport truck's high beams he spoke about the occasion.

"That was probably one of the best experiences I've had in my life. I was able to play in the Under-17 tournament but that was for my province. Being able to wear a Canadian jersey for the first time was surreal. You never know how to put it into words. – Brendan Gaunce

Potting a goal and adding an assist in a 4-1 victory over Team Sweden in the final obviously helped solidify the late summer tournament as a remarkable, never-forget experience.

Both points came during a third period where Canada cemented the win, as Brendan sniped an unassisted insurance goal 40 seconds in, and then grabbed the second assist on Charles Hudon's tally at 12:16.

It's safe to say he was an integral part of the gold medal-winning crew that fed off an ugly 5-1 loss to Sweden in the first game of the tournament to claim the title. He averaged almost a point per game—four in five—and was a key member of what head coach Steve Spott called a superstar-less squad.

After the game, while being interviewed by a TSN reporter, Brendan echoed what his coach previously stated.

"Everyone came together," he says into the camera, "and that's what won us this tournament."

So, there he was, across the world but still very much the same. In the spotlight as a Canadian ambassador, yet as humble and concentrated as ever.

Like in Winnipeg, the international event was another chapter of Brendan's hockey career that pushed him into the public eye. The OHL was aware of his abilities, but the broader hockey community was just beginning to see glimpses.

Also similar to Winnipeg, Brendan's team was one of the favourites heading in. In both circumstances, they capitalized on their breadth of talent and ran over the underdogs (e.g. 7-1 and 6-1 victories over the Czech Republic at the World Challenge and Hlinka, respectively).

From a strictly scoreboard standpoint, the difference between the two outcomes was that following an opening night loss, the Canadian team overwhelmed their supposed stiff competition—the Russians and Swedes—while Ontario was forced to pull out two close calls over Team Quebec and Team West.

In the end, all that mattered was that Brendan and his mates were proud owners of a pair of gold medals.

They fit right in with the dozens of trophies the Markham Waxers captain collected over his minor hockey years.

Brendan's international hockey resume was already noteworthy by the start of his sophomore season in the OHL. It wasn't record-breaking, or in the same realm as world juniors icon Jordan Eberle's, for example, but it was palpable he had done well for himself already.

Just seven months after his first voyage overseas to the Czech Republic, Brendan's number was called yet again by Canada.

The Bulls weren't deep in the playoffs, so Brendan being selected to take part in the 2012 World Under-18 Championship was a no-brainer.

While he was technically 18 at the time, the fact he was a 1994-born player meant he was indeed eligible to participate in the Brno and Znojmo, Czech Republic-hosted event.

"I didn't feel like an older guy, per se, but I didn't feel alone at all since I knew pretty much everyone from before," Brendan says. "I knew some Hockey Canada staff, the coaches, and I think it made me feel more comfortable."

Comfort can go a long way when you're thousands of miles from home, in a foreign country for the sole intent of playing a sport. That reality soothed Brendan's soul.

Denmark, United States, Finland and the Czechs were in Group A with Team Canada. They duelled each aforementioned opponent once in the round-robin, with two of the five teams moving on as Group A representatives in the playoff bracket.

The strongest club on paper was undoubtedly the States.

Not only did they have a capable group of young men born in 1994, they also possessed the distinct advantage of being able to support an entire program devoted to the age group. The development squad played together all year long.

In comparison to other hockey powers, like Canada, Russia and Sweden, the Americans projected to be head-and-shoulders above the rest in the chemistry department. No one could match up in that ever-important regard.

Defeating that force was a tremendous task for the other countries. The Canadians themselves would have to band together instantaneously in order to compensate for the drawback.

Then again, Brendan and his peers weren't exactly strangers to each other.

"I think it's getting easier to get together in a short time span since some of us have now played together a few times. The on-ice mentality, trying to figure out how to play, is the toughest. We are already pretty close off the ice, and come together with the right mindset right away." – Brendan Gaunce

Three of Brendan's 23 teammates at the U-18's—Erie Otters rearguard Adam Pelech, Rychel and Laughton—were also a part of Team Canada at the Ivan Hlinka Tournament and Team Ontario at the U-17 World Hockey Challenge.

The returnee list from August's Hlinka tourney was much more extensive—mainly since both were national teams as opposed to provincial. Aside from Brendan and the three musketeers, there were four others: Red Deer Rebels rearguard Matt Dumba; and three forwards, Medicine Hat Tigers' Hunter Shinkaruk, Owen Sound Attack's Gemel Smith, and Baie-Comeau Drakker's Felix Girard.

The list could have included a few more—such as Athanasiou of London and Monahan of Ottawa, for instance—but they were tied up with the OHL playoffs.

Eight players who have played together for a handful of games was nothing to brag about, but it did provide a core of familiarity that the newcomers could embrace right off the bat.

The coaching staff opted to plop Laughton and Rychel on Brendan's wings to begin the tournament. Recognizing the three had some history together surely played a part in the decision making from up top.

In the opener, Brendan was left off the scoresheet versus the Danes.

The team's power-play inflicted damage on the competition, however, going 2-for-5. Man-advantage goals in the second period allowed Canada to pull away.

In the second match of the tournament, versus the Finns, Canada let themselves go in the middle frame. After shutting out the opposition through the first 20 minutes, goaltender Matt Murray, a Sault Ste. Marie Greyhounds loan, let in three goals on 23 shots.

Yes, 23 shots in one period by one team at an international event. The Canucks were lucky they weren't down 6-1, instead of 3-2.

Somehow the third proved to be a bit of a yawner, with the teams combining for only 11 shots. A goal by Rasmus Kulmala sealed it for the Finns, though, as they waltzed away with a 4-2 victory.

Canada, and Brendan in particular, responded with a vengeance the next time out. They took down the host team by a final score of 6-2.

Rychel and Brendan put on a show, collecting three points each. To boot, a first period goal from Brendan proved to be the game-winner.

The team, as a unit, looked like the real deal versus the Czechs, unlike in the previous match.

So, with a 2-1 record in hand, and only the Americans standing in between Canada and the medal round, things were looking promising.

"Spirits were high with the team at that point," Brendan says, noting the win over the Czech Republic helped boost their confidence. "We knew we still had lots of hockey to play, though."

The final round-robin game was a barn-burner. Tied after the first period, tied after the second.

The Canadians were down by a pair at 4-2 after a minute of third period play, but there was still some fight left in them. A third marker brought back faith, but was soon doused by a Matthew Lane empty-netter. They lost 5-3.

The defeat brought the contingent of 17-18-year-olds Canucks to an even record heading into the playoff round.

They were scheduled to face a formidable opponent in the quarter-finals, the Russians.

For the second game in a row, Brendan did not record a single point. Again, his mates picked up the slack. After a 4-2 victory, they were headed to the semi-final against the favourited Americans.

The red, white, and blue were not exactly a preferred opponent, but it looked as though every team was forced to go through Team USA if they wanted to bring home gold.

Jones would play Canuck killer once again. The 2013 draft eligible forward assisted on both States markers in a 2-1 thriller.

The victory sent the Americans to the gold medal game, while the defeat bounced the Canadians to the bronze match.

"You never want to win bronze but you obviously want to win something," Brendan says a few days after returning to Markham, with the sting of not participating in the gold medal game toned down considerably. "It didn't work out in the semi's but we can't be upset with ourselves."

Brendan missed a penalty shot opportunity in the bronze medal game versus Finland, but redeemed himself with a short-handed tally midway through regulation time. The goal was absolutely massive.

His play in the tournament, in an overall sense, wasn't mind-blowing. His final statistics—three goals, one assist, plus-4, 23 shots on goal—backed that notion up.

He was just solid—nothing less, nothing more.

All the same, after a second appearance wearing the maple leaf, Brendan truly put his fingerprints on the national program.

That Christmas run-in with a fake Hockey Canada letter was a thing of the past. Even though it didn't tug on his emotions too much anyway, the sturdy performance overseas undoubtedly made him feel more secure about missing out on the world juniors experience.

When Brendan looks back—10, 20, 30 years from now—on his major junior hockey career, there will be plenty of brilliant moments that ring a bell inside his head.

Thus far, he's battled the 67's in a six-game series his team didn't belong in prior to the playoffs. The fact he is the assistant captain of his club squad is an accomplishment in itself.

He's also the owner of two gold medals and a bronze medal since graduating minor hockey.

Then there's a couple of other specialty events: The NHL Research, Development and Orientation camp, as well as the CHL/NHL Top Prospects Game. Both are rare honours.

The RDO Camp only lasted two years, and Brendan was fortunate enough to take part in the second edition. The Top Prospects Game, although seemingly a staple of the CHL's inter-league schedule for years to come, is still a once-in-a-career opportunity.

Before being eliminated in the summer of 2012, the RDO Camp represented the first true chance for NHL teams to see draft eligible players strut their stuff. Most have played in the CHL for a year or two already, but the concentration of talent is atypical, especially in mid-August.

The feeling on the other side, from the player's perspective, can be described by one word: Amazed.

"The first day we got there, we were treated like pros. It was like we were the Leafs at the Mastercard Centre. At all of our meetings, we had guys like Brendan Shanahan speak. He was my favourite player when I was younger so listening to him talk to the guys—to see how mellow he was, how good he was in front of a group of people—it kind of showed why I liked him so much on the ice. And then the on-ice, it was just awesome to try out rules the NHL guys were going to use." – Brendan Gaunce

The Markham native was fortunate enough to meet his childhood idol. Not a bad gig after all, Brendan figured.

For three straight days, Brendan and 35 others relished in the spotlight.

National media assembled, picking apart the great frozen game. Newspaper columnists, radio personalities, and TV panellists put in their collective two cents on the ever-debatable no-touch icing idea, for instance.

The pundits weren't gathered with the sole purpose of getting a sneak peak at a new rule change or two. They were hanging around the rinks to amass insight from the 30 NHL general managers summoned to the prospect hot spot.

For the players, they were in front of the right people—their potential employers down the road—and given the gift of flexibility. They were able to stretch the limits, as well, by trying out innovative rules.

The flexibility gave way to a few uneasy moments, however, with each demonstration posing its own form of uncertainty.

"The first game was the most nerve-racking of the four and I think we played nervous because you're trying out new rules and also trying to play well. So, if you screw up a rule, in the back of your mind you think 'ah, I screwed up, they probably think I don't have good hockey sense.'"
– Brendan Gaunce

But, as time progressed over the short camp in Toronto, so did each kid's confidence.

Brendan felt completely comfortable in the mix-and-match dressing room, as Laughton, Subban, summer workout pal and Knights forward Chris Tierney, as well as international teammates like Maidens, all took part in the same hamster-in-a-wheel exercises.

Phoenix Coyotes head coach Dave Tippett walked back-and-forth on Brendan's bench, while opposing players received advice from recent Stanley Cup champion, Pittsburgh Penguins head honcho Dan Bylsma.

Even though—in the big picture—the mini games didn't count towards anything whatsoever, and the coaches weren't providing NHL-calibre pep talks, the experience was everlasting.

Months later, Brendan was still fixated on a few of the try-out rules. The RDO Camp's influence did not grow stale.

"The rule I really noticed was the hybrid icing. I thought that was pretty cool just because you can still have plays where the defenseman puts the puck off the backboards. I think it's pretty smart. I like the smaller circumference of the nets, too. It's only four inches but it makes a big difference. You can make a quick turn or another turn that you wouldn't be able to make with less room." – Brendan Gaunce

And with those words, Brendan's intelligence as a hockey player was shining through off the ice. Clearly he thought the game well, whether you agree with his analysis or not.

He identified with the potential rule changes, and knew most would work in his favour as a power forward.

By this point in his hockey-playing life, he was already able to zone in on any given situation off and on the ice.

Distractions didn't exist in his hockey world. The thousands of cheering or booing fans, the dozens of scouts at each of his games, the NHL general managers, the media—none of it mattered.

Winning took priority, and everything else was a distant second.

"I don't really think about them being there," he says, referring specifically to the scouts. "I'm more worried about what my parents think of my game, to be honest. I do care about scout's opinions in a way, but what my parents say is always completely honest."

Absorbing his family's blessings but politely shushing away the rest. It was a textbook mindset for a teenager on the verge of entering fame.

On every CHL team, there are certain egos that emerge from the pile, peak out from atop the heap of level-headed guys. The majority are extremely grateful for their chance at the Canadian Dream.

A select few? They believe their success gives them a sense of entitlement.

On a game-by-game basis, especially since it was Brendan's draft year, the pressure was constant.

He could have taken the nose-in-the-sky road, and harvested a sense of self-worth the size of the Yardmen Arena ice surface. But he didn't.

Again, the fans, the suits, and the scribes, watched his every move.

"I think this year I've tried to focus myself a lot more before the game," Brendan expresses in mid-January. "I'll take some time to not really look at the crowd, just focus on myself by doing some breathing."

Mental preparation is integral to any athlete's success. Keeping a cool head, spotlighting the circumstance at hand, and leaving every ounce of energy on the playing surface, are all aspects required in order to advance quicker than others in the development process.

Some use music to sync into the atmosphere of the building. Brendan chooses to go with straight-up silence before games. "Away from the rink, I don't really do anything superstitious. When I get to the rink, though, I usually have a longer stretch than the team. I won't tape my stick in the same spot but usually at the same time. I'll get my drinks right after our team meeting. I think I have a couple of rituals. It's nice on the road because it makes you feel comfortable." – Brendan Gaunce

He uses an unassisted method before games, opting for silent treatment. And most often than not it works like gangbusters.

Still, no game, no stretch of time, no half-season, no full season, has and never will be, perfect.

A flubbed pass, case of over-skating the puck, or missed check, during a regular season game may not seem like a big deal at the time. But the draft year pyramid is built brick by brick, stone by stone.

Therefore, it was essential Brendan kept his eyes on the prize, especially during the 2011-12 season.

In February, with the draft about four months away still, he was getting back into the groove offensively after a weak January—case in point: Two four-assists nights in three games—but something else was falling by the wayside.

"For off the ice, when I'm playing well I still need to be doing more homework. On the ice I wouldn't change much, but off it I have to concentrate more on school. I'm still getting good marks but I think my work ethic could be better away from hockey. Some nights after hockey, if I played well, I feel the need to go to bed instead of homework. I'm sure my mom wouldn't like hearing that so I won't tell her but I just feel like I don't have to sometimes." – Brendan Gaunce

Eventually, he turned it around and picked up the slack homework-wise. Win or loss, goal scored or no goal scored, Brendan smartened up and took care of his scholarly responsibilities down the stretch.

One wonders if the persistent OHL schedule, mixed in with a memorable experience in Kelowna at the Top Prospects Game, temporarily altered the 17-year-old's priorities.

"It's definitely something I've been looking forward to for a while," he chimes in on Jan. 28, 2012, speaking about the showcase.

Zharkov and Brendan checked out a Waxers Major Midget AAA game prior to leaving for the west coast. Watching his old hockey friends duke it out is a hobby of Brendan's when he's in the area.

"We leave tomorrow and it's only a three-day thing so it'll go by pretty quick. I'll have to cherish every day, even tomorrow when it's just a practice. I think the first two days are more about taking it all in and just being able to realize you're up there with the top players in your age group. Then gameday will be strictly hockey." – Brendan Gaunce

The premier event engulfed Brendan's emotions, loosened his iron clad strings.

He was usually a tough-to-crack guy. This time around, he was more than willing to relish in the opportunity and seize the experience.

"It's going to be jam-packed but it'll be a neat experience, that's for sure," he adds.

After off-ice testing and a rapid fire media session, the first day was in the books pretty quickly.

Luckily for the 40 players on hand, the backdrop in Kelowna isn't too shabby.

"The scenery in Kelowna is just unbelievable," Brendan says. "I saw that part of North America when I went to Colorado last year to watch Cameron, but I've never really seen mountains up close and in the winter."

The second and third days were far more serious than the opener —on-ice skills evaluations by NHL scouts, skills competition, and the game itself. The mini vacation Brendan was about to feature battles on the ice with some extremely gifted opponents.

Fortunately, a guy by the name of Mark Recchi, who accumulated a cool 1,533 NHL points and three Stanley Cup rings over a Hall of Fame-worthy career, was named head coach of Team Cherry.

In awe of the wily puck veteran, the players just sat back and let the master show off.

Recchi's finger hardware certainly caught the attention of Brendan.

"He brought in his three rings. He had one from the 1980s, 1990s and last year's. The difference from the 80's to nowadays is just ridiculous. It's too big, basically, now. It takes up your whole finger. It kind of looks stupid on your hand because it's so big. It's so glaring, there's so many diamonds." – Brendan Gaunce

Brendan was living in the moment, enjoying his time away from Belleville.

Earlier—only a few weeks prior, actually—Brendan found out he was penciled into the No. 11 spot on the NHL Central Scouting Bureau's North American draft eligible skaters mid-term rankings.

In terms of forwards playing out of the continent, only three others—Nail Yakupov of the Sarnia Sting, Mikhail Grigorenko of the Quebec Remparts, and Radek Faksa of the Kitchener Rangers—ranked higher than Brendan.

At that point in time—January 11th, to be exact—Brendan had tallied 20 goals and 41 points in the first 39 games of the 2011-12 OHL season.

Seeded as the 11th best amongst domestic skaters meant he was considered a first-rounder.

"You would think it would help my confidence, but lately I haven't been playing with as much confidence as I should… No, it was definitely an honour to be ranked that high. When you hear about those things, you start thinking about the draft a bit more." – Brendan Gaunce

Though Yakupov (rated No. 1 on the mid-term rankings) could not make the trip out west for the Top Prospects Game, Grigorenko (2) and Faksa (4) were both in attendance. Five of the seven others players ranked ahead of Brendan—all defencemen—participated as well.

Everett Silvertips Ryan Murray, third on the North American skaters list, captained the Recchi-led Cherry squad, while Colton Sissons of the hometown club, the Kelowna Rockets, wore the 'C' for Team Orr.

Sissons was helped out by two assistant captains: Grigorenko and Barrie Colts forward Tanner Pearson. Joining Murray as chosen leaders of Team Cherry was Brendan, as well as Martin Frk of the Halifax Mooseheads.

Instead of hearing the jolly assistant captaincy news from his agent, coach, or family, a fan let him know first.

"I was on the bus to a game and I just texted my Dad to say whatever. Then I got a mention in a Tweet and it was about me being named assistant," Brendan says, sounding slightly astonished. "So, it looks like technology helped me out."

Sure, the letter on his sweater didn't mean much in the leadership sense of the honour since the team was only together for a single game. But, it was still significant—it symbolized Brendan's promise as a potential stud in the NHL.

It was an absolute honour considering the talent on hand who ended up on the wrong end of the captaincy decision.

The event, as a whole, was another 'showcase' bullet point on the Belleville Bulls star forward's resume.

But would he play up to snuff in the actual game, the reason he was there in the first place?
"I thought I played pretty well in the defensive zone and the neutral zone. One thing I was complimented on was my hard work during the whole game. But, I don't think I really got anything going offensively. I still got a couple of shots. I thought I played a relatively solid game overall." – Brendan Gaunce

Brendan finished the ever-scrutinized match with a rather bland stat line: No goals, no assists, plus-1, no penalty minutes.

Nothing special.

Since it was a relatively tame contest—a 2-1 final score in favour of Team Orr—the majority of Brendan's temporary teammates and foes posted similarly tasteless numbers.

Most of the flash and glamour came from the highly anticipated skills competition, which mirrored the one employed at the annual NHL all-star games.

Fastest skater, hardest shot, shooting accuracy, showdown breakaway challenge—these were the selected events for the January 31st event. There was also a 3-on-3 challenge to top things off.

Pat Quinn's Team Orr managed to pull out an 8-7 victory, with Brendan scoring a 16 in the breakaway challenge.

Before doing his part for Team Cherry, the whole concept of going in on a goaltender, all alone and having the central task of dazzling the crowd, stopped Brendan in his tracks.
"When I was chosen for the breakaway challenge I was dumbfounded, I didn't know what to do. I don't have the skill that the Europeans have, or the skilled domestic players have. I was trying to think of things, and I eventually had two soccer moves in my head. But, they said you can't use any props. So, there goes my idea." – Brendan Gaunce

Wait, what?

A soccer move?

"I was going to take off my hockey jersey so I could wear a soccer one. And I was going to go down, flip the puck onto my stick and hit it with my skate out of the air and into the net. The second one I was going to get Zharkov to stay behind the net, pass it over and I was going to kick it in." – Brendan Gaunce

Sounds like a real crowd pleaser.

Nonetheless, the whole aim of the three-day event is to turn people on to major junior hockey. And if that meant keeping the skills competition away from goofy shenanigans, it was all right with Brendan.

Another can't-miss aspect of the Top Prospects Game each year is the immense media attention. For hockey reporters, there isn't much that trumps a an all-access pass to a multi-day event consisting of the best prospects on the continent.

Each year, players are ushered out to a few media sessions per day. They field the obvious questions about their draft year, upbringing, current situation with Team X, and what they think of the event in general.

Then there's the spectacle-like atmosphere created by the in-house media during play. After all, the fans want an in-depth viewing experience.

"One of the things that really stuck out during the game and at the skills competition is the camera time NHL players and all pro athletes get—there were probably four cameras on the ice at all times—is crazy. It's hard not to laugh and hard not to freak out sometimes. I thought it was kind of media driven more than actual on-ice stuff." – Brendan Gaunce

In one particular moment, Brendan was the centre of attention both inside the Prospera Place in Kelowna, and in thousands of living rooms across the country thanks to the national television broadcast.

Before his turn at the breakaway challenge, Sportsnet's Sam Cosentino, the on-ice personality for the skills competition, asked Brendan what move he was planning on displaying.

As a no frills player with little flash, Brendan didn't know what to say, really. His soccer idea was previously squashed so he was forced to make something up on the go.

On his first try he switched his stick around, using the butt-end to shoot the puck. It appeared to have potential, but the flamboyant effort faltered as he barely got a shot off.

After, Consentino revealed Brendan's secret plan for his second attempt to the eager crowd.

"He told the crowd he wanted me to shoot low stick side," he says. "I was like, 'Oh my gosh, at a skills competition?'"

The goaltender knew exactly what was coming, positioning himself perfectly.

Save.

"He said if I had scored he would give me a 10," Brendan adds, laughing at his poor showing at the skills competition.

***

There's a double bed pressed up against a wall facing the doorway in Brendan Gaunce's bedroom at his family's home in Markham.

A dresser—whose every square-inch is covered by a trophy of some sort—some scattered personal belongings, and a few dated posters also take up considerable space in the rectangular room.

Dust forms on the furniture. The closet is mostly empty. The inhabitant is living in Belleville right now, playing hockey for the Bulls.

Beside the bed are two photos.

One is of his family, a prototypical item in most bedrooms across the globe.

The other, a framed photo of three boys dressed in drag, isn't so representative of a male in his late teens.

"I probably get more nervous for those types of events than a hockey game," Brendan says of his acting career, which, so far, is trademarked by a performance as a middle-aged woman in a performance of the Hairspray, the musical based on a film by cult filmmaker John Waters.

The operative syllable is hair.
Generally speaking, Brendan doesn't appear to have any sentimental attachment to what grows on his head.

In a matter of three years, he has kept his usual clean, short cut for extended periods of time; worn numerous wigs for different occasions, including the aforementioned acting gig; shaved it off in the summer time, once in support of his cancer-battling mother; gone to the salon twice to get a proper 'Bulls playoff run cut', the first time swiping the top off but leaving ample hair on each side, and the second time doing the opposite.

"It's good, I kind of don't notice it anymore," he says dryly about the 2011-12 post-season haircut, which made its way around the Internet thanks to Bulls captain Luke Judson sharing a photo from his cameraphone.

A theme to take away from this rigged timeline of his mop: Brendan does not put too much weight into the opinion of others.

He keeps a deflector up the majority of the time, sidestepping the naysayers and fake boosters.

"Brendan, in all honesty, does not care what people think of him," Julie says, adding he was "painfully shy" before his OHL draft year. "He doesn't care at all. He'll wear whatever he wants, do whatever he wants."

The oddball haircuts, the out-of-left-field acting fascination, the interest in the Harry Potter mega book and film series—it all points to a guy who just doesn't really care to fit into the norms.

The switch from Brendan being humiliated at times as a kid to not bothering to bat an eyelash was largely unexpected, Ally said.

"He used to turn beet red whenever somebody would talk to him," she says of elementary school Brendan. "I don't know what changed it—maybe it was my father always making fun of him in front of everybody—but he has switched big time."

With his rookie season in the rear-view mirror and the prospect of being selected in the first round of the NHL draft fresh in his mind, Brendan's mentality coming into his draft year was to eat up every moment.

This would never happen again, he thought.

His parents, agents, and Bulls coach George Burnett, all believed in his abilities. It was a question of harnessing those talents when it mattered most, then dealing with the rest off the ice.

The entire year would be a giant juggling act, but Burnett and his colleagues sat Brendan down to set things straight.

"We made it clear to him that as much as there's always going to be pressures—distractions and the other different things going into a kid's draft year—I think it's important to enjoy the experience as much as possible," the former Edmonton Oilers head coach says.

It was really the only logical—and probably least stressful—way to approach it.

The distractions will be there regardless. Rankings weren't going to suddenly disappear. His friends weren't going to stop asking which team he'd prefer to play for. The media will not ignore the future of the NHL simply because they feel they are adding to the pool of anxiety.

You may as well embrace it, Brendan decided, because otherwise you're setting yourself up for more problems.

As much as he didn't dwell on other people's opinions on a day-to-day basis, Brendan was still aware of what was going on around him. He knew he had to keep up a certain image, regardless.

Plus, he was smart enough to realize the intentions of other people, the reasons why he was receiving such increased attention as a draft eligible player.

"When you're younger and see draft eligible players, you kind of judge how they treat people," he says, clearly talking about the 1990-born Markham Waxers. "Because of that, at the start of the year I had the outlook of whoever wants an interview or autograph, I'll do it. I don't want to ruin anyone's day or week."

And he lived up to his promise.

After games he'd stop for a moment to ink a signature on a tyke's jersey or puck. He'd also take care of interview requests from the media and NHL scouts. He didn't shy away from much.

"I think the way I look at it is that after 5 o'clock I'm not at the rink anymore so I have that time to talk to people if they want to talk to me. That's a pretty cool feeling that people actually want to talk to you about how you're playing hockey. I'm always open to whatever." – Brendan Gaunce

Since Subban, Zharkov and Brendan were all considered top-end prospects at the beginning of the campaign, the Bulls media relations man, Josh Sweetland, knew he was in for a fair amount of interview requests.

From as far as Los Angeles and as close as Belleville, people wanted to speak to Brendan throughout the season. Of course, demand peaked at the beginning of the season and before the draft, but there was always a constant flow.

Sweetland noted he received an average of 2-3 requests a week to interview Brendan, from media or hockey management outside of Belleville.

"It's 10 minutes a day, I'm doing nothing anyways," Brendan says of the duty of talking to complete strangers on the phone.

The Toronto Star ran a story entitled 'Brendan Gaunce is a star at any position' in his minor midget year. It raved about his ability to excel in both football and hockey while in Grade 10.

The country's largest newspaper spoke to Brendan again during his draft year, this time coming out with a story that zeroed in on his mental maturity and strong hockey genes.

The likes of TSN, Sportsnet, Yahoo! Sports, and Junior Hockey Magazine radio, all chased down Brendan at some point. He, and the rest of the cream of the crop of 2012 NHL draft class, remained hot discussion topics all season long.

And, naturally, the local media were present after every game, looking for answers to questions, good or bad.

"He doesn't forget; he's punctual and doesn't really seem to mind taking phone calls, whether it be from a random blogger or an NHL team," Sweetland adds.

Athletes in all sports and competition levels are more accessible to fans than ever before.

The invention of Twitter has revised the athlete-fan relationship, granting fans the ability to send a 140-character message to an athlete without their consent.

For all intents and purposes, it's merely a way to increase one's profile as a public figure.

Fringe NHLers such as Paul Bissonnette, of BizNasty2Point0 fame, have mastered the social media website. They've created a cult following without being one of the best players in the world.

Brendan mentions that Tweets he receives from fans are mainly positive.

The odd one will be from the other end of the spectrum, though. Which he shrugs off, anyway.

"If I know them, like Mr. Roberts or Mr. Titanic, I'm all ears because they know how I play," Brendan says of his screening system for constructive criticism. "I definitely take the criticism to heart."

As for the media, he generally tries to avoid reading, watching or listening to coverage about himself. Although if it's a high profile article like the two Toronto Star pieces, it's hard to duck away from the attention.

"I think it depends where the article is based out of," he says. "If it's in Toronto, since it's so close to Markham, I'll see it. I'll get a text or something and I'll usually read it then."

This past season posed an interesting relationship with the media, because Subban and Zharkov—whom Sweetland calls "quite the bubbly Russian kid"—were in the same situation. Often times, he was asked about their play, and contributions to the team, on a semi-regular basis.

Most questions surrounding Subban pertained to the influence of his brother P.K., injury woes and incredible season. It's not difficult to chime in about your team's MVP, that's for sure.

With Zharkov, it was a bit different because he wasn't from Canada. The questions were more vague, and the odd time Brendan even played translator for the 6-foot-3, 200-pound St. Petersburg native. "Sometimes when we're in Belleville, they'll ask him a really long question. It'll be 20-30 words and I'll trim it down to a couple of words. I don't know a word of Russian. They must learn English at a young age because when I hear Russian I don't understand it at all." – Brendan Gaunce

In a relatively small market OHL community of Belleville, mistakes can be magnified.

On-ice struggles might end up being front page news of the Bellevlle Intelligencer; an off-ice gaffe the same.

The less populated the surrounding area, the faster word spreads about both positive and negative rumours. The aftermath of being photographed as an under-ager at a bar in, say, Ottawa, is amplified ten-fold in the humble grounds of Belleville.

Keeping a low profile has been key for Brendan.

"You don't want undue attention being drawn to you. In the past, we've had guys go out and mess up," he adds. "Word spreads like wildfire around here."

Being out and about is necessary in order to connect with the casual fan, local businesses, and season ticket holders. Being out and about in the wrong light, however, could doom a player's status and potentially affect their future.

The whole 'bad boy' image is an overused tag these days, but it's always something a person in the public eye needs to be aware of.

Brendan has managed to keep himself out of negative press, the unwanted spotlight, since joining the OHL.

Along with groups of teammates, Brendan participated in many out-reach programs in the 2011-12 season.

Bowling with the Bulls, handing out teddy bears prior to the Teddy Bear Toss game, reading at elementary schools, and playing mini-stick hockey, are all examples of the efforts made by the Bulls to strengthen their bond with their host city.

Though all major junior hockey teams participate in similar events nationwide, it's safe to say not every player enjoys the experience. Some are dragged out to the appearances, unenthusiastically taking part to please management.

Brendan seems to be a part of the majority, the bulk of players. He's grateful for the opportunity.

"I've realized that when you're younger, it's so big to be able to meet any hockey player over the age of 16. Talking to them is easy for me," he says.

Another dynamic thrown into the wheel turning Brendan's draft year was that he was set to battle against buddy Sean Monahan a grand total of 16 times over the course of the pair's second seasons in the league, since the Bulls and Ottawa 67's are eastern Ontario rivals. Two in the exhibition schedule, eight through the regular season, and six storied matches in the playoffs.

The two 1994-born forwards played against each other in minor midget, as Monahan, a native of Brampton who is eligible for the 2013 NHL draft since he was born in October, suited up for the Mississauga Rebels.

The elite talents are most often than not matched up on the ice, even in the OHL. It's rare for a period to go by when they don't clash in the face-off circle or corner.

Over time, they've developed a friendship. Each acted out integral roles on Ontario's Under-17 World Hockey Challenge team, and the Canadian Ivan Hlinka Tournament squad.

After countless confrontations on the ice, they finally met as teammates at an U-17 camp in Guelph. And, according to Monahan, "bonded" instantly.

"He was actually sitting beside me in the change room. We were on the same team at the camp. And we started talking, he seemed like a good guy, and we've been friends ever since. We're pretty competitive in the circle. Facing off against him, knowing we're going to text about it later, makes it even more intense. You know you're going to hear about it if you lose more than you win after the game." – Sean Monahan

Over a 10-minute interview, slick scoring Monahan mentioned Brendan's ability to 'think the game well' more than a few times. Unprompted, he spoke about the importance of such an instinctive and intangible trait.

He noted Brendan is one of the toughest players to get a reaction out of in the entire OHL.

On the ice, the burly centreman is all business. It's hard to figure out what pushes his buttons. Among testosterone-fuelled young men, this is rare, let alone among ones at the top level of an aggressive sport.

Bulls equipment manager, Matt Sands, knows this side of Brendan all too well. His job is an all-access pass to seeing teens at their best and worst.

An equipment manager is usually the first team employee at the rink on gameday, and the last to leave. They greet the players as they arrive, asking about any special requests, and then collect the remnants of a hard-fought battle after the game is complete.

Over his four years with Belleville, Sands has sharpened the skates of P.K. Subban, Shawn Matthias, Eric Tangradi, and more than 100 others.

Out of all of the handful of professional hockey players who have donned the black and yellow while Sands has held his position, Brendan stands out in terms of pre-game preparation and concentration.

"When he's at the rink, he's just so focused," he says. "He won't say much, he'll stick to his routine and his regimes. And I think that's what's special about him."

Adding that Brendan "gets it" when it comes to having a certain preference towards skate sharpness, and stick height and taping, Sands feels at ease when he recalls Brendan's start with the club.

"One of my memories from last year is that we spent a couple months— right in the middle of the season—getting his stick to where he wanted it. He came to Belleville using Bauer but we use Easton. It was a little bit of a crossover period, and that's when I realized he was a special kid. He knew exactly what he wanted and why, what kind of stick, flex, etc." – Matt Sands

That ties into why many believe vaults Brendan into a pool of draft eligible players who have a legitimate chance of turning pro within a couple of years.

Granted, a million and one stars have to align in order for a player to make the NHL. But, it appears Brendan has done his part in checking off many of the requirements.

At the same time, the slightest improper readjustment can send a player off the rails and further away from The Show than ever before. Stranger things have happened.

However, when not only the player himself buys into the notion of laying it all on the line, but his parents do as well, it's difficult to argue against the seemingly inevitable upward trajectory.

"My Dad always said, 'there's going to be scorers in the league. But, it's the guy who can score goals and also stop goals defensively who make it to the NHL.' I think I've had that mindset for the last couple years of my life. Scoring goals is probably the best feeling on the ice but I think stopping a rush or blocking a shot, when you look back at a game, is probably more rewarding." – Brendan Gaunce

Stephen clearly gave his son ample advice by emphasizing the significance of developing a steadfast defensive game. It's a reliable motto to live by when stepping onto the ice as a member of the Bulls, and beyond.

Harnessing that trust in caring about the defensive end can transform into second nature.

That urge to burst up the middle when his winger is awaiting an outlet pass on the sideboards diminished slightly over time. That temptation to forecheck three-deep in the first period dampened as well.

And while this style offers fans a step down in terms of entertainment, it helps teammates and coaches breathe easier on the bench when Brendan's in the play. Those moments are 'less entertaining' because they're responsible and lack flair.

"I think he was always the same player," minor hockey coach Paul Titanic argues. "He's not and never was a flashy guy, but he managed to get a surprising amount of points when Mike Gouglas and I coached him. He's an efficient and effective player, and he's always been that type of player."

In the final moments of Belleville's games in his sophomore season, Brendan was out there 90 per cent of the time.

When Burnett looked at the backs of jerseys while patrolling the bench, the No. 16 stuck out like a sore thumb. In terms of centremen to lean on for a key face-off, the two-way talents of Brendan led the way.

"I think he's so responsible defensively that he doesn't create enough offence sometimes. He's the type of guy that you, as a coach or teammate, recognize their value to the team because they can do so many different things. Whether it's kill penalties, help on the power-play, be out there in the last minute—whatever it might be—and the capability of playing in any situation." – Gary Roberts

An attribute that Roberts seems to notice every time his eyes follow Brendan on the ice is his long reach. His 6-foot-2 height translates into an above-average wingspan, an immediate advantage over small opponents when he cares to lunge.

When you picture a hockey player of Brendan's stature using his sizable reach, you also envision the body movements associated with swiping for the puck and pouncing on opponents. As you move down the torso and towards the lower body, something strikes you.

There is a certain burden to lunging often, to using one's reach effectively throughout a shift, period, game, season: The skating stride is affected.

Brendan—partly due to the precedent set by Cameron, but also because he owns an ugly stride—is widely known as a 'poor' or 'subpar' skater.

Considering the reach he deploys on a regular basis, it's not all that surprising. Nor, at times, is it even a dramatic burden; skating doesn't define a hockey player.

It does, however, comprise a large chunk of scouting reports. Ticks on the clipboard can only come from so many places. Only so many characteristics can be evaluated and ranked. And skating is such a massive part of a player's aesthetic output.

"I think my skating has improved a bunch this year. My first three strides aren't the quickest but they're pretty explosive and strong. That's something I've been working on a lot this year. My mentality towards the game, away from the rink, has changed. If we have a Monday off or something, I'll usually go to the gym. Because you have to push yourself to that next level. You hear stories about guys in the NHL and what they've done, so I try to do some extra things here and there." – Brendan Gaunce

Obviously, Brendan is used to being hounded about his skating style, its perceived inefficiencies and its predetermined faultiness.

It's been a criticism since he waltzed into the spotlight as a sterling OHL prospect in his dominant minor midget season.

Read virtually any media account of Brendan and his skating will be brought up as an underdeveloped skill. Read most scouting reports and you'll find the same rhetoric. It was an inescapable stigma during his draft year.

The most scrutinized year of his hockey life often revolved solely around his skating abilities. Some scouts can't get past it, think it's a deal breaker

"He's a fast guy, but not a quick guy. And, now that I've watched him play, I need to make Brendan Gaunce quicker," Roberts explains, seemingly jotting down the note in his head while he speaks. "He needs to accelerate and be able to change speeds more often. That's our goal now."

Gouglas has seen Brendan play hockey more often than anybody aside from his parents. There's no doubt he knows the burly forward's habits and ways better than any scout from the NHL, or elsewhere.

At the same time, he has built up bias that may or may not taint his view of Brendan.

Interestingly enough, though, Cameron has been able to mend his awkward stride over time. This is something that can't be ignored. "I've seen him out-race guys who have that shorter, choppy-looking stride, in a foot race. Cameron always has that knock on his skating. NCAA coaches would ask me about him and his skating. Both are deceiving though, Cameron and Brendan. Cameron has proved people wrong." – Mike Gouglas

Prototypical top-line NHLers have sufficient speed and a smooth stride. There are exceptions to the rule, but a great majority rely on their feet to lead them to the right place on the ice with and without the puck.

Brendan will probably lag in that department as a pro, barring a dramatic change in his physique or skating technique.

A first line centre job in the NHL will have to come through different avenues, potentially through his excellent playmaking skills, bullet shot, or gritty all-around game.

"I feel like he can be that go-to second line centreman on a good team," Cameron says of his little brother. "I feel like he doesn't have the high-end skill that some of these other guys do, but he still always seems to get the job done. I feel like he's already able to play at the next level."

Cameron's words are honest and unrelenting, just the way Brendan prefers his brother to speak about him.

Anything more, anything less, would be unacceptable. Brendan's just as honest back.

Plus, it's not as if Brendan lives in a fantasy world. Over the course of the 2011-12 season, he chimed in on numerous ocassions about his offensive upside.

He never stated his ceiling is a second line role, but he also admits wholeheartedly that he doesn't have the natural knack of some of his peers. He doesn't consider himself a dance partner with the puck; he'd rather dump-and-chase or take it to the hard areas.

Notching a point-per-game like he did in his second year in the OHL was a massive feat. He didn't have an arsenal of firepower behind him, as Belleville ranked 18th in the entire OHL in goals for.

Instead, Brendan led a team who, plain and simple, struggled to put the puck in the net.

Second line ceiling or not, his captain has his back. Brendan is the ultimate team contributor.

"In the OHL, in general, to have a 17-year-old lead your team is pretty unheard of. There's not many guys who do it, and the guys who do are special talents. He's a guy who will do anything to help the team. He can play on any of the four lines in a pro system. I know he probably wants to be a top-six guy, and I think he can do that. But, if not, he can contribute on line three or line four, as a banger and a crasher." – Luke Judson

There's no perfect science to predicting a prospect's ultimate capability in any sport. If there was, the allure of playing the games and coming through the ranks would lose its pizzazz.

That's why Brendan is a bit of a wild card.

Who's to say his best days in the offensive end, his best days as a skater—his best days as a defender, for that matter—are not to come? No one truly knows.

What educated hockey people can do, though, is make informed decisions. They can pool data, debate its merits, and go on a whim.

"I would never put a line number on him. I think he's going to be a great pro for a lot of years. As I said, tremendous skill and a willingness to play at both ends of the rink is something most players don't have. He's smart and intelligent, and I would think that will help him get to the National Hockey League a bit sooner." – George Burnett

Even within the tight-knit Gaunce camp—coaches, family, trainers, and teammates—there's some discrepancy surrounding certain skill sets.

It's another by-product of being in the limelight. The attention OHLers receive from their inner circle is amplified greatly during their draft year. It's not just the public.

Burnett, for one, was asked about his 2010 second overall pick countless times throughout the 2011-12 season.

Anyone with a hockey pulse wanted to know what was up with that Brendan Gaunce kid.

Was he for real? What type of star power did he have? Was it only a matter of time before he walked off into the OHL sunset, making an AHL or NHL team sooner than expected? What did Burnett think, in general? Was he a wild card at all? How about his personality—does he have character?

In a mid-season interview, the respected junior and pro coach said he would be "foolish" to believe Brendan will don a Bulls sweater in his fourth year of OHL eligibility. At 20, Brendan should be well on his way up the professional hockey ladder, he added.

Then again, the NHL franchise who has his rights need to have a plan for him. The framework of their system is crucial.

"I've dealt with lots of kids in similar situations, kids who are top draft picks, and when I look at those guys—Keith Primeau, Brad May, Nathan Horton, Manny Malhotra—it has a lot to do with the team. It really depends on where they're at and their progression." – George Burnett

Dependable, strong-willed, skilled centreman are hard to come by in the NHL.

Case in point, the squad in Brendan's backyard, the Toronto Maple Leafs, have lacked a legitimate pivot since Hall of Famer Mats Sundin began to wind down. At the other end of the spectrum lies a handful of franchises around the league who are just plain centre-rich (see: Pittsburgh Penguins).

The whole 'fitting into a team's mould' is something completely out of Brendan's control.

All he was in command of was his play as a member of Team Ontario, Team Canada, and the Belleville Bulls.

As a talent under the microscope, comparisons to current NHLers sprout up here and there. They vary, of course, with the evaluation being strictly subjective.

And, in a lot of ways, unfair since he's a teenager and not a professional hockey player yet. Obvious differences include age, body type, mental maturity, and skill development—but the contrast list is incredibly lengthy.

Nevertheless, comparisons are an interesting piece of conversation for fans, media, and scouts. It ballparks potential, if nothing else.

"I think B is somewhat like a Jordan Staal. He covers good territory with minimal effort. He's a relatively reserved guy; a somewhat reserved, somewhat thoughtful guy. I think on the ice he plays a similar game that is helped by his intellectual approach to things. He's a very smart player who understands the intricacies of the game. There's no doubt that off the ice he's similar." – Gary Roberts

Commentator David Foot, another guy who knows Brendan's game quite well, is a little more ambitious—in terms of offensive upside—in his assessment.

The association isn't one shared by the greater hockey community, but he raises valid points.

"He reminds me of Rick Nash," Foot says. "He's one of the best guys on the wall and in the corner. That's where the comparison comes in. They both battle and get into the dirty stuff."

Burnett sees promise in Brendan's underestimated skating, burning desire to win, and difficult-to-handle package.

"Jordan Staal," he says. "Having coached against him, I see that as a pretty solid comparison."

Now that the Thunder Bay native is on a club that truly needs a second line centre—the Carolina Hurricanes—many believe Staal will be a premier player in the NHL.

He's been revered as an upper echelon talent since breaking into the NHL in 2006, but stuck it out in a third line role behind arguably the two best players in the entire league, Sidney Crosby and Evgeni Malkin.

The one characteristic Staal—one-fourth of the legendary brother quartet of Eric (Hurricanes), Marc (New York Rangers), and Jared (Providence Bruins)—is praised for most often is his stability. He has a vibe about him that he doesn't make many mistakes, especially in the defensive end.

Other pundits have thrown out comparables like Ryan O'Reilly of the Colorado Avalanche, Ranger Brandon Dubinsky, and another member of the NHL siblings club, Brayden Schenn.

They all come with a side note, of course, alerting the world that this is merely a rough comparison.

The dots are connected for a reason, though.

All of these players, except for perhaps Schenn, occupy a power forward role. Each is reliable in pressure situations and at the draw. There isn't single aforementioned player that does not have the potential to score 25 goals in the NHL, if given the ice time.

The list goes on and on. They even all shoot left.

But really, what about Brendan: What does he think of being mentioned in the same sentence as Staal and the like?

"I'm Brendan, not Jordan. That's an honour—trust me—but I'm no one but myself."

5

FINALLY

At 18, Brendan Gaunce has still never participated in a 'real' job interview.

He's been fortunate enough to avoid entry level part-time jobs in the fast food, landscaping, retail, and grocery industries. He's successfully leapfrogged that awkward chapter of the adolescent textbook.

Brendan's never been too lazy or too proud to search for some weekend and evening hours at a local Canadian Tire, Loblaws, or other local business.

Instead, it was actually a bi-product of a system set up by Stephen and Julie, which allowed Brendan to finish high school on time, despite taking only six classes during the regular school year because of his time commitment to hockey.

From Grade 9 onwards, this meant summer school was on the horizon right after the year's books were closed for good. School year round.

While his peers moaned and groaned about receiving the worst possible hours, wages, and tasks since they were the 'new guys' at their part-time gigs, Brendan packed his lunch for summer school and did his own thing.

On the surface, this set-up—this lack of 'real' interview experience—appears disastrous.

Over the course of Brendan's draft year, NHL scouts pulled him aside after games.

The nerves associated with a first interview—even if for a petty job—is off the charts for most. Finding someone breathing easy when their mom drops them off for their initial run-in with the real world would be a gigantic chore.

Now, whether Brendan was prepared or not, the NHL Combine presents the top 100-plus prospects with a rapid fire interview schedule. League officials don't screen you out if you've chosen the books over the mop in previous summers; you're going to be interviewed, plain and simple.

At the yearly event, all 30 teams are granted the opportunity to sit down with kids, examine their body language, attitude, and general habits, while prying about any reported injuries or scuttlebutt they want to clear the air about.

It's rare for a player to be tied up by interviews by 30 clubs at the Combine, but it's happened before. At its basic roots, teams use the event to get some face-to-face interaction in; they crave a chance to actually see a kid out of his equipment, talking, smiling, and put under pressure.

Even in a digitally overwhelming culture, employers still put a ton of value on the human experience of sitting down with a potential employee and feeling them out.

In Brendan's case, on top of the rigorous fitness tests, 24 franchises felt the need to stare him in the eye from across the table.

They had an urge—an inkling of some sort—that they couldn't pass up on learning more about the Markham stud before slotting him into their top secret final rankings sheet.

"I think there's no doubt about that," minor hockey coach Paul Titanic said when asked in January if Brendan would excel during Combine interviews. "More 1-on-1 and exposure to certain teams will help him get drafted earlier because he's an impressive person. They'll be able to see he's a coachable kid."

Each year the media compiles lists dedicated to the wackiest inquiries fielded by prospects at the Combine.

NHL teams will look to throw off a prospect, even only for a laugh or two. It's quite comical, except when you're the confused receiver of the questions.

What's your best score on the golf course? How long would it take you to climb Mount Everest? What's your favourite beer (a trick question in most cases, except in Montreal)? What's your wife's name (also a trick question in most cases)?

That's just a sample of the bizarre and irrelevant questions players in Brendan's position have faced in the past, took in this year, and will continue to absorb in the future.

"I wouldn't say I'm worried, but I wouldn't say I'm really that comfortable," Brendan says prior to departing home for a stay at a

Toronto hotel where he'll room with Malcolm Subban during the Combine festivities. "I've heard they go off topic from hockey a lot, a lot off topic from family—all that sort of stuff. I'm kind of just going in there with an open mind, and hoping to come back with quick answers that make sense."

Though it wouldn't have been a huge burden if he was paired up with a stranger, it was certainly a plus Brendan was able to bunk with a guy he spends plenty of time with during the hockey season.

Along with the other specialty events throughout the year, such as the Top Prospects Game and various international tournaments, familiarity with your surroundings can make the world of a difference.

That whole 'feeling out' experiment was reserved for the Combine chats, not in the hotel room, Brendan explained.

"It definitely helped. I wouldn't have had a problem meeting someone new at an event like this, but I was comfortable. It's huge for your confidence. You can just be yourself and not have to worry about getting to know someone when you're concentrated on the Combine." – Brendan Gaunce

After a stressful two days of interviews with prospective employers, he admitted there were no "weird" questions thrown his way.

He was off the hook. No sweat-induced moments, nothing to make him feel self-conscious or require a stutter-filled answer; he got the long end of the stick.

How anti-climatic.

That lack of 'real' interview practice turned out to be quite a non-factor, after all. Brendan felt he passed with flying colours.

And it would be hard to argue the opposite since his presence in media interviews is largely uncontested in his draft class. That's not to say he's head and shoulders above the rest in off-ice composure, articulation, and maturity, but consensus does say he's an astute fellow.

Scouts, media, and fans alike seem to rave about his ability to appear unruffled by a tough question, look the other way when criticized, and answer in a wise, thought out tone that exudes confidence but not arrogance.

Since his OHL draft day in Belleville, Brendan has been considered a 'good interview' for reporters and team execs. He rarely gives one-word answers and it's uncommon for him to stumble through his sentences. He's got that charisma about him, too, that 'don't sweat it, I know what I'm doing' swagger.

The Combine is a different monster than the rest of the year, though, and Brendan was prepared for that. He was ready to turn on his charm for two straight days.

It helped he had Cameron, an invaluable resource who could feed him advice from time to time during the 2011-12 season, slowly but surely groom him for the most crucial moments.

In a conversation on Friday, June 22nd—Day 1 of draft weekend —Brendan spoke about what stood out about the Combine interview sessions.

"They asked a lot about how I can be a top six forward in the NHL. People seem to be saying that I can only be a third or fourth line player. Some teams have been saying that, too. Obviously I disagree with that, but that's their opinion. Then other teams had more confidence in me and think I can be whatever I want to be in the NHL." – Brendan Gaunce

In Brendan's mind, the top six forward knock—which will inescapably hover over his head until he plays his first shift as a first or second line player as pro—is merely another motivational point on his way to hopefully cracking a big league roster.

By continuously working on his foot speed and creativity with the puck, the plan is to slowly chip away at the perceived inefficiency, Brendan said.

He knows the flash of, Nail Yakupov and Alex Galchenyuk, for instance, is something that will probably never come. But, he believes there are components of his offensive game that can be refined.

Being a top six forward in the NHL is an immense accomplishment. If you do the math, there are only 180 players in the entire world at a given time who can stake claim that they are currently a member of one of the top two lines on an NHL squad.

Nevertheless, Brendan's goals are lofty and settling for a third or fourth line role isn't on his immediate objectives list.

Doubts have always been few and far between when discussing Brendan's play in the defensive end. Critics have trouble pin-pointing an own-zone deficiency.

Brendan figured out the tricks of the defensive trade at a young age and never allowed his peers surpass him in that department. He's always harnessed the required energy to act out the role of a two-way player, and takes pride in contributing away from the other team's net.

He's not perfect by any means, but you'd be hard pressed to find a head coach in the OHL that wouldn't be content having Brendan out on the ice when ahead by a goal in the final minute of a contest. He's just reliable that way.

This loyalty and understanding of defensive responsibilities could very well be why teams were hungry for more Brendan after the Combine interviews. They needed to have that guy—that centreman with an NHL-ready frame and good head on his shoulders—come tour the city.

Four teams approached Brendan's agent, Paul Capizzano of MFIVE Sports, to ask if the recent member of Team Canada's Under-18 Championship squad could make a pit stop in their city prior to the draft.

Boston Bruins. Buffalo Sabres. Chicago Blackhawks. Dallas Stars.

All of them showed increased interest towards the projected first-rounder.

Brendan flew to Boston, Buffalo, and Chicago. Dallas held a camp in the GTA and invited him out. Together, they eventually—after trades—represented the 12th (Buffalo), 13th (Dallas), 14th (Buffalo), 18th (Chicago), and 24th (Boston) picks in the draft.

HockeyProspect ranked Brendan 18th overall, unintentionally aligning him with the Blackhawks leading up to the draft.

The opportunity to work out in front of some of the more influential people in an NHL team's organizational structure was a little more up Brendan's alley. In comparison to the Combine, Brendan felt much more comfortable sweating through lifting and cardio tests in an intimate setting.

Those who expressed their gratitude towards Brendan make up a rather envious group.

The names are highly recognizable, and their championship total averages out to 2.75 per team. They're not necessarily all from the Original Six or have hoisted the Stanley Cup the past four years, but it's a solid pack considering there's 30 teams in the league.

On draft day—even with all the rankings and lists and predictions and personal hunches and rumours and straight up pot-stirring conversation in the past—it ultimately comes down to where the dominoes fall.

As much as the private workout requests displayed the teams' concentration on Brendan, it didn't mean he was a guaranteed lock to join one of the franchises at the draft.

Brendan learned over the course of the 2011-12 season that paying attention to politics—Who will go where? Who will pick who?—is not worth the stress.

"I haven't gotten too into it with my agent," he says on draft day. "Some guys want to know, but it just puts more pressure on the situation if you think a certain team is going to pick you. I actually don't even know. I don't want to have my hopes up anyway."

From the moment the Bulls stepped on the ice for their opening night date with the Ottawa 67's on September 23rd, 2011, Brendan's year-long audition began.

The end of the road in late June—the spectacle that is the NHL draft—felt a million miles away back then.

Luckily for the baby-faced kid, there were little droppings along the way, small scoops of ice cream to keep his draft taste buds happy.

And although they seemed rather tedious in the moment, the NHL team-administered tests helped keep Brendan's mojo going.

An OHL season has many rolling hills and swooping valleys, so taking time to reflect and remember what you're going through is vital. At times, these evaluations would allow him to do so.

He soaked it all in.

Brendan sat his desk in Belleville after a night's worth of homework and grind away. Or, he made the long bus ride home from road trips into a mini questionnaire filling out period.

These evaluations were personality tests, nothing too obscure. They served a purpose, of course: To gather psychological information about the prospect that can't be observed through viewings or face-to-face interviews.

Some took up to two hours, which had Brendan thinking, 'I didn't sign up for this…' Especially since most questions weren't based around hockey. Lots of brain teasers and situational queries took up space on the page.

It's not as if he was being singled out or anything. He was being treated like all blue-chip prospects.

Brendan was just doing the draft year thing, chugging along game by game, interview by interview, test by test.

By mid-to-late March, or when the Bulls were about to be eliminated from the OHL playoffs, Brendan began admitting to having persistent interest from about seven NHL franchises.

"They've been telling me that they like how I play, like my character," he notes. "They say, 'If we can draft you, if you're there, we wouldn't think twice about taking you.'"

In the months previous, there were more who reached out to chat after a game or took him out for dinner.

"I've done probably 10 or 11 with teams," he says in November of 1-on-1 interviews with team scouts. "I've had a bunch as of late. I've had at least 3-4 over the past couple of weeks. I think it's their first look at a player off the ice and out of their hockey domain."

The conversations, Brendan added, were "pretty casual" and "nothing was really like, 'we want you, we want to pick you if we can.'"

It's interesting how curiosity in a prospect's services changes over the course of the year.

It's almost like a live auction, where the item up for sale jolts in value as soon its held in high regard. Then, after buyers play a short game of chicken, the number of suitors drops. But, the drive to obtain the item keeps increasing to the ones left; they can't face defeat.

In a very odd way, Brendan and his peers are surrogates for antique lamps, speed cars and trips to Dubai. They're pursued by a strong field from the start of the bidding war, yet only one leaves with the grand prize.

The whopper to Brendan, the team his heart skips a beat for, has always been the Toronto Maple Leafs.

"I've always been a Leaf fan," he says in September. "Living in Toronto, they're my favourite."

As the season wore on, Brendan took a grander approach to the question every media type and casual friend felt obligated to ask: 'Who would you prefer to be drafted by?'

Deep down he couldn't ignore the die-hard Leafs fan inside. However, the default answer is always 'any team in the NHL' for most prospects and he should probably be politically correct, he said.

In a conversation in June, Brendan didn't necessarily stray from the norm, but offered a nugget of insight into the human element of the situation.

"If you asked me that question two years ago—when I was in minor midget—it would probably be a certain answer. But, as you get a little closer to the draft, you look at each team as an opportunity for yourself. And obviously each team has different needs. I don't think there's one, in general, that I would like to go to. There's so much parity in today's NHL, anyway." – Brendan Gaunce

There aren't too many 18-year-old kids, in hockey and otherwise, who would willingly use the phrase 'you look at X as an opportunity for yourself.'

Who cares about that type of stuff at that age, right?

Wrong.

"With the evolution of the NHL, every team is on equal ground. From ownership down, it's not that big of a difference from one team to another. On draft day, it won't really matter what number I go. I'll be just as thrilled either way. But, I think, it does matter for a bit, just to yourself. For pride, obviously. The only number I'm really worried about is 50, because that's where my brother was picked." – Brendan Gaunce

That late statement was obviously a half-joke, but charming nonetheless.

Eternal bragging rights could be obtained if his name was called before the No. 50 pick, where Colorado chose Cameron in 2008. Brendan could have that edge, that extra ammunition, in paltry fights and casual taunting.

When you take a second to think about it, Brendan and Cameron were in a pretty rare situation during the 2011-12 season.

After the '08 draft, which was held in Ottawa, the older Gaunce brother was officially the No. 50 prospect in his age group at the time. That, in itself, is a tremendous accomplishment for a family of five.

To have Brendan go earlier or around the 50th pick mark would cement the Gaunces as a legitimate hockey family, one that produced two cream of the crop players in their respective classes.

And considering they only had two chances to do so, with Ally being a female and all, Stephen and Julie did all right for themselves in the hockey player-producing department.

Even though there are a handful of current brother combinations in the professional hockey realm—the Staal name comes to mind immediately—it would be an extraordinary feat if both were drafted and drafted high.

In NHL history, there's been only about 100 siblings who have played in the league.

Cameron has 11 games of experience under his belt from his call-up during the 2010-11 campaign. There's the first checkmark.

Plenty in that select group have been fortunate enough to be drafted, traded, or signed by the same team at some point. Playing in the greatest hockey league in the world with your brother is one thing—playing alongside him is another.

From a generic parent's perspective, it's a no-brainer: 'Join the same team, please, because I don't want to cheer for two clubs.'

The image of battling against each other in front of 20,000 people is tempting—think of all those whack-it-out sessions in the Gaunce garage back when Cameron and Brendan were kids—but certainly not ideal. In most cases, brothers would prefer to wear the same colours.

When questioned about the topic in January, Cameron gave the unselfish answer.

"I think I'd prefer—to tell you the truth—if he got drafted somewhere else. He should forge his own path. I don't want an organization to have any pre-conceived notions about Brendan before he comes in. Don't get me wrong, it'd be awesome to have him in the Colorado organization, but it'd be nice to see him do his own thing. That first training camp, and stuff like that, is something you'll always remember." – Cameron Gaunce

It's an approach not every older brother has, but Brendan and Cameron were never a typical tandem.

Brendan didn't follow Cameron's lead by taking a year off before making the NCAA or OHL decision. On the ice, they don't play an identical game.

They also have pretty distinct personalities. They're not attached at the hip like some brother duos; Brendan's actually closer with his sister. And so on.

It was all out of Cameron's hands, anyway.

In reality, there was a 1-in-30 chance of a double Gaunce connection in Denver—so why even pretend it's bound to happen?

As well, Colorado's first pick of the 2012 draft was a good 20 spots (41st overall in the second round) from where Brendan was pegged by most prognosticators. Originally, they held the 11th overall selection but decided to swap it with the Washington Capitals.

This alteration lessened the probability of Stephen and Julie cheering for the same NHL squad night in and night out.

Now, although Brendan and Cameron took divergent routes to the NHL draft—Brendan second overall in OHL draft, Cameron passed on first year of OHL; one more offensively minded than the other, the other more physical; one considered of first round quality, the other second round—anxiety doesn't select its owners.

The only real difference is that the ups and downs of a draft year are amplified when you're a more valued stock like Brendan. The same basic feelings are present inside the most hyped star, the kid who slides into the seventh round out of no where, and all the talent levels in between.

Each and every player in the NHL draft picture is under immense scrutiny; whether they want to admit it or not is another thing.

The whole concept of potentially realizing the Canadian dream was overwhelming at times for Brendan.

Then, in other instances, you could barely tell he felt the glares of being under the microscope, just going about his business as if he were trying out for the Markham Waxers as a returning captain.

About two weeks before the draft—June 6th, to be exact—it wasn't so much the attention getting to him, but rather the entire experience.

His life was about to change, and he didn't want his other side—post-draft Brendan—to be a cocky version of his normal self.

"Right now, it's just all been adding up to one big point. I think this will be the climax to everything. Having Cam going through it for me, it's pretty helpful. He was a perfect example of staying level-headed, taking things in stride. I'm pretty sure of myself, that the draft won't change much in regards to how I act. I'm pretty confident in myself that I won't change just because of the draft—that's the outlook I have." – Brendan Gaunce

The draft lined up almost perfectly with the conclusion of Brendan's Grade 12 year, his goodbye to high school.

In fact, the two schedules were eerily aligned, with his very last exam of high school falling on the Monday right after draft weekend. A pair of monumental events were gently placed two days apart.

"I don't think anything with hockey is," Brendan says of what's been creating tension in his mind and body at the beginning of the most important month of his life. "Just the school work, it's been tough to catch up. The end of Grade 12 is hard as it is, and with the lost time— from going on road trips and the Combine and flying out to NHL cities— it's not any easier."

Having the opportunity to graduate at St. Brother Andre Catholic High School, with all of his childhood friends, created another fascinating element to the mix.

In grades nine and 10, before his OHL-playing days, Brendan went to Markham District High School. When he left town for Belleville, however, his ties were more or less cut at MDHS.

So, when it came time to figure out how he would finish off Grade 12, the Gaunces felt Brendan should temporarily enrol at Brother Andre to wrap things up.

"It just made more sense. It was an easy choice, really," Brendan says of the decision to attend a third high school in four years.

While his peers were gleaming with the expectation of leaving home in the fall for the university or college dorm life, the best athlete in school wasn't thinking twice about anything non-sports related.

His chosen career path didn't require a certain level of education. Neither did his unofficial Plan B.

The acting gigs he revelled in, the drama classes he received quality marks in, and the realization that he enjoyed to put on a show— these all factored into his 'back-up plan.'
"I think if I weren't into hockey—or another sport—so heavily, I would have given acting a real try. I like the whole experience. I get more nervous for that than anything else. But it's a fun, good nervous. If not that, probably something along the lines of a sports psychiatrist." – Brendan Gaunce

His enjoyment with the acting stream began back in Grade 7. His introduction to psychiatry didn't come until his high school years, however.

Stating it would be "pretty neat" to have such a "hands-on" job, Brendan said he is drawn to the social sciences—and more specifically psychiatry—since its related to how the brain works.

Let's call it Plan C.

Employers in the psychiatry field certainly need to see more than a high school diploma. Because of that, and just for a safety net in general, Brendan will attend Queen's University in the 2012-13 school year.

The Kingston-based institution is one of the finest universities in the country and the OHL is willing to pay his tuition, so why not?

Plus, Brendan's a thinker, an intellectual type when he wants to be.

Out of the 1994-born NHL draft class, Brendan was right up there with the smartest of the bunch. His general smarts, poise, and composure, weren't unparalleled, but he stood out from the crowd in terms of being able to effectively think the game on and off the ice.

Throughout the season, his focus rarely steered away from what needed to be done hockey-wise. He wasn't concerned about a possible career in helping others get through challenging psychology times; he had his own battles to fight.

During a lengthy conversation in late October, without being prompted by a particularly specific question, Brendan rambled on—in a sharp, concise manner, mind you—about the weight of living up to people's expectations.

"I was talking to my parents one night and my dad said whatever the rankings are it doesn't matter: 'Even if you're not on the NHL Central Scouting Bureau's top list, it doesn't matter in November.' I think both years I have come in with the same mentality. Obviously every player says they don't want to think about the draft but it is hard not to. I'll be honest with that. It's hard not to think about the draft and the people at the games. Being able to play the sport that I love makes it a lot easier. If it is my job in the future, it'll probably be the best part of my life. And if not, I'll always be able to cherish these years, which calms the nerves down a bit." – Brendan Gaunce

At that point, Brendan was only a month into his sophomore season as a Belleville Bull.

There were hundreds of shifts to be played on the ice, and a handful of marquee extra curricular events to attend off it.

Grasping the situation in the way he did, though—really understanding that this was a special circumstance, one many dream of—was imperative.

He was being realistic about the heaviness of the 2011-12 season as a whole. It was one he would never forget.

It was his chance to turn the key and open a door into the heralded realm of professional hockey. All he needed to do was find a way to be gentle and calm down the stretch, and the rest would work itself out.

"Everyone is asking if I'm excited, what teams I'd rather be drafted by, if I drafted Toronto would it be cool," Brendan says in an early June conversation. "Most of the questions surround the same stuff. I'm not used to it, in a way, but I've been trying to say the same things to everyone."

Like a looming storm cloud ready to burst with precipitation, the draft was in the immediate forecast.

It was nearly here.

"It's definitely something I'm looking forward to," he adds. "Hopefully I get drafted decently early so I can soak in whatever happens afterwards. I'm just going to have fun with it. You only experience it once, so you really have to take it in."

***

Anxiety is a peculiar thing.

It's laid out eloquently in the dictionary as "distress or uneasiness of mind caused by fear of danger or misfortune." Yet, it embodies so much more than that.

For those who experience its wrath on a daily basis, it becomes an inescapable fact of life. It's like stepping over a trap door in a phone booth; you can't flee its suffocating nature.

For those lucky enough to only experience anxiety when an overwhelming situation presents itself, the distress comes in a similar form but isn't at all familiar.

Brendan Gaunce's draft day anxiety began about nine hours before he woke up on Friday, June 22nd.

The forthcoming biggest day of his life was too far away; the final block of time in between him and his dream stretched all mental boundaries. He could not sleep.

At about 2 p.m., after being awake for a good five hours, he sat down for a wrap-up interview before facing off against the toughest opponent he's ever encountered: The NHL draft.

"Last night I wanted to go to bed, but just couldn't," he says, shaking his head in frustration. "I just wanted to sleep so it could come quicker, but it wasn't working out."

Shortly after wiping the remnants of sleeplessness from his eyes, Brendan headed downstairs for breakfast.

Perhaps feeling the effects of running on empty, or maybe just a complete coincidence, Brendan looked like a bit of a goof as he sat down for the first meal of the day.

"I went to go sit down and I got caught on the table," Brendan says, re-enacting the embarrassing scene.

He spilt three glasses of water on himself. On the most important day of his life.

As usual, Brendan quickly shrugged it off, joking about the incident with family and friends in the hours that followed. It looked as though he wet his pants, but in the way he told the story you wouldn't have guessed it brought about humiliation.

All he could do was laugh it off, really.

What a way to start off a nerve-racking day, he bantered.

The last couple of days in Pittsburgh had been bittersweet.

He dipped into the city's attraction list by attending a Pirates game and hitting up a few local shopping centres. On Thursday, the eve of the draft, he joined fellow MFIVE sports clients for a dinner event at the Hard Rock Café.

It was a bunch of artificial tomfoolery, however.

An 18-year build up was about to culminate. Other events in the Pennsylvania hub were background noise to the real reason he was in town.

Overall, he did whatever he could to take his mind off the inevitable fretfulness that the first round of the NHL draft is puts on premier prospects.

"I don't really know what's going on now—through my head and stuff," he says, looking straight ahead. "I'm excited for it, but also nervous. I rarely have that feeling."

All of the advice in the world—from his brother, mentors like Gary Roberts and Steven Stamkos, older teammates like Joseph Cramarossa—could not prepare him for the authenticity of actually being hours away from fulfilling a massive life goal.

Every ounce of energy spent on and off the ice in the name of hockey snowballed up until this point. Ultimately, it's a once-in-a-lifetime opportunity, experience, and a feeling Brendan knew he will never forget.

"Guys like my brother, who have been drafted before, have been telling me it's the most exciting weekend of your life. I've never been through something like this, so it's hard to say how I should be acting or feeling towards the situation. I'm just trying to take it all in. Once my name gets called, it's going to be a relief … if it gets called it'll be a relief." – Brendan Gaunce

After the mini shopping spree and casual lunch, Brendan heads upstairs in the hotel. He was going to try his best to keep busy as anticipation mounts towards leaving to the site of the draft, the Consol Energy Centre, at around 5 p.m.

Inside the hotel room, Cameron and his bubbly girlfriend Andrea sat on one bed. They're the only ones who stayed put for the entire afternoon, cracking jokes and conversing over this and that.

Hockey wasn't brought up often. Even when one of Brendan's former teammates, Brandon Panteleo and one of Cameron's former teammates, Dan Titanic, were in the room.

The Panteleo and Titanic families both made the trip to Pittsburgh to be there for Brendan. Three minor hockey coaches—Mike

Gouglas, Paul Titanic, and Scott Badali—couldn't miss the watershed moment either. This is their big day, too.

Unfortunately, Brendan's four grandparents didn't make the trek from New Brunswick. They were the only ones missing.

"Without those people," he says, almost in a whisper, "I wouldn't be here, to be honest."

In total, there were 17 people in Brendan's camp.

Each person lessened the circulating anxiety associated with draft day. The more comfort surrounding him, the less exposed he felt to draft day jitters.

As Brendan, Cameron, and Andrea meandered through the afternoon, people come in and out the room. Some stopped for a quick chat, others stayed for hours.

The constant throughout the afternoon hangout was Cameron's incredible wit.

"I'm pretty sure the range from 40th to 50th overall is where you want to get picked," he says to Brendan. "That's where all the studs are."

Of course, he was just tooting his own horn for some comic relief. Brendan was overtly nervous, and Cameron knew humour goes a long way.

And although they're five hours south of the GTA, Cameron made sure his little brother still felt at home in Pennsylvania.

Over by the window was a standard cooler. It wasn't filled with celebratory booze or sandwiches prepared for the trip down, though. Instead, there's about a dozen pre-assembled meals for the two hockey devotees.

Cameron made sure they wouldn't miss a beat on their diet. The mentality drilled into their heads by trainer Roberts has no boundaries. They can't take a weekend off no matter where they are—it could ruin everything.

The fitness aspect was arbitrary on draft day. The packaged meals consisting of chicken, spinach, sweet potatoes, and other goodies, served another purpose: They helped keep routine.

Each day spent in Pittsburgh was focused on harnessing habits and not allowing the immense pressures tumble down was a task in itself. Brendan did his absolute best to block out the draft weekend racket.

That kid that just wanted to fit in on Penny Crescent—the one who jumped into his OshKosh car so he could play zamboni driver for the big kids—he was now a man.

Even the toughest men, the most durable, unbreakable men can't escape fear at certain moments of their lives. Everyone has a tipping point on the nerve scale.

In this case, even the Belleville Bulls power forward couldn't put on a mask of confidence and honour.

"I'm finally getting nervous," he says to his mom quietly while waiting for an elevator inside the hotel.

It was 4:22 p.m. on draft day and Brendan was unquestionably overwhelmed.

***

Brendan Gaunce cranks his neck up in the direction of the hanging, four-sided scoreboard. He stares for a few moments before his hands gravitate towards each other to form a clap. The claps don't stop for about 10 seconds.

After, he looks at the pop-stained floor, trying to find a space within his scanning area that is not filled with a disappointed expression. The nine people to his direct left are all avoiding eye contact.

The lack of eye-to-eye glances is a blessing in disguise—he doesn't want to see them and they don't want to see him.

A nervous smile unwittingly appears on his face about every 15 minutes. It's a forced expression. It only comes at the start of the clap session; he's doing his absolute best to be a good sport.

Like a father playing with his toddler kid, Brendan's legs rumble up and down, vibrating the anxiety out of his system but picking it back up with every new beat. They jiggle but are as hard as a rock.

He snaps his fingers, picks a cut on his face.

Rinse and repeat.

"He looks down a lot when he's trying to get prepared or nervous," Stephen says. "Then you see him kind of hold his fingers. He's done that since he was little kid."

The show is half over: 15 picks are off the board and as many teams have left Brendan in the dust.

The Brendan Gaunce Fan Club has taken up two partial rows in the Consol Energy Centre's lower bowl since about 6 p.m.

It's now 9:15.

In Section 112, Row Q, the supporting cast of family friends made themselves comfortable.

Four seats ahead, in Row M, the following influential people, in order from left to right, staked out in anticipation: Brendan, Ally, Cameron, Stephen, Julie, Cameron's girlfriend Andrea, Ally's husband Jason, childhood best friend Brandon Pantaleo, and minor hockey coaches Scott Badali and Mike Gouglas.

Those restless hours leading up to the draft—the time spent lulling around the hotel because there was nothing better to do—now feel like a fast forward movie. The first round is an absolute marathon for prospects.

Each team has 15 minutes to choose their crowned jewel of the 2012 draft class. And most push the threshold.

At this point in time, all but two of the teams who expressed serious interest—enough to invite Brendan to a private session in their city—have passed on the two-way centreman.

After the draft class' elite—the Nail Yakupovs and Ryan Murrays —were long gone, the tension really ramped up in Brendan's camp.

At 12th, Buffalo took Mikhail Grigorenko. The next pick, Dallas', proved to be a charm for Kitchener Ranger Radek Faksa. The Sabres second and final choice of the opening round was in the No. 14 spot, and they called Zemgus Girgensons' name.

Chicago's 18th and Boston's pick at 24 remained.

"When the few teams we thought he'd go to passed, it was like, 'uh, oh,'" Julie says.

At 15, the Ottawa Senators went with the hometown kid, defenceman Cody Ceci.

A player cut from a similar cloth as Brendan, Thomas Wilson, was scooped up by the Washington Capitals next. There goes No. 16.

Officially into the second half now, Tomas Hertl of the Czech Republic went to the San Jose Sharks at 17th.

Next was the Blackhawks, a club hot on Brendan's case leading up to the draft.

Before entering the arena that night, Brendan's agent, Capizzano, made sure the Gaunces realized he was likely to go in between picks 15 and 25. He also put an asterisk on the wise words, noting there were no guarantees Brendan would be a first round pick since the draft is highly unpredictable.

The note about potentially falling out of the first round was included in Capizzano's pep talk for a reason. Other than a handful of players, there was a slim chance the rest of the consensus top 30 could slide into the second day.

Stranger things have happened.

"I didn't look over a lot but Julie did a few times and, as a mother can, she sensed he was getting more worried," Stephen says, describing the scene in Section 112, Row M, after each member of Brendan's camp realized that every passing pick meant one less chance for glory on Day 1 of the draft.

The chatter was minimal all the way from Brendan on the far left to Gouglas on the far right.

The congratulatory claps and short wisecracks came and went but, for the most part, the row's inhabitants remained painfully silent. If it weren't for the other 10,000 people in the same facility, it would have been an unbearable scene.

One of those fellow draft-goers, Finnish winger Teuvo Teravainen, heard his name called by Chicago at 18. Another spot gone.

As much as pre-draft meetings with teams can essentially be tossed out the window on the draft floor, it still stings like a you-know-what when the words 'Brendan' and 'Gaunce' are not uttered by its GM.

Especially in such tense moments.

Gripping onto the hope that Team X is super high on Brendan's package only provides temporary relief. And it's synthetic because the NHL draft is all about reacting to what's in front of you.

At the same time, each franchise's philosophy is widely different in regards to the sort of player types, characters, and positions needed at a particular draft.

In the state of Pennsylvania alone, the Philadelphia Flyers and Pittsburgh Penguins, holding the 20th and 22nd picks, respectively, don't traditionally ice players of the same breed.

The Flyers aren't nicknamed the Broad Street Bullies without a back story; forward-wise, they seek gritty, two-way enforcer types who can put the puck in the net. Conversely, the Penguins set their table nicely by taking ultra talents like Sidney Crosby and Evgeni Malkin.

At pick 20, Philadelphia had a decision to make.

Would they take a goalie like Malcolm Subban or Oscar Dansk? Would they fulfill some needs on the blueline with the selection of an Olli Maatta or Brady Skjel? Or, would they stick to their traditions and pick up a standard piece by choosing a gutty forward such as Brendan or Scott Laughton?

They went with the Oakville native, Laughton. He of 53 points and 101 penalty minutes in 64 regular season games for the Oshawa Generals during the 2011-12 season.

"He's a prototypical Philadelphia Flyer," Stephen says after the draft, remembering being happy for Brendan's long-time running mate.

Again, Brendan was looked over.

The magic number was now done to 10. Friday's first round was dwindling and it was time for the butterflies to sputter wildly.

"Other than the top five, I was thinking there was a chance I could be taken," Brendan explains post-draft. "I don't think there was serious thought, though, until about 20-25. That was the point, heading into the draft, I figured I would get nervous at."

The next team on the digitalized draft was the Calgary Flames.

They grabbed someone right out of left field, taking a Quebec high school student-athlete, Mark Jankowski, with the 21st overall selection.

How could this be, Brendan kept thinking, his eyes jolting from the ground at his feet, to the back of the seat directly in front of him, to the general direction of the draft floor, and back.

His mouth was drying up more and more by the minute, and the nerves were unfortunately replaced with boundless worries.

After both the Penguins (Maatta) and Florida Panthers (Michael Matheson) took a pair of defencemen with the next two picks, the group accompanying Brendan really needed to step up.

"The more you think about it, the worse it gets. So, you just don't think. It's easy to say now, of course. After pick No. 23, my daughter leaned over and said, 'Dad, I don't have a dress to wear tomorrow.' It kind of broke us all up, got us out of our nervous funks." – Stephen Gaunce

Ally, Brendan's No. 1 fan since his road hockey days, helped pop the bubble momentarily—albeit in a minor and volatile way.

A joke from her, however, wasn't able to produce the happiness associated with being a first round NHL pick. It was a blimp, a small flicker in the strenuous confines of the Consol Energy Centre.

Only the general managers of the remaining seven teams on the board could offer a break from what felt like the longest time spent in a doctor's office waiting room.

Antsy and uncertain, praying for positive results but aware the prayers don't really have an affect this late in the game.

Realistically, the evil thoughts going in and out of Brendan's brain—Am I really on the verge of possibly not getting picked tonight? What did I do wrong? Was it an on-ice blunder? Maybe something I said in the interviews?—were a bit overboard.

All credible mock drafts notched Brendan as a first rounder. His package—the natural talent, the frame, the attitude—ranged from above-average to exemplary when put up against fellow draft eligibles.

The kid was a surefire top 30 prospect. But this deep in, it was just a matter of personal hunches.

OK, so here we go. No. 24 is up and 25 on deck.

Boston was his last chance at going to a 'very interested' squad. They were the final ones to be checked off the 'strong arm suitors' list.

Bruins general manager Peter Chiarelli might have been conscious of the fact that two Belleville Bulls were anxiously awaiting the highly anticipated phrase, "From the Belleville Bulls…" because when he stepped up to the podium he just came out with it, avoiding the team tag.

"Most importantly, we'd like to announce our selection," Chiarelli says. "And it's Malcolm Subban."

Of the 250-plus draft hopefuls in the 2012 class, Brendan admired Malcolm the most. He was a true friend, first and foremost, and the fact he went above him in the draft barely mattered.

Arguably the most talented members of the Bulls bonded over—among other things—the perceived shadows they were behind because of their older brothers' successes in hockey.

They shared an equal amount of respect for the game and thankfulness for the opportunity. They lived through their brothers vicariously, and now it was finally their turn to ignite the family members.

"For the kids, it's just built up so much," Julie says. "For the last couple of months, between the Combine and trying to get school done, interviews with teams, rankings coming out, lists coming out—it's a lot."

Indeed. It was a lot.

And for Malcolm, it was finally time to celebrate.

As for Brendan, the 25th selection was up next.

Would St. Louis be his fateful destination? Only the Blues knew.

For another 15 minutes, Brendan thanked god he was on the aisle seat. He couldn't bear to sit beside a stranger. Ally to his left was comforting, but another body to his right would have been suffocating. He needed space to look, a spot to breathe a sigh of relief without being in plain sight.

Now five whole picks from the start of where he was 'supposed to' go, his brain was beginning to play tricks.

"After 20, I was thinking about a lot of scenarios. As a kid touted to go in the first, I wanted to go then. I'm not going to lie. I wasn't nervous in the sense that I wasn't going to get drafted at all, but going Friday was important from that standpoint." – Brendan Gaunce

The Blues would be a suitable destination.

Hot off a 109-point, Central Division title-winning season. Former stomping grounds for Brett Hull. Chance to win the franchise's first Stanley Cup. Young, character-rich core. Somewhat close to home.

St. Louis was a suitable landing spot for Brendan. s

But Doug Armstrong and Company had the United States on their mind, selecting a defenceman one inch taller but 27 pounds lighter than Brendan.

Jordan Schmaltz, a good ole Wisconsin kid from the Green Bay Ramblers of the USHL, was their prized first-rounder.

All eyes were now on the Cup finalists a year prior, the Vancouver Canucks.

Brendan fell in love with the bursting beauty of Kelowna—a mountain city located less than five hours from British Columbia's most populated hub—at the Top Prospects Game. In comparison to the other NHL cities remaining—Phoenix, New York, Newark, and Los Angeles— Brendan was only slightly more familiar with Vancouver.

The Canucks are a world-class organization with a whole lot going for them. Their upward trajectory through the turn of the century climaxed in 2011 with a Stanley Cup Finals experience.

Unlike the majority of his fellow GMs, Vancouver's Mike Gillis —and his trusty assistant GM Laurence Gilman as well as senior advisor Stan Smyl—opted to forego the intense waiting period in between picks.

After only a few minutes of chit-chat at the table, the Canucks brass stood up, tucked in their draft table chairs, and made the rounds on their way to the stage.

Gilman is the chosen one to announce the team's selection at No. 26.

He makes the traditional toasts, thanking the host city and congratulating the recent Stanley Cup winner, then proceeds to offer a touching prelude. Smyl, a Canuck through and through, was the initial member of the organizer's number retiree club.

The year aligned with Smyl's magical No. 12 and the club wanted to seize the opportunity to honour the 34-year employee for his tireless dedication.

Then Gilman begins.

"It is with great pleasure that we make our selection for the 2012 NHL Entry Draft ... from the Belleville Bulls of the Ontario Hockey League ... Brendan Gaunce."

Cue the hysteria.

The hugs.

The love.

The pure joy.

Brendan Gaunce is officially an NHL draft pick.

A lifelong dream accomplished; a world instantly turned upside down; and a feeling completely indescribable.

"I think it was more of a 'I don't know what's going on' feeling than anything else. You always watch the draft and the guys in it don't know how to describe the feeling. I'm with them now. At the time I was thinking—as the picks were going off the board—that the next one was going to be me. But, obviously that didn't happen. Then it turned out to be Vancouver, which is a great fit for myself because they're low on centremen in their program. I'm very happy with it." – Brendan Gaunce

As Brendan hugs each of the devotees in Section 112, Row M, the smile on his face grew.

The siblings, the parents, the in-laws, the best friend, the hockey coaches—they all contributed to his moment of untainted glory.

After making the 20-stair trek down to the draft floor, Brendan meets the team's manager of media relations and publications, Stephanie Maniago, who takes his blazer and walks him up to the stage.

You hear many prospects say it: It starts to feel real when Gary Bettman shakes your hand.

"Hey, congratulations!" Bettman pipes when Brendan extended his hand for the monumental exchange.

He finally did it.

After going through the lineup, shaking every member of the Canucks brass gathered on stage, Brendan slips on a National Hockey League jersey.

Smiling straight ahead, the kid they call B is on top of the world.

Back at their seats, Stephen and Julie converse over the tremendous feat. First Cameron, now Brendan; they have produced two NHL-worthy talents.

"Your first thought is excitement. Your second is relief. Then it's 'Wow.' In all honesty, that's what it was," Stephen says a couple of days after the draft. "You almost say, 'Yes!' under your breath. And then it's 'Oh my god, I can breathe,' then it was 'Good for you, buddy.'"

Then, a hurricane of emotions take hold of both parents.

One thing they couldn't get past was the fact that Vancouver, a Canadian team with sound management and an enviable core of players, chose Brendan.

There are a few other franchises that compare to the Canucks, both in terms of the on-ice possibilities and the other stuff.

As Brendan makes his rounds, talking to TSN's James Duthie beside Gillis, and then shaking each scout's hand at the franchise's draft table, the humbled parents discuss what had transpired.

"When he was walking up there to accept the jersey, I turned to Julie and said, 'Did you know that Vancouver was even interested?,' and she said 'No!?' But, did it matter? Absolutely not."

In the hour following his triumph, Brendan is whisked around the bowels of the Consol Energy Center by the Canucks public relations staff.

He makes stops inside the promotional photography area to flip some pucks and pose awkwardly for the camera. He greets the media for the first time in Vancouver green and blue, decked out in his brand new digs. He even takes some time to provide exclusive behind-the-scenes footage for CanucksTV, which is run by the team itself.

Through it all, the 18-year-old consistently described as a talent 'mature beyond his years' is living a truly childhood daydream.

"When I was walking around with the jersey on," Brendan says in astonishment of achieving one of his highest aspirations in life, "I still felt like it was on me because I bought it in the store. It was so surreal."

He is an NHL hockey fan no more; instead, a certified member of the NHL draft picks club.

"Hockey's our biggest sport in Canada, so being drafted to a Canadian is definitely extra special. They have such a strong fan base, so much media, and just a winning tradition," he adds.

While it turns out the Canucks themselves hadn't articulated their interest in him over the course of the 2011-12 season, their sights were set on scooping the Markham native up, if possible.

With a position late in the first round, however, it wasn't looking too promising heading into Friday's festivities.

If Brendan was going to be a Canuck by the end of the night, they would have to garner some serious luck.

"We had Brendan much higher on our list than the 26th position. We knew that the draft was so deep in defencemen that there were going to be a lot of them taken in front of us. As the picks began to go on the board and Brendan was still there, we got excited. We felt optimistic about the fact that we could possibly get him. As it really evolved, getting closer to our pick, we had St. Louis in front of us, Boston in front of them, and he was still there." – Laurence Gilman

Truth be told, Gillis and Gilman—the true decision-makers at the team's draft table—were so keen on Brendan's offerings that they were willing to tinker with their entire draft strategy in order to call his name at the podium.

It wasn't a matter of maybe getting their guy; they were going to get their guy. They were in love with his intangibles, and saw security in his tangible attributes.

After the 23rd choice was in the books, there were two teams the Canucks felt would bite on the best player available theory and, hypothetically, snatch up Brendan.

"If Brendan wasn't going to be there, we had framed a deal to trade down to get an additional pick in the second round. It was all predicated on whether Brendan would be there or not. Then, Boston took the goaltender Malcolm Subban and St. Louis took defenceman Jordan Schmaltz. Right away we were really excited that Brendan was going to be there. So, we notified the other teams that we were actually not going to trade down and were going to make our selection." – Laurence Gilman

Gillis, the NHL's 2010-11 General Manager of the Year, was a fifth overall draft choice himself back in 1978.

Since beginning his tenure in April of 2008, he had been given the opportunity to pick three first rounders. Ironically, his initial choice as GM was Cody Hodgson, one of Brendan's idols growing up.

Unfortunately, thanks to a bitter divorce between Hodgson's camp and the club on his way out via trade to the Buffalo Sabres, Brendan wasn't able to give the fellow Markham Waxer alumni a jubilant 'Hey, man! We're teammates now' call.

In a post-first round media scrum, it was clear Gillis had put the Hodgson saga behind him.

The former Canuck's strong link to Brendan didn't factor into the decision whatsoever. In fact, Gillis was very found of Brendan's office situation, including the irreplaceable influences of Stephen and Julie.

"Everything about him is good," Gillis tells reporters. "Good parents, good potential, and good leadership."

As for specifics, the 53-year-old executive said Brendan brings a "raw" piece to their puzzle, but is also made up of "captain material."

"In all of the testing that we did—not at the Combine, but our own testing—he scored at the very top in terms of character and analysis and cognitive awareness," Gillis adds.

The Western Conference powerhouse obtained a sturdy, two-way centreman who doesn't have a bad bone in his body off the ice. He was is a Ryan Kesler Jr., some could say.

Take one look at the squad's depth cart immediately after the draft and it's easy to see why Vancouver targeted Brendan. From a positional standpoint, down the middle is arguably their weakest area.

On their present roster, it's looking pretty healthy, with the likes of Henrik Sedin, Kesler, Maxim Lapierre and Manny Malholtra holding down the top four centre spots. When you peel back the layers of their system though, things get thin in terms of NHL-bound pivots.

"We would be extremely happy if it turns out that Brendan evolves into a bonafide everyday second line centreiceman in the National Hockey League. He's big in stature; strong on the puck; tenacious, can forecheck extremely well; and obviously a kid with tremendous character. Championship organizations are built with players like that. And, for us, to have the opportunity to draft a player like that and bring him into our organization is obviously a great thing for us." – Laurence Gilman

Spontaneously in the scrum, Gillis compares Brendan to Nicklas Jensen of the Oshawa Generals, the Danish winger drafted by Vancouver in the first round of the 2011 NHL Entry Draft, 29th overall.

Both are adept defensively, can put the puck in the net, have large frames and, perhaps most importantly to the Canucks, show marvellous promise.

Together, they represent an important packet of the future, a look at what's to come for Canucks fans. Each will surely take time to develop, but it appears they're virtual locks to become NHLers over the next few seasons.

"I would say that the biggest factor was that he was a big, strong centreiceman," Gilman says when asked what really turned them on to Brendan. "Whether he's a safe pick or a risky pick, it didn't factor into our thinking. We coveted a centreiceman with the exact qualities that Brendan possesses."

In terms of what they aren't particularly found of about Brendan's game is the usual: His skating. Noting they don't believe his speed, acceleration, or first few strides are in a "detrimental" state, Gilman still insisted it's an area of focus moving forward.

"One of the most critical areas is his skating. It's a game of speed at this point in time, and that's how our hockey club is built, so we're going to want to see his foot speed improve. And we think that is something that will come naturally." – Laurence Gilman

The skating rag has been tossed in Brendan's direction before, and there isn't anything that motivates him more.

Nevertheless, skating was as a worry for another day for both parties.

It was time to embrace the moment.

Plus, there were six rounds remaining.

Other uncertainties, such as getting the Bulls into the playoffs again and winning a playoff series, were put on hold immediately. Some were even diminished altogether.

Case in point, in Brendan's mind, being drafted 26th overall—as opposed to 15th or 21st, for instance— didn't really register as a negative or a damaging tag.

The whole 'rankings matter, to an extent' rhetoric he spoke about on Friday morning was zapped out of mid air when the words 'Brendan Gaunce' amplified through the Consol Energy Centre speakers.

Who cares about the number, Brendan stated to the media, it was about which team obtained his rights. In the end, he was a first round pick to a Canadian team who sincerely admired his worth as a player and person.

Finally, after a painfully long draft day, Brendan and the Brendan Gaunce Fan Club retired to the hotel for some well-deserved celebrations.

After a short rest, they were raring to go again in the early morning, heading to the arena for Day 2 of the 2012 NHL draft. Brendan sat with his family for the second and third rounds before setting up shop in the Canucks private suite.

There, he interacted with team management and a couple of the members of the Canucks 2012 draft class who also made the trip to Pennsylvania.

When it was all said and done, Brendan was coupled with the 57th (Alexandre Mallet of the Rimouski Oceanic), 147th (Ben Hutton of the Nepean Raiders), 177th (Wesley Myron of the Victoria Grizzlies), and 207th (Matthew Beattie of Philips Exeter Academy) overall picks.

Vancouver took a player from the OHL, QMJHL, Central Canada Hockey League, British Columbia Hockey League, and New Hampshire High School hockey loop.

By opting to usher in four forwards and a defenceman, the Canucks showed great trust in their goaltending depth.

"I think he could have gone in the top 10," Brendan says of Subban, who now has the Bulls bragging rights locked up. "He's a special talent. That's pretty cool we could share the first round experience."

He felt the Bruins pulled off a major steal and the Edmonton Oilers did swell by picking up Daniil Zharkov 91st overall.

About 100 spots later, the fourth and final Bull to hear his name called at the 2012 NHL draft, Brady Austin, was selected by the Buffalo Sabres with the 193rd pick.

"I texted Austin when he got drafted," Brendan recalls, laughing. "We had a bet going that he was going to go this weekend. I thought he would and he didn't. Looks like I'm a little richer."

Despite having a subpar season as a collective in 2011-12, Belleville's OHL team fared swimmingly in Pittsburgh—Subban and Brendan went in the first; Zharkov in the third; and Austin in the seventh.

Back at home in Markham, a couple of days following draft weekend—having just finished his final exam as a high school student—Brendan was in a particularly good mood.

He was about to go mini-putting with some friends, relax for the first time in about a month. Tomorrow was a travelling day to the west coast. His first NHL camp, the Canucks six-day development gathering, was here.

It was less than a week after the day he'll never forget—June 22, 2012—and it had already sunk in for Brendan. It took a few days of getting used to, of course, but the way the Canucks welcomed him at the draft, was key in allowing him to come to terms with the fact that he was property of an NHL team.

"It's starting to make sense to me now. I'm a Vancouver Canuck. It feels good," Brendan expresses.

Understandably, Stephen and Julie were still caught up in the madness of it all. They weren't the ones up in Vancouver's suite, taking it all in alongside Brendan's brand new employers.

They are adults who have things to do on weekdays, too, distracting them from really sitting down and absorbing the fantastic accomplishment.

"I was driving home today thinking that I haven't even seen him walk to the stage, or really be presented with the jersey," Stephen says on the 28th, six days after the first round. "It was a weird thing to realize."

Still, it's not difficult to sum up how it felt to see Brendan reach such a massive milestone in his young life.

As a parent, it's not hard to talk about your kids and their successes as a whole, so this was a cinch.

"I don't know if proud is the right word sometimes. As a parent, you just get so happy and excited when your kids are doing something that they love, do well at it—whether it be hockey, marriage, parenting, their job—that's where the joy is. You're not prouder of one kid than the other, either. We're pretty blessed to be in this situation, and sometimes you just don't want that bubble to burst." – Stephen Gaunce

***

Sometimes innate object can be emblematic of the grandest, most prolific things.

Take a plastic spinning top, for example.

It's so loosely constructed, one of millions of mass-produced toys created per year. It's not perfect in any way, or unique either. It's just kind of there, as a piece of material.

But when it gets going, when momentum overruns gravity, the top becomes magical. It turns at a speed previously inconceivable to the person spinning it. Those in attendance marvel at the achievement, then reset for another go-around, and another, and another.

However, most often than not, the effort put forth by the person sees no result. The spinning top just tilts to one side before wobbling to an eventual stop. It's an imperfect object that cannot possibly please on every attempt.

The technique used to put the spinning top in motion is necessary in order to see any sort of success. Without precision, the art of the spinning top is lost.

The subsequent rotation period, when a lengthy twirling period is accomplished, leaves spectators in awe of the thrower.

In a lot of ways, the plastic top and its actions emulate the life and times of a family.

There's plenty that has to go right in order for the clan to unite, flourish, and conquer.

Each family member gets their turn at the spinning top, snapping their wrists ever so gently in order to snap the $1 item a few inches off the air.

The watching period is that member's time to shine, their sterling moment in the spotlight as the other snicker and smirk along.

At the NHL draft, Brendan Gaunce was on the heels of a pretty incredible twirl.

The entire lead-up to his handshake with Gary Bettman—early morning practices, battles in the corners on the ice, bag skates, extreme workout sessions—has been a direct result of keeping the momentum going.

Four years earlier, Cameron was on quite the tear himself. It hasn't let up either, with the chance of cracking the Avalanche in the fall definitely in the picture.

Ally's been doing her own thing, finishing school and getting married. In early September, Jason and her will welcome a new person into the world. At the draft, she was about seven months pregnant, with the sex purposely unknown.

Friends, family, and acquaintances all rave about the Gaunce siblings and their down-to-earth nature. They're known as quality people who give a damn about the right things.

"As a parent, I'm just happy they're doing what they want to do," Stephen says.

Stephen and Julie's attempt to keep the proverbial spinning top moving at a steady force has been victorious since meeting back in the 1980s. They've trekked through the years, providing for their children as best they can. There's no doubt Brendan, Ally, and Cameron have adopted their parents' blueprint for success in life.

Together, they're a five-person unit with their own turns at keeping the symbolic spinning top moving at ample speed.

"Being a grandparent in early September will be amazing if everyone is healthy," Julie says.

Breast cancer stunned the family back in the spring of 2011.

Julie assures the world she is fine. And she is.

"I'm back to normal. It didn't take long," she explains. "All of the hockey distractions in the winter actually helped a lot, it made me get out of the house and keep going."

A week before the draft, in mid June, she went in for mammogram, which turned out "clear and good." The doctor appointments have gone from weekly to monthly to tri-monthly, meaning her journey back to full health is well on its way.

Then why the "if everyone is happy" remark? What's that supposed to mean?

As Julie began to fully enjoy life again back in March, Stephen's mother was diagnosed with colon cancer.

She's still ill.

One of Brendan's grandmothers from New Brunswick, who is in her late-70s, went in for surgery in April 2012. She's undergoing five months of chemo.

As you can tell, the spinning top sometimes falls off the table and onto the ground, stalling any momentum.

The other members of the unit have to cheer on the fallen, do anything in their power to get that plastic thing moving at full speed.

In some of Julie's darkest days dealing with cancer, Stephen, Brendan, Cameron, and Ally were there. The boys shaved their heads, Stephen played around-the-clock caretaker, and Ally provided a feminine touch. They were fully behind the household's biggest cheerleader.

On this birthday, June 24th, Stephen received a two-way plane ticket to the east coast from his three kids. The gift sent him to see his ailing mother for the upcoming weekend.

The gift givers knew Papa Gaunce needed it. More than most, they know exactly what it feels like to hear the word "cancer" associated with your mother.

That's two close family members diagnosed with the disease in less than a year.

"From last fall to this spring and everything since, it's just been a little hectic," Julie says after a deep breath. "We never have a boring moment. There's always something going on. It's been a crazy year, a really crazy year."

The spinning top can't work its magic 24/7. There's poor twirls here and there, bumps in the road along the way.

The pillars holding up Brendan, Cameron and Ally's lives—their parents—are all too important to them.

Being drafted to the NHL, playing in the NHL, as well as getting married and having a child, are all tremendous endeavours.

They're all young and successful, paving individual paths through life.

Brendan, in particular, is at a bit of a crossroads. He's an 18-year-old who has finished high school, been drafted by the Vancouver Canucks, and could potentially be named the next captain of the Belleville Bulls.

The next few years of his life will inevitably be shaped by his play on the ice. He could end up playing a regular shift in the NHL in a year or two or, like many have before him, toll in the minors for a while before getting a kick at the can. There's even a minute possibility he will fall of the rails and exit from the professional hockey pursuit.

Anything can transpire.

Who knows.

The one thing Stephen and Julie do know is that Brendan is coming into his own as a person.

On June 27th, the eve of the Canucks development camp, Julie and Brendan spent a few hours together. He had a plane to catch in the afternoon, and a few errands needed to be taken care of beforehand.

First they went to the bank. Then they dropped by Brother Andre High so Brendan could tie up some loose ends in order to graduate.

Toronto Pearson International Airport was the final destination of the day.

As they approached the parking lot, Brendan asked if his mom could just drop him off. He wanted to do the travel thing on his own for once.

It was a small, yet telling moment.

"He said he'd text me telling me he's OK and on board. So, I went to a nearby Ikea and looked around for a bit," Julie says.

It's not as if Brendan found his mother particularly irritating, suffocating, or anything along those lines. He simply felt the need to be a grown-up.

And it's not like the NHL draft automatically changed him into a more mature, independent guy.

He just knew he could handle it.

He wasn't the 'little guy' strapping on the Penny Crescent pads anymore.

He wasn't the captain of the Markham Waxers 1994-born AAA club anymore.

He wasn't the wide-eyed 16-year-old walking in front of a camera, answering questions about the Bulls organization shortly after being selected second overall anymore.

At the same time, he was all of that and more—combined.

His first NHL camp was a plane ride away.

It was Brendan's turn once again.

He wanted to toss the plastic spinning top all by himself.

THE OTHER STUFF

Player Report (2012 NHL Draft Black Book)

Brendan Gaunce – LC – Belleville Bulls, 6'2.0" 215

Gaunce joined the Bulls after a very prolific offensive campaign with the Markham Waxers Minor Midget AAA team. Despite coming to a team deep with more experienced forwards, Brendan took this in stride and developed into a very skilled two-way player. We were extremely impressed throughout the 2010-2011 season with the way that Gaunce constantly matched up against older, skilled players and shut their line down. As well, the 16 year old centre was a constant presence on the Bulls penalty killing unit. While this role partially hindered his ability to put up points he still put up fairly impressive numbers.

Going into the 2011-2012 season, we were well aware of his defensive skills and were ready to see him show off his ability to raise his offensive game to the next level. Gaunce got off to a good start with his performance at the Ivan Hlinka tournament. Team Canada put him in a situation where he was expected to contribute both offensively and defensively. The result - Brendan was easily one of the best forwards in that tournament and was a big impact player for his team. Gaunce showed outstanding vision and creativity that simply wasn't present often enough in his rookie season. After rejoining the Bulls he assumed more of a leadership role, and took the opportunity to help the team more at both ends of the ice.

Offensively, Gaunce has excellent vision that allows him to quickly react to plays as they develop. This ability also allows Brendan to thread some passes through defenders, and he has done so fairly regularly. He has an excellent shot with a very quick release. However at times he will choose to shoot from lower percentage areas. Gaunce is effective along the walls and the boards, and wins a large percentage of battles. Positionally he always seems to know where he needs to be on the ice, and his play without the puck is very strong. On the forecheck, Gaunce anticipates well and consistently applies strong pressure on opponents. This combination has seen him force an inordinate amount of turnovers. Gaunce has long, powerful strides in his skating, and has shown us on several occasions the ability to rush the puck very well up the ice, choosing good options if skating lanes break down.

Defensively, Gaunce just continues to get better, if that's even possible. His willingness to block shots is key in the penalty kill role, and his good positioning helps with pass interceptions. Although we're not fans of comparisons, it's hard not to compare Brendan to Jordan Staal. Another former OHL'er, that played a very similar style of game. However. Gaunce may have a little more in the area of playmaking in contrast to Staal's goal scoring. We strongly feel Gaunce would be an excellent option for a team looking for a centre that plays a great two-way game.

Game Reports

Oct. 22, 2011 – Belleville Bulls vs. Sarnia Sting (OHL)

BEL #9 LD Adam Bignell (2012) - Bignell did well jumping up and anticipating the play, and creating turnovers for his team. His vision is very good, and he reads plays well.

BEL #16 LC Brendan Gaunce (2012) - Gaunce is a powerful skater with an excellent frame. Carries the puck up the ice effectively. Displays exceptional hockey sense, and really explodes in races for the puck. Mix of determination and size helps him in any close call involving possession of the puck. Very effective along the boards. Hard worker out front of the net, and it translated in a huge goal for Belleville in this game.

SAR #10 Nail Yakupov (2012) - Utilizes teammates much better than he ever did before. Made excellent give and go play while driving to the net for a goal.

SAR #1 G Brandon Hope (2012) - Hope had great positioning, and excellent leg movement. Rebound control needs to improve. Gave up a soft goal in the 3rd period of a close game, but responded with 6 or 7 great saves through the remainder of regulation and overtime.

SCOUT NOTES:

In a bit of a back and forth contest, it appeared the Bulls had pulled one out. However Reid Boucher (New Jersey) who has been largely inconsistent so far this year, buried two goals within the final 10 minutes to send this game to overtime. Rookie blue liner Jordan Subban (2013) was strong offensively later on in the game. He notched a goal in regulation, then pulled off an unbelievable move in the 4th round of the shootout to score the winning goal. Garret Hooey (2012) appeared to have improved his skating over the summer. It still looks awkward but is much smoother and quicker than he was before. Anthony DeAngelo (2014) Displayed good puck rushing ability and went end to end on a few occasions.

Nov. 13, 2011 – Belleville Bulls vs. Oshawa Generals (OHL)

BEL #9 LD Adam Bignell (2012) Bignell's mobility is excellent, and very technically sound however he doesn't get enough power when trying to generate speed.

BEL #16 LC Brendan Gaunce (2012) Can rush the puck very well from end to end. Chooses his options really well between rushing/passing in his own end as well as the neutral zone. Solid passing ability, seems to always land tape to tape. His hockey sense is at a very high level and reads the game very well.

BEL #30 G Malcolm Subban (2012) Subban's movement in his crease is outstanding, and he has quick reflexes. Subban's positioning in correlation to the net is good, however he will sometimes come off the post too early which cost him, and leaves some very open spaces at times.

OSH #21 LC Scott Laughton (2012)Used in all game situations. Has a decent shot but missed the net in close a few times. Good hands and skates down the wing well.

SCOUTS NOTES:

A very tight defensive game to wrap up the weekend between these two rivals. Belleville's Malcolm Subban (2012) played absolutely outstanding putting together a 65+ minute performance to get the overtime win for the Bulls. Kevin Baillie (2012 re-entry) also looked very good tonight keeping the Generals in it and bringing home the single point. Cole Cassels (2013) a player who we felt had a lot of room for improvement going into this season appears to have noticeably improve his skating ability at least in reference to his north/south skating. It took 10 shooters, but Jason Shaw (2012 re-entry) scored the big winning goal in the shoot-out wrapping up a solid performance by him.

Nov. 17, 2012 – Belleville Bulls vs. Peterborough (OHL)

BEL #9 LD Adam Bignell (2012) Bignell shows very smooth skating and body positioning. He handled one on one's well. Clears the front of the net surprisingly well for size. Tends to turn the puck over too much.

BEL #16 LC Brendan Gaunce (2012) Good jump, long powerful strides, can beat anyone 1 on 1 with a combination of hands and puck protection. Lightning quick release on his shot.

BEL #17 LW Daniil Zharkov (2012) Zharkov competed well, works hard, and made a lot of smart simple plays. Went to the front of the net a lot on the power play, took a beating and hung in there.

PET #29 LD Slater Koekkoek (2012) Played man on man exceptionally well. Good skating ability. He's not explosive, but his skating looks very smooth. Very difficult to play against on the penalty kill. Will block shots, and positionally strong. Solid power play QB. Chooses his passing options extremely well. Usually uses a wrist shot from the point and it finds it's way through. Used excessively in every game situation.

PET #16 LD Trevor Murphy (2013) Already getting penalty kill time, was more well known in minor midget for his offensive contributions. Quick reactions and appropriate to the play. Broke down plays in his own zone.

PET #21 RW Stephen Nosad (2013) Explosive and rushes the puck, driving the net whenever possible. Used on the penalty kill and is very responsible and positionally sound. Makes plays happen offensively on a regular basis using his speed and skill. Solid puck protection ability.

SCOUT NOTES:

Not the most exciting game we've seen so far this year, Peterborough took control early, and didn't really look back. Not quite as physical as other match-up's we've seen from these two teams in the past as they hold a good divisional rivalry. Dylan Corson (2012) played a depth role for the Bulls tonight. He showed good work along the boards, and made a great pass to set up the Bulls' only goal. Nicholas Ritchie (2014) has made a smooth transition to the OHL. He looks exactly like his older brother Brett in terms of style. However Nicholas seems to have a bit more explosiveness and becomes physical more frequently on opposing players.

Feb. 10, 2012 – Belleville Bulls vs. Kingston (OHL)

BEL #4 RD Jordan Subban (2013) Subban looked excellent on the power play. He made several great plays at the line to keep the puck in the zone, as well as some nice moves when coming in from the point to shoot the puck.

BEL #16 LC Brendan Gaunce (2012) Looked great in his own zone consistently showing strong positional play and engages quickly and intelligently. He has an incredibly quick release on his shot that can sometimes catch the opposition off guard. Very dangerous short handed can take the puck and get up ice in a hurry. He works hard and battles for that second chance after he was stopped. He had the presence of mind to bank the puck off the goaltender who was out of position for a big goal.

BEL #17 LW Daniil Zharkov (2012) Zharkov has been noticed this game a lot for his tendency to float and become uninvolved in the game. However as it got progressively more physical, Zharkov elevated his physical game.

BEL #24 LW Garrett Hooey (2012) Seemed to wander a bit in the offensive zone and lost his positioning. If he maintained it it's very likely he would have had a goal on one particular play. Hockey sense and his decision making with the puck were very questionable tonight. He lost battles along the wall not battling hard enough or disengaging too early from the battles. Took a very undisciplined penalty with the game close. Willing to shoot the puck, and has a good shot on him, but passed up on some very good passing opportunities to shoot.

KGN #4 RD Alex Gudbranson (2012) Utilized on the power play although he's not a big offensive defenseman. He chose the right options and complete his passes. Really struggled with the puck when he was heavily pressured and turned the puck over. He looks a lot better tonight than he did earlier in the year defensively.

KGN #7 LD Warren Steele (2012) Made some very good plays in one on one situations. He made some great plays at the line on the power play, to keep the play going and chose the right options with the puck on the power play. Made some risky plays at the line to keep the play in the offensive zone, but they were successful.

KGN #17 LC Ryan Kujawinski (2013) Ryan looked a little uncoordinated out there at times, but still got the job done. Made a beautiful pass which lead to him being able to score a great goal when the puck was sent back to him. Ryan was really a leader offensively for Kingston creating a ton of scoring chances.

KGN #23 LW Jack Nevins (2012) Nevins landed some absolutely devastating hits. Goes right to the net in the offensive zone, and seems to know his role and his position very well. Landed a ridiculous amount of hits this game and just punished the Bulls players all night long. Has a good shot, but was able to make the right choice and complete some good passes. Looks like a low risk, low reward player. Jack is incredibly strong, and excellent checker, and does enough at both ends of the ice to contribute a little bit in those areas.

SCOUTS NOTES:

Excellent rivalry game went down at the K-Rock Centre tonight as the Bulls and Fronts played a very tight game throughout the night. A lot of back and forth action in terms of momentum saw this game go to overtime. Jake Worrad (2012 re-entry) scored the overtime winner less than 30 seconds in to take a valuable two points for the Bulls. This game was extremely physical and both sides delivered some huge hits throughout this one.

RAPID FIRE GET-TO-KNOW

Favourite...

Shootout move: Low-stick or high-glove

Pump-up music: Don't listen to music before games

Ice cream: Cookies and cream

Animal: Dog

Video game: NHL 12

City: Kelowna, some places in New Brunswick

OHL rink: London, Oshawa

Superhero: Used to be Batman, don't really have one anymore

Dish: Steak with sweet potato fries

Colour: Blue

Draft season...

Low point: Personal slump and team slide (15 losses in 18 games)

High point: Player of the week and team streak (12 wins in 14 games)

LOOSE ENDS

... ON THE TWO SIDES OF BRENDAN GAUNCE

SEAN MONAHAN:

"Off the ice, Brendan is a real nice kid. Kind of soft. But then when you get on the ice he's real mean and competitive so there are a lot of differences."

... ON FORWARD CONNOR CRISP PLAYING GOAL FOR ERIE OTTERS

BRENDAN:

"It's not like he isn't playing in the best semi-pro league in the world or anything. It's not like it's some pick-up league in Markham. It's the real deal."

.... ON THE END OF HIGH SCHOOL

BRENDAN:

"I don't know why people always say they want to leave high school. It's so secluded; it's so much easier than the real world. It's a huge step in my life though, especially since I want to go to university."

... ON THE IMPORTANCE OF A STRONG FAMILY

GARY ROBERTS:

"If you meet his parents, if you meet Steven Stamkos' parents, if you meet Jeff Skinner's parents – they've very, very grounded people who have done a great job raising their children. Through their successes, they haven't changed as people. For me, that's a huge element at this age — not that you can't get there if you didn't have a good childhood — to becoming a leader."

... ON LIVING IN THEIR BROTHERS' SHADOWS

MALCOLM SUBBAN:

"We always joke with each other, about our brothers. We're kind of in the same boat there. We have a lot of similarities. I think it's brought us together more. It's helped each of us handle the pressure better."

... ON HIS FAVOURITE OHL RINKS

BRENDAN:

"I like playing in Peterborough. It's an older rink and I've also had some success in there. Peterborough and Oshawa, having rivalries against those teams helps. Even rinks like London, Kitchener and Windsor, who have huge fan bases, allows you to feel like a pro playing in front of 8,000, 9,000 fans."

... ON THE 2011 VERSION OF THE SHOW '24/7'

BRENDAN:

"I love those kind of shows. I definitely watched all four episodes. That's the kind of stuff that makes you get what goes on away from the rink and the persona guys bring to work. It shows they're actual people, like you and I. A prime example is Michael Del Zotto. They did a couple big features on him since he's been having such a great year for New York. It was kind of weird seeing them video-tape him when he was driving because I've known him for a long time. People all around the world watching what he does with his life was kind of strange. When Michael got hurt, the guys were laughing because he said he felt like a 51-year-old man and all the guys were saying it was all a lie. But that's exactly how he is and I wouldn't be surprised if that's how he was actually feeling."

... ON THE INFLUENCE OF '90-BORN WAXERS TEAM

PAUL TITANIC:

"We were able to keep the core together for many years. That consistency was a big factor, that continuity was a big factor with that team. I know Brendan was at an awful lot of those games. I think part of learning the game is by watching."

EXTRAS

2011–12 regular season statistics

68 Games (most on team; tied with 2 others)

28 Goals (5 PP; 4 SH; 4 GW; 2 IG)

40 Assists (most on team)

68 Points (1.0 per game)

+4 Rating (1 of only 8 plus-ratings on team)

68 Penalty Minutes (5th most on team)

*Source: OntarioHockeyLeague.com

2011–12 post-season statistics

6 Games

1 Goal

2 Assists

3 Points

–2 Rating

2 Penalty Minutes

*Source: OntarioHockeyLeague.com

Statistics from Brendan Gaunce's 10-game intervals throughout 2011–12 season

First 10 (September 23rd–October 21st)

Goals: 5 (0 PP; 2 SH; 3 GW; 1 IG)

Assists: 4

Plus–minus: +3

Penalty Minutes: 18

Team Record: 5–5

Second 10 (October 22nd–November 16th)

Goals: 5 (1 PP; PK; 2 GW; 0 IG)

Assists: 7

Plus–minus: Even

Penalty Minutes: 8

Team Record: 8–2

Third 10 (November 17th–December 9th)

Goals: 8 (3 PP; 0 PK; 1 GW; 1 IG)

Assists: 5

Plus–minus: +10

Penalty Minutes: 16

Team Record: 6-4

Fourth 10 (December 10th-January 12th)

Goals: 3 (0 PP; 0 PK; 0 GW; 0 IG)

Assists: 6

Plus-minus: -6

Penalty Minutes: 13

Team Record: 3-7

Fifth 10 (January 14th-February 10th)

Goals: 3 (1 PP; 1 PK; 0 GW; 0 IG)

Assists: 4

Plus-minus: -4

Penalty Minutes: 2

Team Record: 3-7

Sixth 10 (February 11th-February 29th)

Goals: 4 (0 PP; 0 PK; 0 GW; 0 IG)

Assists: 9

Plus-minus: +3

Penalty Minutes: 9

Team Record: 5-5

Seventh 10 (March 2nd-March 23rd)

Goals: 1 (0 PP; 1 PK; 0 GW; 0 IG)

Assists: 6

Plus-minus: -2

Penalty Minutes: 2

Team Record: 5-5

Final four (March 25th-April 2nd)

Goals: 1 (1 PP; 0 PK; 0 GW; 0 IG)

Assists: 1

Plus-minus: -2

Penalty Minutes: 2

Team Record: 2-2

*Source: OntarioHockeyLeague.com

2011-12 Eastern Conference Coaches Poll

Most Underrated Player

1.   Sam Carrick, Brampton Battalion tied Joey West, Peterborough Petes (18)

3.   Josh Leivo, Sudbury Wolves (14)

Most Improved Player

1.   Tanner Pearson, Barrie Colts (34)

2.   Jamie Wise, Mississauga St. Michael's Majors (13)

3.   Igor Bobkov, Kingston Frontenacs tied Frank Corrado, Sudbury Wolves (10)

Smartest Player

1.   Michael Sgarbossa, Sudbury Wolves (37)

2.   Riley Brace, Mississauga St. Michael's Majors (12)

3.   Ryan Strome, Niagara IceDogs (11)

Hardest Worker

1.   Boone Jenner, Oshawa Generals (24)

2.   Luke Judson, Belleville Bulls (22)

3.   Alex Friesen, Niagara IceDogs (17) - finished first in voting in 2009-10

Best Playmaker

1.   Michael Sgarbossa, Sudbury Wolves (41)

2.   Ryan Strome, Niagara IceDogs (23) – finished first in voting in 2010-11

3.   Brendan Gaunce, Belleville Bulls (7)

Most Dangerous in the Goal Area

1.   Tyler Toffoli, Ottawa 67's (32) – finished second in voting in 2010-11 and third in 2009-10

2.   Michael Sgarbossa, Sudbury Wolves (23)

3.   Mark Scheifele, Barrie Colts (9)

Best Skater

1.   Ivan Telegin, Barrie Colts tied Shane Prince, Ottawa 67's (25)

3.   Jesse Graham, Niagara IceDogs (13)

Best Shot

1.   Tyler Toffoli, Ottawa 67's (36) – finished second in voting in 2010-11

2.   Christian Thomas, Oshawa Generals (16) – finished first in voting in 2010-11 and second in 2009-10

3.   Michael Sgarbossa, Sudbury Wolves (13)

Hardest Shot

1.   Cody Ceci, Ottawa 67's (21)

2.   Jamie Oleksiak, Niagara IceDogs (15)

3.   Josh McFadden, Sudbury Wolves (13)

Best Stickhandler

1.   Ryan Strome, Niagara IceDogs (26) – finished tied for first in voting in 2010–11

2.   Michael Sgarbossa, Sudbury Wolves (25) – finished third in voting in 2010–11

3.   Riley Brace, Mississauga St. Michael's Majors (10)

Best on Face-Offs

1.   Alex Friesen, Niagara IceDogs (24) – finished tied for third in voting in 2010–11 and first in 2009–10

2.   Boone Jenner, Oshawa Generals (18)

3.   Mark Scheifele, Barrie Colts (11)

Best Body Checker

1.   Cameron Wind, Brampton Battalion (25)

2.   Anthony Camara, Barrie Colts tied Alex Cord, Mississauga St. Michael's Majors (13) – Camara finished first in West voting in 2010–11

Best Shot Blocker

1.   Jamie Oleksiak, Niagara IceDogs (22)

2.   Zach Bell, Brampton Battalion (15)

3.   Cody Ceci, Ottawa 67's (14)

Best Defensive Forward

4.   Alex Friesen, Niagara IceDogs (31) – finished third in voting in 2010-11

5.   Joey West, Peterborough Petes (15)

6.   Josh Leivo, Sudbury Wolves (10)

Best Penalty Killer

1.   Jamie Wise, Mississauga St. Michael's Majors tied Alex Friesen, Niagara IceDogs (25) – Friesen finished first in voting in 2010-11

3.   Luke Judson, Belleville Bulls tied Frank Corrado, Sudbury Wolves (11)

Best Offensive Defenceman

1.   Dougie Hamilton, Niagara IceDogs (45) – finished first in voting in 2010-11

2.   Cody Ceci, Ottawa 67's (17)

3.   Josh McFadden, Sudbury Wolves (10) – finished third in voting in 2010-11

Best Defensive Defenceman

1.   Cameron Wind, Brampton Battalion (24)

2.   Dougie Hamilton, Niagara IceDogs (19) – finished third in voting in 2010–11

3.   Frank Corrado, Sudbury Wolves (15)

Best Puck Handling Goalie

1.   Mark Visentin, Niagara IceDogs (32)

2.   Brandon Maxwell, Mississauga St. Michael's Majors (26)

3.   Malcolm Subban, Belleville Bulls tied Kevin Bailie, Oshawa Generals (7)

Best Shootout Shooter

1.   Tyler Toffoli, Ottawa 67's (31)

2.   Mark Scheifele, Barrie Colts (28)

3.   Mathew Campagna, Sudbury Wolves (14)

Best Shootout Goalie

1.   Malcolm Subban, Belleville Bulls (26)

2.   Mark Visentin, Niagara IceDogs (19)

3.   Petr Mrazek, Ottawa 67's (14)

*Source: OntarioHockeyLeague.com

2012 Top Prospects Game
(February 1, Kelowna, B.C.)

Team Cherry

Forwards
-Tim Bozon, Left Wing / Kamloops Blazers (WHL)
-Dane Fox, Centre / Erie Otters (OHL)
-Martin Frk, Centre / Halifax Mooseheads (QMJHL)
-Brendan Gaunce, Centre / Belleville Bulls (OHL)
-Coda Gordon, Centre / Swift Current Broncos (WHL)
-Scott Laughton, Centre / Oshawa Generals (OHL)
-Andrew Ryan, Centre / Halifax Mooseheads (QMJHL)
-Gemel Smith, Centre / Owen Sound Attack (OHL)
-Dominik Volek, Centre / Regina Pats (WHL)
-Tom Wilson, Centre / Plymouth Whalers (OHL)
-Mike Winther, Centre / Prince Albert Raiders (WHL)
-Daniil Zharkov, Centre / Belleville Bulls (OHL)

Defensemen
-Mathew Dumba, Defence / Red Deer Rebels (WHL)
-Nick Ebert, Defence / Windsor Spitfires (OHL)
-Dillon Fournier, Defence / Rouyn-Noranda Huskies (QMJHL)
-Brett Kulak, Defence / Vancouver Giants (WHL)
-Ryan Murray, Defence / Everett Silvertips (WHL)
-Damon Severson, Defence / Kelowna Rockets (WHL)

Goaltenders
-Matt Murray, Goaltender / Sault Ste. Marie Greyhounds (OHL)
-Brandon Whitney, Goaltender / Victoriaville Tigres (QMJHL)

Team Orr

Forwards
-Andreas Athanasiou, Left Wing / London Knights (OHL)
-Francis Beauvillier, Centre / Rimouski Oceanic (QMJHL)
-Raphaël Bussières, Centre / Baie-Comeau Drakkar (QMJHL)
-Radek Faksa, Centre / Kitchener Rangers (OHL)
-Mikhail Grigorenko, Centre / Quebec Remparts (QMJHL)
-Tomas Hyka, Centre / Gatineau Olympiques (QMJHL)
-Scott Kosmachuk, Centre / Guelph Storm (OHL)
-Tanner Pearson, Left Wing / Barrie Colts (OHL)
-Colton Sissons, Right Wing / Kelowna Rockets (WHL)
-Chandler Stephenson, Centre / Regina Pats (WHL)
-Lukas Sutter, Centre / Saskatoon Blades (WHL)
-Branden Troock, Right Wing / Seattle Thunderbirds (WHL)

Defensemen
-Gianluca Curcuruto, Defence / Soo Greyhounds (OHL)
-Matt Finn, Defence / Guelph Storm (OHL)
-Adam Pelech, Defence / Erie Otters (OHL)
    -Derrick Pouliot, Defence / Portland Winterhawks (WHL)
-Griffin Reinhart, Defence / Edmonton Oil Kings (WHL)
-Dalton Thrower, Defence / Saskatoon Blades (WHL)

Goaltenders
-Chris Driedger, Goaltender / Calgary Hitmen (WHL)
-François Tremblay, Goaltender / Val-d'Or Foreurs (QMJHL)

*Source: HomeHardwareTopProspects.ca

2012 Under-18's
(April 12-22, Czech Republic)

Forwards
-Hunter Shinkaruk, Left Wing / Medicine Hat Tigers (WHL)
-Anthony Mantha, Left Wing / Val-d'Or Foreurs (QMJHL)
-Brendan Gaunce, Centre / Belleville Bulls (OHL)
-Branden Troock, Right Wing / Seattle Thunderbirds (WHL)
-Kerby Rychel, Left Wing / Windsor Spitfires (OHL)
-Scott Kosmachuk, Right Wing / Guelph Storm (OHL)
-Mike Winther, Centre / Prince Albert Raiders (WHL)
-Félix Girard, Centre / Baie-Comeau Drakkar (QMJHL)
-Gemel Smith, Centre / Owen Sound Attack (OHL)
-Troy Bourke, Left Wing / Prince George Cougars (WHL)
-Scott Laughton, Centre / Oshawa Generals (OHL)
-Sam Reinhart, Centre / Kootenay Ice (WHL)
-William Carrier, Left Wing / Cape Breton Eagles (QMJHL)

Defensemen
-Darnell Nurse, Defense / Sault Ste. Marie Greyhounds (OHL)
-Ryan Pulock, Defense / Brandon Wheat Kings (WHL)
-Damon Severson, Defense / Kelowna Rockets (WHL)
-Josh Morrissey, Defense / Prince Albert (WHL)
-Warren Steele, Defense / Kingston Frontenacs (OHL)
-Mathew Dumba, Defense / Red Deer Rebels (WHL)
-Adam Pelech, Defense / Erie Otters (OHL)

Goaltenders
-Spencer Martin, Goaltender / Mississauga Majors (OHL)
-Brandon Whitney, Goaltender / Victoriaville Tigres (QMJHL)
-Matt Murray, Goaltender / Sault Ste. Marie Greyhounds (OHL)

*Source: HockeyCanada.ca

2011 Ivan Hlinka
(Aug. 8–13, Czech Republic/Slovakia)

Forwards
-Andreas Athanasiou, Left Wing / London Knights (OHL)
-Hunter Shinkaruk, Left Wing / Medicine Hat Tigers (WHL)
-Brendan Gaunce, Centre / Belleville Bulls (OHL)
 -Scott Laughton, Centre / Oshawa Generals (OHL)
-Charles Hudon, Left Wing / Chicoutimi Sagueneens (QMJHL)
-Mathew Campagna, Centre / Sudbury Wolves (OHL)
-Kerby Rychel, Left Wing / Windsor Spitfires (OHL)
-Gemel Smith, Centre / Owen Sound Attack (OHL)
-Matia Marcantuoni, Left Wing / Kitchener Rangers (OHL)
-Sean Monahan, Centre / Ottawa 67's (OHL)
-Jarrod Maidens, Centre / Owen Sound Attack (OHL)
-Félix Girard, Centre / Baie-Comeau Drakkar (QMJHL)
-Thomas Wilson, Right Wing / Plymouth Whalers (OHL)

Defense
-Adam Pelech, Defense / Erie Otters (OHL)
-Slater Koekkoek, Defense / Peterborough Petes (OHL)
-Morgan Rielly, Defense / Moose Jaw Warriors (WHL)
-Griffin Reinhart, Defense / Edmonton Oil Kings (WHL)
-Michael Matheson, Defense / Lac St-Louis Lions (LHMAAAQ)
-Mathew Dumba, Defense / Red Deer Rebels (WHL)
-Derrick Pouliot, Defense / Portland Winterhawks (WHL)

Goaltenders
-Daniel Altshuller, Goaltender / Nepean Raiders (CCHL)
-Domenic Graham, Goaltender / Drummondville Volts (QMJHL)

*Source: HockeyCanada.ca

@BrendanGaunce16 Twitter feed
Bio: "Like to play hockey"

2011

Jul 11 — Counting down until a big part of my life is over.....the last saga of Harry Potter is out in Canada on Friday

Jul 14 — Never been so bored in my life, what can I do other then a movie or xbox tonight...I guess there is always the intellectual route in reading

Jul 22 — Piranha's may be the stupidest movies I have ever watched. Whoever the director was they have to figure out a plot for their horror movies

Aug 12 — Big win tonight, sorry Zharkov I will have bragging rights this season. Finals tomorrow versus Sweden #cantwait

Aug 14 — Very happy to land in Canada, only a week left of summer until back to Belleville

Aug 21 — Just watched Home Alone 3 with @saucethedog, classic movie.#thisismytown

Aug 25 — Hospitals always creep me out, a couple sick upgrades in the Markham hospital #ifonlyIcouldeattimhortons

Aug 29 — Back to Belleville for the year, all ready for country music and a whole lot of xbox..#herewegoagain

Sept 3 — Shark week 3D is up there with piranhas as the worst movie I have ever seen. They had such good potential but ending up brutal.#rattled

Sept 11 — I got my first car last night, I always knew the libs wanted to have me behind the wheel and not Cam, you found your home baby#treatmewell

Sept 20 — Warrior is the best movie I have ever seen. Lucky for Cam we play hockey and don't do MMA fighting, id put ya in the sleepa hold#out

Sept 25 — Family guy season premiere was hilarious, has to be the funniest show on tv. "Also, I left a poo on your desk, goodbye" #classic

Sept 28 — Happy birthday to my one and only brother in-law. I don't know how you put up with my sister, but you do. #justkiddingyourlucky

Oct 5 — Great win tonight! Even better I got to see my grandparents, always say I played well even if I didn't..number 2 fans #onlybehindmysister

Oct 6 — Leafs come up with a huggge win! Sorry habs you're gonna have to wait for that first win #teammidgets..oh ya and I forgot about #optimusreim

Dec 11 — One of the hardest things to do in life....sleep on a bus. So many distractions and smells lingering around #howmuchlonger

Dec 17 — Just had a gift exchange with my billets, always like giving....receiving is not that bad either #besttimeoftheyear

Dec 18 — One thing I missed when I was away....not being able to play with my dog #rocky #tougherdog

Dec 21 — Happy birthday to my good buddy @MalcolmSubban! #goodgoalie #somesayfranchise @SteveSilas

Dec 27 — Christmas break is over once again! Back to Belleville to start our playoff run!

Dec 31 — Nice to have a day off, especially on New years eve! Still going to bed before 12 though, 2012 will be there when I wake up....I hope.

2012

Jan 5 — Another Markham member on the bulls, @Cramberry16! Cya soon

Jan 13 — Crazy day outside. Most people think about driving and cringe, @simmer25 lives for this weather! #nascardriver #wouldyoulikeadonutwiththat

Jan 21 — Does anyone know how to fix the computer screen size after you plug it into a smart board? Mine is stuck in half screen and magnified #help

Feb 7 — Don't you hate when you are hungry and the food you ordered isn't coming as quick as normal. #alreadyfinishedmydrink #Illbeparched

Feb 8 — When you aren't the person in the class talking, it is so weird to listen to how crazy some peoples conversations are #stoptalkingaboutcults

Feb 12 — The grammy's is unreal, but what is wrong with Lady Gaga? You already have millions of dollars and followers, be normal again #creepyoutfit

Feb 20 — Wishing my good buddy @delsauce21 luck tonight. Game 7 is always the best feeling, wish I could have gone...dukc dome will be rocking.

Feb 28 — "I can dunk when I'm standing still, but can't when I'm running, is that weird?" @simmer25

Mar 2 — Wow, unreal day in belleville, feels like april already. Now only if gas prices would go down...#alligatorarms

Mar 7 — First day for shorts this year. It is finally feeling like March should,now just need to wait until march break to really enjoy it #sosoon

Mar 15 — Just saw two ladies casually sliding along the side of the street on elliptical's? Good to get some fresh air but wow that looks awful...

Mar 18 — 21 Jump Street was the funniest movie I have seen in a while. I recommend you go see it as soon as you can, especially you @saucethedog....

Mar 19 — Happy Birthday to my brother Cam! 22, getting pretty old #halfwayto44

Mar 22 — Finally, playoffs.

Mar 25 — Had a good day today, thanks for the wishes. Jimmy with the classic mario party 2 hockey celly on the winner. Good seeing the family after!

Mar 27 — Love when teenagers stare and laugh at my hair when I still have a better hair cut then them. You have your sisters coat and haircut bud.

Mar 31 — Welcome back @Krychs to twitter! 40 goal scorer in the OHL should have 1000 followers I'd say. #slapshotworksbest

Apr 2 — Had another great year in Belleville. Bad way to end it but nevertheless it was a blast. We had a great group of guys that made it special!

Apr 24 — When someone farts and the dog thinks it's someone knocking on the door. #hellosqueaker

Apr 30 — Weird being back at the gym so soon. Body definitely needs to get back in work out mode though, sore already and summer just started....

May 8 — Steam rooms are so hot I feel like I'm suppose to be getting a tan. I really wish that was the case #badgenes #pale

May 10 — How does someone get rattled even before they have to go to school? Must be from missing the highlights this morning, that's what it is.
May 13 — Happy mothers day to everyone and especially mine! Really appreciate everything you do!

May 27 — That quite possibly could have been the best celebration I have ever seen. Taking out the ref, and throwing your gear into the crowd.
May 29 — First day of interviews done, now out to dinner with Cam for a nice meal. The real question is will he make us split the bill... #pleaseno

June 3 — Watching Mystery Alaska for the first time, recommended by Cam. Let's hope it lives up to the hype.

June 4 — I wish the Yardman would use Cartman as the jumbotron spokesperson, would make stoppages a lot more fun.

June 10 — This time of year is exciting and all from the hockey standpoint, but this end of the year school work is making this month way to stressful

June 15 — Just watched a police car run a red light while talking on his phone and looking at his computer. How does that work?

June 17 — I don't know how that 17 year old is doing it at the US open. I couldn't even think about that, guess he doesn't have to do exams though...

June 19 — One more day of school then off to Pittsburgh tomorrow morning. Finally it's here.

June 23 — Thanks everyone for the support last night! It was great to be drafted by the Canucks, looking forward to going to Vancouver next week!

*Source: Twitter.com

2012 NHL Scouting Combine Official Results
(May 28-June 2; Toronto, Ontario)

PEAK POWER OUTPUT - ANAEROBIC FITNESS
PLAYER TEAM (LEAGUE) Watts/kg
1. Alex Galchenyuk Sarnia (OHL) 15.6
2. Matthew DeBlouw Muskegon (USHL) 15
Matia Marcantuoni Kitchner (OHL) 15
4. Thomas Wilson Plymouth (OHL) 14.9
5. Chris Calnan Nobles (HIGH-MA) 14.8
6. Ludwig Bystrom Modo Jr. (SWE-JR.) 14.6
7. Cristoval Nieves Kent School (HIGH-CT) 14.5
8. **Brendan Gaunce Belleville (OHL) 14.4**
9. Sebastian Collberg Frolunda (SWE) 14.4
10. Slater Koekkoek Peterborough (OHL) 14.4
AVERAGE   13.2

MEAN POWER OUTPUT
PLAYER TEAM (LEAGUE) Watts/kg3
1. Chris Calnan Nobles (HIGH-MA) 11.4
2. Cristoval Nieves Kent School (HIGH-CT) 11.3
3. Slater Koekkoek Peterborough (OHL) 11.2
Daniel O'Regan St. Sebastian School (HIGH-MA) 11.2
5. Thomas Wilson Plymouth (OHL) 11.2
6. Mathew Dumba Red Deer (WHL) 11
7. Matthew DeBlouw Muskegon (USHL) 11
Ludwig Bystrom Modo Jr. (SWE-JR.) 11
Mitchell Moroz Edmonton (WHL) 11
10. Mark Jankowski Stanstead College (HIGH-QC) 10.9
AVERAGE   10.1

FATIGUE INDEX
PLAYER TEAM (LEAGUE) % DROP-OFF FROM PEAK
1. James Melindy Moncton (QMJHL) 32.3
2. Olli Maatta London (OHL) 35.6
3. Erik Karlsson Frolunda Jr. (SWE-JR.) 39
4. Zachary Stepan Shattuck-St. Mary's (HIGH-MN) 39
5. Kevin Roy Lincoln (USHL) 40

6. Jordan Schmaltz Green Bay (USHL) 40.1
7. Henrik Samuelsson Edmonton (WHL) 40.4
8. Devin Shore Whitby (OJHL) 41.1
9. Teuvo Teravainen Jokerit (FIN) 41.5
10. Griffin Reinhart Edmonton (WHL) 43
AVERAGE   49.7

VO2 MAX – AEROBIC FITNESS
PLAYER TEAM (LEAGUE) (ml/kg/min)
1. Tomas Hertl Slavia (CZREP) 65.7
2. Ryan Culkin Quebec (QMJHL) 65.7
3. Brian Cooper Fargo (USHL) 65.5
4. Sebastian Collberg Frolunda (SWE) 64.4
5. Kevin Roy Lincoln (USHL) 64.1
6. Anthony Stolarz Corpus Christi (NAHL) 62.7
7. Patrick Sieloff USA U–18 (USHL) 62.6
8. Thomas Wilson Plymouth (OHL) 62.4
9. Ben Johnson Windsor (OHL) 62.4
Mathew Dumba Red Deer (WHL) 62.4
AVERAGE   55.9

VO2 MAX TEST DURATION
PLAYER TEAM (LEAGUE) MINUTES
1. Hampus Lindholm Rogle JR. (SWE–JR.) 14:40
2. Ryan Murray Everett (WHL) 13:32
3. Henrik Samuelsson Edmonton (WHL) 13:25
4. Thomas Wilson Plymouth (OHL) 13:11
Brian Hart Exeter (HIGH–NH) 13:11
6. Martin Frk Halifax (QMJHL) 12:53
7. Anthony Stolarz Corpus Christi (NAHL) 12:46
8. Ben Johnson Windsor (OHL) 12:41
9. Devin Shore Whitby (OJHL) 12:37
10. Nail Yakupov Sarnia (OHL) 12:25
Max Iafrate Kitchener (OHL) 12:25
AVERAGE   10:31

WING SPAN – ANTHROPOMETRY
PLAYER TEAM (LEAGUE) INCHES
1. Anthony Stolarz Corpus Christi (NAHL) 81
2. Jon Gillies Indiana (USHL) 80.25
3. Malcolm Subban Belleville (OHL) 79.5

4. Brandon Whitney Victoriaville (QMJHL) 79
5. Matt Tomkins Sherwood Park (AJHL) 78.5
6. Andrey Vasilevskiy Ufa 2 (RUS–JR.) 78
7. Stefan Matteau USA U–18 (USHL) 77.75
Radek Faksa Kitchener (OHL) 77.75
Jujhar Khaira Prince George (BCHL) 77.75
Cody Ceci Ottawa (OHL) 77.75
Mikhail Grigorenko Quebec (QMJHL) 77.75
AVERAGE   74.4

SUM OF SIX SKINFOLDS
TEAM PLAYER (LEAGUE) mm
1. Matt Tomkins Sherwood Park (AJHL) 35
Kenton Helgesen Calgary (WHL) 35
3. Frank Palazzese Kitchener (OHL) 38 4.
4. Michael Matheson Dubuque (USHL) 39
5. Mark Jankowski Stanstead College (HIGH–QC) 39
6. Francis Beauvillier Rimouski (QMJHL) 39
7. Christophe Lalancette Acadie–Bathurst (QMJHL) 40
Kevin Roy Lincoln (USHL) 40
9. Matthew DeBlouw Muskegon (USHL) 40
10. Cristoval Nieves Kent School (HIGH–CT) 41
AVERAGE   61.4

YUHASZ BODY FAT
PLAYER TEAM (LEAGUE) %
1. Kenton Helgesen Calgary (WHL) 7
Matt Tomkins Sherwood Park (AJHL) 7
3. Frank Palazzese Kitchener (OHL) 7.3
4. Michael Matheson Dubuque (USHL) 7.4
5. Mark Jankowski Stanstead College (HIGH–QC) 7.4
6. Francis Beauvillier Rimouski (QMJHL) 7.4
7. Christophe Lalancette Acadie–Bathurst (QMJHL) 7.5
Kevin Roy Lincoln (USHL) 7.5
9. Matthew DeBlouw Muskegon (USHL) 7.5
10. Cristoval Nieves Kent School (HIGH–CT) 7.6
AVERAGE   9.6

HAND–EYE COORDINATION
PLAYER TEAM (LEAGUE) SECONDS
1. Francois Tremblay Val-d'Or (QMJHL) 21.4

2. Robert Baillargeon Indiana (USHL) 22.2
Tomas Hertl Slavia (CZREP) 22.2
4. Chris Calnan Nobles (HIGH–MA) 22.6
5. Artur Gavrus Owen Sound (OHL) 23.5
6. Ville Pokka Karpat (FIN) 23.8
Calle Andersson Farjestad Jr. (SWE–JR.) 23.8
8. Mathew Dumba Red Deer (WHL) 24
Andrey Markov Saskatoon (WHL) 24
10. Matt Tomkins Sherwood Park (AJHL) 24.7
Christophe Lalancette Acadie–Bathurst (QMJHL) 24.7
AVERAGE   28.6

STANDING LONG JUMP – MUSCULOSKELETAL LOWER
BODY
PLAYER TEAM (LEAGUE) INCHES
1. Michael Matheson Dubuque (USHL) 119
2. Jake McCabe U. of Wisconsin (WCHA) 119
4. Patrick Sieloff USA U–18 (USHL) 115
5. Andreas Athanasiou London (OHL) 114.5
6. Mathew Dumba Red Deer (WHL) 114
Francis Beauvillier Rimouski (QMJHL) 114
8. Cody Ceci Ottawa (OHL) 113
9. Chris Calnan Nobles (HIGH–MA) 112.5
10. Brady Skjei USA U–18 (USHL) 112
Filip Forsberg Leksand (SWE–2) 112
AVERAGE   103.8

VERTEK VERTICAL JUMP PAUSE
PLAYER TEAM (LEAGUE) INCHES
1. Chris Calnan Nobles (HIGH–MA) 32.5
2. Andreas Athanasiou London (OHL) 31.5
3. Brady Skjei USA U–18 (USHL) 29.5
Jake Paterson Saginaw (OHL) 29.5
Malcolm Subban Belleville (OHL) 29.5
6. Jake McCabe U. of Wisconsin (WCHA) 28.5
7. Mathew Dumba Red Deer (WHL) 27.8
8. Francis Beauvillier Rimouski (QMJHL) 27.5
9. Matt Tomkins Sherwood Park (AJHL) 27.3
10. Brian Cooper Fargo (USHL) 27
Brendan Gaunce Belleville (OHL) 27
AVERAGE   23.5

VERTICAL JUMP NO PAUSE
PLAYER TEAM (LEAGUE) INCHES
1. Chris Calnan Nobles (HIGH–MA) 32.5
2. Andreas Athanasiou London (OHL) 32
3. Jake Paterson Saginaw (OHL) 30.5
Malcolm Subban Belleville (OHL) 30.5
Jake McCabe U of Wisoncin (WCHA) 30.5
6. Matt Tomkins Sherwood Park (AJHL) 29.8
7. Brady Skjei USA U-18 (USHL) 29.5
8. Francis Beauvillier Rimouski (QMJHL) 29
9. Mathew Dumba Red Deer (WHL) 28
Brendan Gaunce Belleville (OHL) 28
Matia Marcantuoni Kitchener (OHL) 28
AVERAGE   24.7

VERTEK LEG POWER PAUSE AVG (LEWIS)
PLAYER TEAM (LEAGUE WATTS)
1. Brendan Gaunce Belleville (OHL) 1684
2. Chris Calnan Nobles (HIGH–MA) 1673
3. Brady Skjei USA (U–18) 1666
4. Malcolm Subban Belleville (OHL) 1656
5. Thomas Wilson Plymouth (OHL) 1653
6. Henrik Samuelsson Edmonton (WHL) 1639
7. Stefan Matteau USA U-18 (USHL) 1626
8. Griffin Reinhart Edmonton (WHL) 1611
9. Cody Ceci Ottawa (OHL) 1606
Brian Hart Exeter (HIGH–NH) 1606
AVERAGE   1387

VERTEK LEG POWER NO PAUSE AVG (LEWIS)
PLAYER TEAM (LEAGUE) WATTS
1. Jake McCabe U. of Wisconsin (WCHA) 1757
2. Brendan Gaunce Belleville (OHL) 1714
3. Thomas Wilson Plymouth (OHL) 1687
4. Malcolm Subban Belleville (OHL) 1686
5. Griffin Reinhart Edmonton (WHL) 1675
6. Chris Calnan Nobles (HIGH–MA) 1673
7. Cody Ceci Ottawa (OHL) 1670
8. Henrik Samuelsson Edmonton (WHL) 1667
9. Brady Skjei USA U-18 (USHL) 1666

10. Stefan Matteau USA U-18 (USHL) 1659
AVERAGE   1421

VERTEK LEG POWER PEAK PAUSE (SAYERS)
PLAYER TEAM (LEAGUE) WATTS
1. Chris Calnan Nobles (HIGH-MA) 6818
2. Brady Skjei USA U-18 (USHL) 6523
3. Malcolm Subban Belleville (OHL) 6516
4. Andreas Athanasiou London (OHL) 6443
5. Brendan Gaunce Belleville (OHL) 6371
6. Thomas Wilson Plymouth (OHL) 6286
7. Jake Paterson Saginaw (OHL) 6170
8. Brian Hart Exeter (HIGH-NH) 6060
9. Griffin Reinhart Edmonton (WHL) 6040
10. Morgan Rielly Moose Jaw (WHL) 6034
AVERAGE   5428

VERTEK LEG POWER PEAK NO PAUSE (SAYERS)
PLAYER TEAM (LEAGUE) WATTS
1. Jake McCabe U. of Wisconsin (WCHA) 6835
2. Chris Calnan Nobles (HIGH-MA) 6818
3. Malcolm Subban Belleville (OHL) 6667
4. Brendan Gaunce Belleville (OHL) 6525
5. Brady Skjei USA U-18 (USHL) 6523
6. Andreas Athanasiou London (OHL) 6522
7. Thomas Wilson Plymouth (OHL) 6437
8. Griffin Reinhart Edmonton (WHL) 6348
9. Morgan Rielly Moose Jaw (WHL) 6344
10. Cody Ceci Ottawa (OHL) 6336 AVERAGE   5621

4 JUMP (MAT) MODE - GROUND TIME
PLAYER TEAM (LEAGUE) SECONDS
1. Andrey Markov Saskatoon (WHL) 0.3
2. Patrick Sieloff USA U-18 (USHL) 0.4
Malcolm Subban Belleville (OHL) 0.4
4. Brian Hart Exeter (HIGH-NH) 0.44
5. Derrick Pouliot Portland (WHL) 0.49
Colton Sissons Kelowna (WHL) 0.49
7. Olli Maatta London (OHL) 0.5
8. Devin Shore Whitby (OJHL) 0.5
9. Dane Fox Erie (OHL) 0.54

Jacob Trouba USA U-18 (USHL) 0.54
AVERAGE   0.68

JUMP (MAT) MODE – AVG. JUMP HEIGHT
PLAYER TEAM (LEAGUE) INCHES
1. Brady Skjei USA U-18 (USHL) 24.9
2. Mathew Dumba Red Deer (WHL) 24.2
3. Thomas Wilson Plymouth (OHL) 24.1
4. Jake McCabe U. of Wisconsin (WCHA) 23.8
5. Michael Matheson Dubuque (USHL) 23.6
6. Cristoval Nieves Kent School (HIGH-CT) 23.4
7. Branden Troock Seattle (WHL) 23.3
8. Malcolm Subban Belleville (OHL) 23
Francis Beauvillier Rimouski (QMJHL) 23
10. Jacob Trouba USA U-18 (USHL) 22.8
Chris Calnan Nobles (HIGH-MA) 22.8
AVERAGE   20.4

RIGHT HAND GRIP- MUSCULOSKELETAL UPPER BODY
PLAYER TEAM (LEAGUE) POUNDS
1. Morgan Rielly Moose Jaw (WHL) 167
2. Francis Beauvillier Rimouski (QMJHL) 161
3. Mitchell Moroz Edmonton (WHL) 160
4. Brendan Gaunce Belleville (OHL) 159
5. Samuel Kurker St. John's Prep (HIGH-MA 155
6. Matthew DeBlouw Muskegon (USHL) 154
7. Jake McCabe U. of Wisconsin (WCHA) 151
Matia Marcantuoni Kitchener (OHL) 151
9. Andrey Vasilevskiy Ufa 2 (RUS-JR.) 150
10. Chris Calnan Nobles (HIGH-MA) 148
Francois Tremblay Val-d'Or (QMJHL) 148
AVERAGE   128

LEFT HAND GRIP
PLAYER TEAM (LEAGUE) POUNDS
1. Andrey Vasilevskiy Ufa 2 (RUS-JR.) 155
Chris Calnan Nobles (HIGH-MA) 155
3. Morgan Rielly Moose Jaw (WHL) 150
4. Matia Marcantuoni Kitchener (OHL) 148
5. Michael Matheson Dubuque (USHL) 147
6. Brendan Gaunce Belleville (OHL) 146

Kenton Helgesen Calgary (WHL) 146
8. Jake McCabe U. of Wisconsin (WCHA) 144
9. Malcolm Subban Belleville (OHL) 143
Damon Severson Kelowna (WHL) 143
AVERAGE   123

BENCH PRESS – NUMBER OF REPS
PLAYER TEAM (LEAGUE) 150 lbs
1. Mike Winther Prince Albert (WHL) 17
2. Cristoval Nieves Kent School (HIGH–CT) 15
3. Chandler Stevenson Regina (WHL) 14
4. Morgan Rielly Moose Jaw (WHL) 13
5. Phillip Di Giuseppe U. of Michigan (CCHA) 12
Jujhar Khaira Prince George (BCHL) 12
Thomas Wilson Plymouth (OHL) 12
8. Oscar Dansk Brynas Jr. (SWE–JR.) 11
Max Iafrate Kitchener (OHL) 11
Brian Hart Exeter (HIGH–NH) 11
Colton Sissons Kelowna (WHL) 11
Ben Johnson Windsor (OHL) 11
Slater Koekkoek Peterborough (OHL) 11
Andreas Athanasiou London (OHL) 11
Daniel O'Regan St. Sebatstian School (HIGH–MA) 11
Lukas Sutter Saskatoon (WHL) 11
Dylan Blujas Brampton (OHL) 11
AVERAGE   7

BENCH PRESS
PLAYER TEAM (LEAGUE) lb/lb body weight
1. Mike Winther Prince Albert (WHL) 14.8
2. Cristoval Nieves Kent School (HIGH–CT) 11.7
3. Chandler Stevenson Regina (WHL) 11.1
4. Morgan Rielly Moose Jaw (WHL) 9.8
Daniel O'Regan St. Sebastian School (HIGH–MA) 9.8
6. Andreas Athanasiou London (OHL) 9.3
7. Phillip Di Giuseppe U. of Michigan (CCHA) 9.2
8. Jujhar Khaira Prince George (BCHL) 9.1
9. Slater Koekkoek Peterborough (OHL) 9
10. Colton Sissons Kelowna (WHL) 8.8
AVERAGE   5.1

PUSH–UPS
PLAYER TEAM (LEAGUE) MAX NUM.
1. Chandler Stevenson Regina (WHL) 52
2. Jake Paterson Saginaw (OHL) 48
3. Kenton Helgesen Calgary (WHL) 46
4. Kevin Roy Lincoln (USHL) 45
5. Michael Matheson Dubuque (USHL) 41
6. Thomas Wilson Plymouth (OHL) 39
Tanner Richard Guelph (OHL) 39 8.
Mathew Dumba Red Deer (WHL) 38 9.
Daniel O'Regan St. Sebastian School (HIGH–MA) 37
Samuel Kurker St. John's Prep (HIGH–MA) 37
AVERAGE 30

PUSH–UPS x BODY WEIGHT
PLAYER TEAM (LEAGUE) POUNDS
1. Chandler Stevenson Regina (WHL) 9880
2. Jake Paterson Saginaw (OHL) 8448
3. Kenton Helgesen Calgary (WHL) 8234
4. Thomas Wilson Plymouth (OHL) 7995
5. Samuel Kurker St. John's Prep (HIGH–MA) 7423
6. Michael Matheson Dubuque (USHL) 7289
7. Brendan Gaunce Belleville (OHL) 7245
8. Kevin Roy Lincoln (USHL) 7020
9. Mathew Dumba Red Deer (WHL) 6992
10. Cody Ceci Ottawa (OHL) 6970
Ville Pokka Karpat (FIN) 6970
AVERAGE 5096

PUSH STRENGTH
PLAYER TEAM (LEAGUE POUNDS)
1. Jake Pateson Saginaw (OHL) 333
2. Chandler Stevenson Regina (WHL) 320
3. Thomas Wilson Plymouth (OHL) 313
4. Lukas Sutter Saskatoon (WHL) 303
5. Matthew Finn Guelph (OHL) 302
6. Samuel Kurker St. John's Prep (HIGH–MA) 285
7. Francis Beauvillier Rimouski (WHL) 282
8. Ryan Murray Everett (WHL) 276
9. Jacob Trouba USA U–18 (USHL) 274
Brian Cooper Fargo (USHL) 274

AVERAGE   222

PUSH STRENGTH
PLAYER TEAM (LEAGUE) lb/lb body weight
1. Jake Paterson Saginaw (OHL) 1.89
2. Chandler Stevenson Regina (WHL) 1.68
3. Francis Beauvillier Rimouski (QMJHL) 1.56
4. Scott Laughton Oshawa (OHL) 1.54
5. Thomas Wilson Plymouth (OHL) 1.53
6. Matthew Finn Guelph (OHL) 1.52
7. Micahel Matheson Dubuque (USHL) 1.51
8. Brian Cooper Fargo (USHL) 1.49
9. Jacob Trouba USA U-18 (USHL) 1.47
10. Devin Shore Whitby (OJHL) 1.45
AVERAGE   1.14

PULL STRENGTH
PLAYER TEAM (LEAGUE) POUNDS
1. Thomas Wilson Plymouth (OHL) 312
Branden Troock Seattle (WHL) 312
3. Cody Ceci Ottawa (OHL) 309
4. Samuel Kurker St. John's Prep (HIGH-MA) 304
5. Brendan Gaunce Belleville (OHL) 300
Chris Calnan Nobles (HIGH-MA) 300
7. Francis Beauvillier Rimouski (QMJHL) 297
8. Henrik Samuelsson Edmonton (WHL) 295
9. Morgan Rielly Moose Jaw (WHL) 291
10. Jacob Trouba USA U-18 USHL) 288
AVERAGE   251

PULL STRENGTH
PLAYER TEAM (LEAGUE) lb/lb body weight
1. Francis Beauvillier Rimouski (QMJHL) 1.64
2. Branden Troock Seattle (WHL) 1.61
3. Chris Calnan Nobles (HIGH-MA) 1.6
Gemel Smith Owen Sound (OHL) 1.6
5. Kevin Roy Lincoln (USHL) 1.58
6. Artur Gavrus Owen Sound (OHL) 1.57
7. Matthew DeBlouw Muskegon (USHL) 1.56
Jake Paterson Saginaw (OHL) 1.56
9. Jacob Trouba USA U-18 (USHL) 1.54

10. Thomas Wilson Plymouth (OHL) 1.52
Samuel Kurker St. John's Prep (HIGH-MA) 1.52
Trevor Carrick Mississauga St. Michael's (OHL) 1.52
Ludwig Bystrom Modo Jr. (SWE-JR.) 1.52
AVERAGE   1.28

UPPER BODY POWER 4 KG BALL
PLAYER TEAM (LEAGUE) INCHES
1. Dane Fox Erie (OHL) 253
2. Brendan Gaunce Belleville (OHL) 235
Daniil Zharkov Belleville (OHL) 235
4. Andreas Athanasiou London (OHL) 232
Jujhar Khaira Prince George (BCHL) 232
6. Thomas Wilson Plymouth (OHL) 230
Mitchell Moroz Edmonton (WHL) 230
Patrick Sieloff USA U-18 (USHL) 230
9. Pontus Aberg Djurgarden (SWE) 227
10. Brandon Whitney Victoriaville (QMJHL) 222
AVERAGE   198

*Source: NHL.com

First round of the 2012 NHL Entry Draft
(June 22, 2012)

No. Team   Player   Junior Team   Position

1 — EDM — Nail Yakupov — Sarnia Sting (OHL) — F
2 — COL — Ryan Murray — Everett Silvertips (WHL) — D
3 — MTL — Alex Galchenyuk — Sarnia (OHL) — F
4 — NYI — Griffin Reinhart — Edmonton Oil Kings (WHL) — D
5 — TOR — Morgan Rielly — Moose Jaw Warriors (WHL) — D
6 — ANA — Hampus Lindholm — Rogle J20 (Swedish Elite) — D
7 — MIN — Mathew Dumba — Red Deer Rebels (WHL) — D
8 — PIT — Derrick Pouliot — Portland Winterhawks (WHL) — D
9 — WPG — Jacob Trouba — US Develop. Program (USHL) — D
10 — TBL — Slater Koekkeok — Peterborough Petes (OHL) — D
11 — WSH — Filip Forsberg — Leksands IF (Swedish Elite) — F
12 — BUF — Mikhail Grigorenko — Que Remparts (QMJHL) — F
13 — DAL — Radek Faksa — Kitchener Rangers (OHL) — F
14 — BUF — Zemgus Girgensons — Dubuque Saints (USHL) — F
15 — OTT — Cody Ceci — Ottawa 67's (OHL) — D
16 — WSH — Thomas Wilson — Plymouth Whalers (OHL) — F
17 — SJS — Tomas Hertl — Slavia Praha (Czech Extraliga) — F
18 — CHI — Teuvo Teravainen — Jokerit (SM-liga) — F
19 — TBL — Andrey Vasilevskiy — UFA 2 (Russia) — G
20 — PHI — Scott Laughton — Oshawa Generals (OHL) — F
21 — CGY — Mark Jankowski — Stanstead College (Que HS) — D
22 — PIT — Olli Maatta — London Knights (OHL) — D
23 — FLA — Michael Matheson — Dubuque (USHL) — D
24 —BOS — Malcolm Subban — Belleville Bulls (OHL) — G
25 — STL — Jordan Schmaltz — G Bay Gamblers (USHL) — D
26 — VAN — Brendan Gaunce — Belleville (OHL) — F
27 — PHX — Henrik Samuelsson — Edmonton (WHL) — F
28 — NYR —Brady Skjei — US Development Team (USHL) — D
29 — NJD — Stefan Matteau — Development Team (USHL) — F
30 — LAK — Tanner Pearson — Barrie Colts (OHL) — F

*Source: NHL.com

Vancouver Canucks selections at the 2012 NHL Entry Draft

Round — Player — Junior Team — Position
1 (26) — Brendan Gaunce — Belleville Bulls (OHL) — F
2 (57) — Alexandre Mallet — Rimouski Oceanic (QMJHL) — LW
5 (147) — Ben Hutton — Nepean Raiders (CCHL) — D
6 (177) — Wesley Myron — Victoria Grizzlies (BCHL) — LW
7 (207) — Matthew Beattie — Exeter (NH-High) — LW

*Source: NHL.com

Vancouver Canucks depth chart as of June 25, 2012

Left Wing	Centre	Right Wing
Daniel Sedin	Henrik Sedin	Alexandre Burrows
Chris Higgins	Ryan Kesler	Jannik Hansen
David Booth	Maxim Lapierre	Zack Kassian
Mason Raymond	Manny Malholtra	Dale Weise
Aaron Voltpatti	Andrew Ebbett	Steve Pinizzotto
Bill Sweatt	Jordan Schroeder	Anton Rodin
Prab Rai	Alex Friesen	Andrew Gordon
Steven Anthony	Stefan Schneider	Kellan Tochkin
Darren Archibald	**Brendan Gaunce**	Nicklas Jensen
Alexandre Mallet	Taylor Matson	Alexandre Grenier
Ludwig Blomstrand	Pathrik Westerholm	Matthew Beattie
Wesley Myron	Joseph Labate	
Ilya Kablukov	Mats Josten-Froshaug	

Defense	Goaltenders
Alexander Edler	Cory Schneider
Dan Hamhuis	Roberto Luongo
Jason Garrison	Eddie Lack
Kevin Bieksa	Joe Cannata
Chris Tanev	David Honzik
Keith Ballard	
Andrew Alberts	
Yann Sauve	
Kevin Connauton	
Adam Polasek	
Peter Andersson	
Frank Corrado	
Patrick McNally	
Jeremy Price	
Henrik Tommernes	
Ben Hutton	

*Source: Forecaster.**TheHockeyNews.com**

Belleville Bulls award winners

2010-11

Don Foster Award — Luke Judson
Top Scorer Award — Andy Bathgate
Nina Chapman Memorial Trophy — Joe Underwood
George MacIntyre Memorial Trophy — Luke Judson
Bob Ricketts Memorial Trophy — Stephen Silas
Ron Smith Memorial Award — Malcolm Subban
Rookie of the Year Award — **Brendan Gaunce**/Malcolm Subban
Unsung Hero Award — Brett Mackie
The "RUT" Award — Brett Mackie
Most Improved Player Award — Scott Simmonds
Dr. H.F. Williamson Memorial Award — Braeden Corbeth
Tom Gavey Media Good Guy Award — Mike Mascioli
Jake Gilmour Award — Luke Judson
Ivan Tennant Award — Adam Bignell
Roger Neilson Award — Braeden Corbeth
Bobby Smith Award — **Brendan Gaunce**

2011-12

Don Foster Award — Malcolm Subban
Top Scorer Award — **Brendan Gaunce**
Nina Chapman Memorial Trophy — Brady Austin
George MacIntyre Memorial Trophy — **Brendan Gaunce**
Bob Ricketts Memorial Trophy — Stephen Silas
Ron Smith Memorial Award — Joseph Cramarossa/Michael Curtis
Rookie of the Year Award — Daniil Zharkov
Unsung Hero Award — Michael Curtis
The "RUT" Award — Luke Judson
Most Improved Player Award — Brady Austin
Dr. H.F. Williamson Memorial Award — Michael Curtis
Tom Gavey Media Good Guy Award — Luke Judson
Jake Gilmour Award — Luke Judson
Ivan Tennant Award — Scott Simmonds
Roger Neilson Award — Malcolm Subban
Bobby Smith Award — **Brendan Gaunce**

*Source: BellevilleBulls.com

ABOUT JOHN MATISZ

John Matisz is a journalist based in London, Ontario. Currently, he is employed by Metro News, Canada's most read national daily newspaper, covering the Ontario Hockey League's London Knights - among other things. Since graduating from Brock University in 2011, his work has also appeared in the Hockey News magazine, on TheScore.com, and in the St. Catharines Standard.

ABOUT HOCKEYPROSPECT.COM

HockeyProspect.com was founded in 2004 by Mark Edwards. At the time, Mark was coaching Wayne Simmonds in Midget AAA.

Mark thought that Wayne had some special talent and he wanted to create a medium to give some publicity to players who, like Wayne, who had been missed.

HockeyProspect.com, is an independent hockey scouting service dedicated to producing scouting reports and draft rankings. All of our scouts are chosen based on their hockey background, integrity and dedication to the sport.

Mark has coached for 19 years with the bulk of that coaching at the Midget and Junior 'A' levels. He has coached players currently playing in the NHL and others on their way up the ladder. Mark has been scouting since 2003.

PHOTO CREDITS:

As always thanks to CHL Images for the use of their outstanding photos.

Cover: CHL IMAGES

www.ingramcontent.com/pod-product-compliance
Lightning Source LLC
Chambersburg PA
CBHW061430040426
42450CB00007B/976